The Truth Shifters are the outsourced waves of very powerful Deceptions and Manipulations, the schemes of a Stronghold Bonded Union that are actively searching to be able to captivate the Human Mind within its powerful desires, to Influence and Control the active Consciousness of Humanity's robust Spiritual, Political, and Economic characteristic behaviors....

© Copyright 2023-MIHAI ILIOI - All rights reserved.

It is not legal to reproduce, duplicate, or transmit any part of this document electronically or in print. Recording of this publication is strictly prohibited.

Table of Contents

Dedication 3
Introduction 5
Chapter One: Understanding Truth 7
Chapter Two: Absolute Truth 11
Chapter Three: Relative Truth 19
Chapter Four: Projective Truth 33
Chapter Five: Truth vs. Realities 43
Chapter Six: Truth vs. Thoughts 62
Chapter Seven: Shifting Shadows 80
Chapter Eighth: Transcendental Realm 103
Chapter Nine: Truth Shifters 147
Chapter Ten: Deceptive Platforms 232
Conclusion 298
About Author 308

Dedication:

I want to dedicate this book to all my family and friends and to all the people who, regardless of their cultural background, environment, and belief systems, are on their journey through life.

For those who are always striving, always searching, and always seeking a breakthrough in their life pursuit of understanding freedom, whether it is freedom of religion, political freedom, or economic freedom, and for those who are pushing forward relentlessly and striving to achieve their purpose and goals, and seeking to break through any obstacles and any powerful challenges that may come their way while they are actively searching for the truth and the freedom this book is dedicated to you.

This dedication is for those searching for freedom and overall well-being that exists in all its forms, be it religious, political, or economic. It is for those who endure suffering and pain in their lives while, at the same time, they are navigating the turbulent waters and mighty waves for their life's survival amid all circumstances.

This dedication is especially for those who, in their search for reaching and understanding the accurate process of freedom and liberty, have become prey to many influences and powers that are actively feeding their existences from the very pain of humanity's brokenness and sadness and yet never giving up and continue to rise and persevere.

May the messages and the insightful information from the pages of this book inspire you to keep searching and striving for natural comfort, peace, and strength to overcome any adversity that comes your way.

May you find solace in the understanding and the knowledge that you are not alone in this temporary journey of your life, and by your side, there are multitudes upon multitudes of people just like you who are searching and striving for a better life and a better place. Still, more than anything else, please know that our Almighty God will provide guidance and support along the way, and his everlasting love and faithfulness will sustain you.

To all those who are navigating the journey of life, this book is for you.

With this dedication, I also express my sincere thanks and gratitude to all the readers of this book, and I want you to know that your comments and feedback are critical and appreciated.

Sincerely,
Mihai Ilioi

Introduction

John 8: 32

"Then you will know the Truth, and the Truth will set you free."

We are living in challenging times when the apparatus and the receiver of our information and their module systems, and the processor of our synchronized minds, are showing signals of solid and real palpitation of its pulses and its active modes that are continually beeping confusion in the heart and the soul of the humanity. All over the world, people are currently being actively exposed to different movements and various manifestations, and many other multiple revelations in their search for freedom. On the life journey of their active search and regardless of the many aspects of their freedom they are searching for, freedom of Religion, Economic freedom, or Political freedom, their results will produce the same solid effects. It will have the same impact on people's lives if their search has been clouded and influenced by the currents and the winds of deceptions and manipulations that are active and that have been controlling humanity from the very first moment when the world and time came into existence.

To understand the root of deception and the will of manipulation flowing into the lives of sincere people searching for the Truth so they may be set free, we need to understand what is behind it and what is fueling its desire to exist as a living entity.

Deception and manipulation at the very corrupt core of their existence have only one set goal in common: to feed themselves with solid power, control, and domination, and they will stop at nothing in their desire to achieve it.

We all know the old saying" A Match Made in Heaven" when we talk about how sometimes things look good, sound good, and feel good.

When it comes to the subject of this book, this saying will best describe it something like this:" Deceptions and Manipulations are a Perfect Match that is made within humanity's Mind. Their powerful advances will never stop by using their waves of solid influences and desires to achieve and have power, control, and dominance over society and humanity's living soul.

As I mentioned at the beginning of this introduction, the result is almost identical. It will produce the same fruits of corruption, regardless of the living platforms of life where their deceptions and manipulations may be actively working and forth activated, on a religious platform and structure, an economic forum and system, or even on a political platform and design. The power and the control they seek to achieve in their search for complete dominance over people have no drawing borders for their quests, and any humanitarian barriers do not limit the powerful desires they all possess.

Their webs and real powerful tentacles can cross into any aspect of humanity's life at ease if they are not resisted and pushed back. May the absolute Truth that it is the Word of God and the peace of God that transcends all understanding surround us, protect us, and Guard our Hearts and Minds in Christ Jesus.

Chapter One:
Understanding Truth

John 18 vs. 37-38:" So Pilate said to Him," Then you are a King?" Jesus answered," You say correctly that I am a King, and for this is why I was born, and for this, I have come into the world to testify to the Truth. Everyone who is of the Truth (who is a friend of the Truth and belongs to the Truth) hears and listens to my voice. Pilate said to Him, "WHAT IS TRUTH?

Accepting the Word of God guards us against the elemental spiritual forces of this world that are trying to bring forth their solid waves of deception and manipulation against the works and the power of Truth in our life, and it will help us to be able to process an accurate understanding of Truth. Reading the Word of God, these passages where Jesus Christ spoke with Pilate before His death at the Calvary brought forth an entirely new perspective of how to look and search for Truth.

Pilate shows us that we can be influenced in life by not being able to recognize the Truth, not being able to understand the Truth, and not being able to grasp the Truth even when the Truth is staring us in the face.

In trials, prosecutors and judges often ask questions from the defendants, and they expect an answer before moving on with their decision to pursue their case further.

Here, we see Pilate asking Jesus Christ these questions in the physical realm, face to face, or like one of the old saying phrase "eye to eye": What is Truth?

After asking this question, he tried to dismiss the charges against our Lord and Savior Jesus Christ by telling the accusers," I find no guilt in him" (no crime, no cause for accusation).

Based on what I mentioned above, Pilate was sincere in his quest to understand the Truth. And because of that, when he asked this question regarding the Truth verbally, I do believe that he did receive his answer deep inside his own Spirit, Heart, Mind, and Soul, and then, without hesitation, he tried to set Jesus free.

When we are ready for God's Truth to be revealed to us, to bring us to His understanding of the Truth, we need to genuinely open ourselves up to the opportunity that our answers and what we are looking for sometimes will be revealed and received in our spiritual being, deep inside into our dwelling place where the soul resides. Sometimes, in our search for Truth, we try hard to discover and understand what Truth is. We start this journey not knowing and unable to grasp the very idea that we as human beings have actively been very blessed and wired with the ability to comprehend robust logical, physical, and spiritual ideologies. The accurate information and the actual manifestation of the power of the Truth in our life can be truly captured and processed by our Mind for our human being's temporary expression and our human being's eternal Soul benefits.

For this reason and only this reason alone, the real battle and the real war that humanity is facing daily on the multiple war frontlines for control of society and its desires, happening on the major platforms of humanity's Religious, Political, and Economic structures, is the fight for the control over the power of the Mind.

The spiritual forces that are all around us are fighting against our humanity and our humanity's real purpose in life by sending continually and without interruption their agents of misinformation, deceptions, and doubts that will try to cloud the human Mind and hold it in their robust misconceptions and deceits schemes, purposely making the human Mind at times not being able to perceive and understand the Truth, even when the infinite Truth has been actively revealed and exposed to our mere human Minds. We may talk about how we do things and how we take actions in life with a clear mind, but for us, talking about having a clear mindset, or even wishing that we have a clear perspective, wanting to have an evident attitude, and having and operating our daily reality of life through the processes of a clear mindset, are all attributes factors that are actively working, in separated planes of information that are producing different results.

I am making this point very shortly that we need to be able to differentiate between the many attributes of our life's functions when we are searching to captivate the power of the Truth within and to sincerely distinguish the properties of a Clear Mind and Clean Mind.

Receiving robust information and revelations of Truth inside our Minds; if we cannot acknowledge and differentiate the mechanism power of our processor through which we can disseminate the information received or the revelation of the Truth within, we will be exposed to errors as we move to release the processed data to our hearts, via our emotions, and feelings that will eventually affect our souls, our beliefs, and our faith.

I pray that the readers of this book will search for themselves and bring their findings to the light of the Word of God, which will allow them to realize if they are living the

Word of God in their life revealed to them in the Truth and by the power of the Truth, with a Clear Mindset or with a Clean Mindset attribute function.

Having a clear understanding of the information that our very Mind is actively processing while being exposed to a myriad of solid and influenceable thoughts daily, reading and studying the Word of God, and trying to understand what the Truth is, the way Pilate wanted to understand what Truth is, in that moment when he asked Jesus Christ about it, is not a true definite answer to our search and quest to find the Truth. Because of that, we can be very clearly wrong in how we process and assert the Power of Truth within our lives.

UNDERSTAND THE TRUTH WITH A CLEAN AND WITH A PURE MIND.

Chapter Two:
Absolute Truth

John 1:1, "In the beginning was the Word, And the Word was with God, and the Word was God.2)" He was with God in the beginning. 3)" Through Him all things have been made, and without Him, nothing was made that has been made. In Him was life, and that life was the light of all humankind".

For us to be able to understand the foundation and the existence of the Absolute Truth that will never be changed, restricted, or minimized, regardless of the daily assault on the very fiber of its revelation to humanity by critics that are at their profound core influenced by spiritual forces of the world, we need to open our spirit and soul, and understand it, in the light and guidance of what the Scriptures are telling and teaching us about it.

Absolute is the adjective of something that exists independently in its expression, manifestation, and revelation. It is not about other things or depending on anything else; the Absolute is beyond human control. Absolute will never be relative to any other outside influences; it is not limited or constrictive by any laws, regardless of whether these influences are spiritual, celestial, or natural laws, and the Absolute Truth is the definition of infinite perfection and completeness.

Jesus Christ was asked by Pilate Pontus, before His death

at the hands of Roman soldiers, handed to them by His people, "What is Truth"? What caught my attention in the wording of his question was that he did not ask, "What is the Truth? Or who is the Truth?

This question arose during the communication and the words exchanged between Jesus and Pilate when the Lord said:" I was born, and I came in this world to testify to the Truth."

Truth is the base and foundation of the spoken Word of God.

The sound of His manifestation that came forward in its expression and revelation from the beginning of Creation has been revealed and manifested from within the Absolute All to sustain the Heavens and the Earth, including all things created in Heavens and made on Earth. Jesus Christ came into this world to testify to the Truth, to witness to the Truth, and to reveal the Truth. By accepting his testimony, humanity may be able to enter the embrace of Truth so that the Truth may set them free and save them from the influencers of darkness that are working overtime to confuse people and hold them in their grip, fueled by corruption and manipulation that is the fruit of deception.

There is only one Absolute, the creator and sustainer of life by the power of its spoken Truth, that holds together the block and time of life, and the name of the Absolute Truth is God, the creator of Heavens and Earth.

Isaiah 45:18 "For this is what the Lord says- He who created the heavens, He is God, and He who fashioned and made the Earth, He found it; He did not create it to be empty but formed it to be inhabited-and He says" I am the Lord and there is no other.

This passage of the scriptures comes like a lightning

strike revelation of this powerful testimony about the nature of Jesus Christ that testified before Pilate hundreds of years later, the Absolute Truth. Our Lord and Savior Jesus Christ -The Lord -is testifying about the Father God, He who created Heavens, He is God, then by the end of the verse, he says," I am the Lord, and there is no other."

In the future, the subject of Absolute Truth opens right before our own eyes, a door of understanding, and we realize that the expression of the Absolute and the revelation of the Truth are working together in One. No other elements, natural forces, or spiritual realms will be able to come in between the Absolute and the Truth to affect or influence the expression of the Absolute or the revelation of the Truth.

John 14:5-6" Thomas said to Him:" Lord, we don't know where you are going, so how can we know the way?' Jesus answered," I am the Way, the Truth, and the Life. No one comes to the Father except through me.

What is Truth? Pilate asked about the Truth in that very moment when Jesus Christ stood before him at his trial. In our desire to search for the Truth that we may be set free for salvation and eternal life, we do need to pay very close attention to the Absolute Truth and to our Creator's living Word that will protect us from being exposed to powerful waves of deception and strong winds that are trying to keep us in bondage within their chains of manipulations.

Our Lord and Savior Jesus Christ, when praying for His disciples to the Father, asked for them to be protected and live in unity; in His prayer, He asked the Father" John 17:17" to Sanctify them by the Truth; your Word is Truth.

Hallelujah to the Lamb of God. The Absolute Truth in

His grace and mercy revealed His expression of love in the entire Creation that was brought into existence and to life by the power of His Truth revealed to humanity by his living and spoken Word.

Absolute is our God Almighty, the creator of the Heavens and Earth. Truth is the Word of our God Almighty, spoken in Heaven and Earth.

Absolute Truth is the Word of our God Almighty.

We need to understand that Absolute Truth was before the beginning and the existence of any dimensional form of planes and parallels that are being actively power manifested within time, space, and matter, and before any realms of spiritual movements and events that are surrounding us, in the material world or the spiritual world.

Because of that, Absolute Truth is not sustained or influenced by any outside forces working around us, being visible or invisible powers that manifest at the core of every expressed element and block of created life.

On the other hand, everything that exists, that moves, that has the breath of life is being sustained and influenced, and it is pulling its beginning and its existence from the source and from the revelation that came forth from the Absolute Truth. When the power of God's love was expressed in the vast Creation of the Absolute, everything that came into existence became part of the Complete All.

This is not a mistake or a grammar misspelling that I wrote, but it is my strong core belief that God exists in All, and All that ever express, and manifest exist in God.

What is Truth? I am the Truth, said Jesus Christ, and everything that has existence and lives is breathing and living its manifested expressions because of me, the Truth.

The Truth was from before the beginning; there was the Absolute Truth before anything was created and formed.

Hallelujah. Our Lord and Savior Jesus Christ is the Word of God, and He testified and revealed to His disciples that He is the Truth.

In Genesis, the scriptures tell us that before everything else, before the existence of the Creation and before anything that has been formed and brought forth to life, God was, "In the beginning God" ….

We already know that the Truth of the Almighty God is the Word of the Almighty God, and they are One. *In the beginning was the Truth, and the Truth was with God, and the Truth was God. The Truth was with God from before the birth of the beginning. Through Truth, all things have been formed and made; without Truth, nothing was made that has ever been developed and created. In Truth, it was life, and that life was the light of All humankind. * Mankind in the realm of its former existence, Earth in its physical domain of reality, and all its dimensional planes and parallels of the Creation that defines it, including the Heavens and their existence, are part of the expression of Love, Power, and Absolute that exploded and outburst forward from the divine depths of Truth.

God -Truth, being the source of All, is not bound and not subject to any limitation of Time, Space, and the Matter of their core Elements of Existence or their Elements of Creation that control it, like Earth, Water, Fire, Air, Wind, Mountains, and all these powers that sustain the sole core of their Creation, are drawing and pulling their existence from within the Truth.

God-Truth, being the source of All, is not bound and not

subject to any limitation, or to any perceived or to any unlimited attributes of Heavens and Thrones, or Dominions and Powers and Principalities, and any other spiritual creations that are also pulling their existence from within the Absolute Truth. Everything that has been birthed and conceived in any surrounding realms, and in the comprehension of the wisdom understanding power that emanates from the Truth being Heavens or Earth, and the things in heavens or the things on Earth, must be genuinely perceived for a better knowledge of the expression of God's unlimited love, through the power processor of a mind, that is connected directly into the very river flow of the revelation power that comes forth, from God's Absolute Truth.

God's Truth is the Majestic Sound expressed by the spoken Word and will always come forward in His Spirit's manifestation and revelation to encapsulate humanity's divine purpose within the self.

For the mind to be connected and remain connected to the river of revelation power of the Absolute Truth, its desire must be clean and free from all other created material or created spiritual forces that, from the beginning of their existence, continually are trying to minimize the authority and the power of the revelation, manifestation and the expression of God's Truth, that will never be changed, shaken or altered, regardless of if there are acceptors or deniers of the Absolute Truth.

In its complexity of receiving information, disseminating the information received, and releasing the correct output signals for active movements that follow for the proper manifestation of its functions and the control over the human being's characteristic attributes, the mind must be plugged and connected within the power of Truth. Some of the new age thinking and teaching that are slowly crawling inside the churches today, and in some movements that are arising today all around the world, their teachings are borderline influenced by witchcraft philosophy.

In the later chapters of this book, I will write more about the dangerous ideology that propagates the power of self, the idea that the mind itself is subject to be controlled and manipulated by the very intentions and by the wishes of its very own motives and active desires.

To be able to receive the clean and unaltered Truth that the mind is actively releasing to the human's expressions for proper function and for connectivity that must work correctly, the way it is supposed to work between the body and the mind, we do need to understand where we stand and if what we are searching for is the freedom that comes from the Truth.

God-Absolute Truth is speaking to His people, releasing the Word through the Prophet Isaiah, and in Chapter 45 of the book, in the last part of vs:18," I am the Lord. There is no other, vs. 19" I have not spoken in secret, from somewhere in a land of darkness, I have not said to Jacob's descendants 'Seek me in vain ', the Lord, Speak the Truth; I declare what is right.

He speaks the Truth because He is the Truth. Still, what happens deep inside our mind when we receive the Word of the Lord, the Truth of God, to process the revelation received from the fountain of Truth, and then we are fast releasing this information in many different forms and interpretations away from the Truth?

It is because our mind's apparatus processing, disseminating, and allocating the information received is being actively pursued and influenced by other structures of strong thought-infused scales that operate deeply within the structural frames of our human's very own Consciousness, Sub-

Consciousness, Self-Consciousness, or Confused Consciousness levels of expressions?

    We must bring our mind and submit it with all its operative and functional groups of our mind's Complete Consciousness attributes functions to the Power and the Authority of the Word of Living God, the Absolute Truth.

Chapter Three:
Relative Truth

2 Peter 2:1-2" But false prophets also arose among the people, just as there will be false teachers among you, who will secretly bring in destructive opinions. They will even deny the Master who brought them swift destruction on themselves. Even so, many will follow their licentious ways, and because of these teachers, the Way of the Truth will be maligned."

We are embarking on this journey in search of the freedom that can come forward in people's lives through the power of the Truth. In our previous chapter, we brought to light, according to the scriptures, that there is only one authority and only one Absolute Truth that can give humanity freedom and liberty, that they may be set free of any false teachings and false truths that are running wild around the world, by luring followers into their nets of deceptions, to dominate and control their life under the pretext of freedom, when what they do is nothing more than subjugate them with no help in sight. Freedom and liberty come only from Absolute Truth, the Lord God Almighty, the Creator of Heavens and Earth, and all the created things beings in Heavens or beings on Earth, including humankind in His Image and Likeness. False truths, in their meaning of the expression, have no place to be in the same sentence, but I chose to write one next to another to bring forward the reflection of how bad this sounds and how bad this looks, considering that false is the opposite of the Truth and vice versa. I firmly believe this is how it looks in the eyes and the presence of the Almighty God when winds of corruption and deceptive waves attach themselves to the people's hearts and minds, setting them up for failure while promising them freedom contrary to the Word of God.

The Relative, Alternative, and Projected truths all have an excellent appeal with attractive words and sounds but lack the power of transformation. They can't help changing the lives of people searching for freedom. Teaching people and leading them into false promises that are influenced by the elemental spiritual forces of this world and passing them to their followers the ideology of something relative, alternative, and, or projective opinions, as the true Word of God that is the only Absolute Truth, it is difficult as both the teacher and the follower are exposed and subjects to failures and together they will bypass the much-needed understanding of the Truth that can set them free in life.

Jesus Christ, in the passage of scriptures in Luke 6:39, says, "Can the blind lead a blind? Will they not both fall into a pit?" The example that our Lord Jesus Christ gave us about two thousand years ago regarding the dangerous situation of deception and what will be the result when a blind human starts leading another blind human today is ringing indeed true, like never before, when the so-called teachers of the Truth of God are bypassing the truthfulness and the testimony of the Word of the Lord. In their eagerness to fulfill their spiritual desires, their hearts become greedy. Blindness is setting in, darkening their eyes with veils of idolatry and pride that will make them immune to the Absolute Truth, thus not being able to differentiate between the Absolute Truth and between something relative or even sometimes that comes against us as a distorted alternative to the Truth.

Relative Truth, in its definition and at the core of its

existence, is building itself up as a truth warrior, advertising itself as channels that can flow from within its revelation, that can bring forth freedom for those that are seeking to be set free from the blindness and the corruption of their oppressed systems, but in reality, the followers of the relative Truth and their leaders, are working on all fronts and forms of deception to minimize and to deny the power of God and His Absolute Truth.

The relativities and the relations that arise in the existences of God's majestic and manifold creation, brought forth by the power of His expression and revelation of His Word, between the physical realm and the spiritual realm inside one's expressed and connected thoughts, manifested within the very Mind's processor chambers, that are being experienced and expressed by different groups of people, and also at the individual level of one, being at the level of spirit knowledge or physical knowledge, will never be able to influence or alter the true origin of their foundations that still actively are coming forward into existence from the Absolute Truth. However, all these created elements of life and their expressions are subject to it.

By definition, a relative truth experienced by someone, once or multiple times, in a physical realm of the matter form and inside its own mind space of comprehension thought, or a relative truth experienced by someone once or multiple times in its spiritual realm form and inside owns mind space of its comprehension thought, considering that both realms, the physical realm, and the spiritual realms, are subjected, and submitted to the Absolute Truth.

The Mind, in all its Conscious ability to process information, if indeed it is brought into the understanding and submission of God's Truth, will be able to process the data, the revelations, and the experiences that are flowing from both realms from the spiritual realm at the spirit level and the physical realm at the body and its function level. We need to know that the power of corruption and the influence of the enemies of our souls and bodies will try at all costs to keep us away from our Creator, from the flowing energy of His Absolute Truth, and from the freedom that the truth brings.

For a complete understanding of the dangerous influences that are continually at odds with God's eternal Truth, which is able and will transform people's lives, we need to stay sharp and focus our search on the refreshment and revelation that comes from the Word of God. Let's take the word "Understanding" and try to describe its meaning, function, and application in its terminology of having insight or a revelation about a subject, a comment, a theory, or a fact, about something that can be influenced by its perspective of seeing it, feeling it, or even manifesting it, then acting on that insight. We often hear these words passed around in churches, meetings, and gatherings circles.

I "Understand how you feel," but in fact, you don't understand how I feel because if I am under the feeling of an emotional or even a spiritual process manifested within, being a pain, grief, sorrow, or happiness, celebration, and joy, and just because you had experienced the same method of emotional or spiritual manifestation at one time or another in your life, it does not elevate itself to a typical result, even if the expression and the touching of the spiritual process were the same within us, and if its effect was the same. The result of my relative Truth is accurate to me in my own experience and results, and your relative Truth is true to you in your own experience and outcome. Regardless of our relative truths, I am making this analogy to reflect and expose the temptation that can knock deep inside the hearts of people confused and blinded by their power trip and grip to control others.

We need to know that our experiences and manifestations fueling our lives, concerning one another and together about God's Word, are true to us. Still, we will be exposed to error if we start preaching and leading people into false teachings, telling them that our relative Truth and our own experiences and results have authority over others.

We begin bypassing the absolute Truth that comes genuinely only by the revelation of the Word of God in exchange for a temporary benefit.

The relative truth that can become true to you, based on the results of your lived experiences in both physical and spiritual manifestations, and the relative truth that becomes true to me, because of my own lived experiences in both physical and spiritual expressions, are both fueled by the same source, from the Absolute Truth's wellspring, thus making our relative truths irrelevant to each other's outcome. Because they are unrelated, we must find a way to outsource our relative facts as accurate in their resolve only through the light and revelation from the Word of God. We cannot just start bringing followers into the circles of our own temporary and short-lived experiences of our relative truths and keep them away from the absolute Truth for our benefit.

Doing so will be a deception for us and those who listen to our teachings, and instead of calling them to follow the Word of God in Truth, we are calling them to follow our own experiences, testimonies, and convictions. In the later chapters, I will cover this dangerous and corrupt ideology that manifests itself in many movements worldwide, including inside many churches. I am not talking about the times when we come together in fellowship to speak to each other about the blessings of God, and doing so, bringing forward the testimonies of our own life-changing experiences that happened in our own life by the grace of God and by His amazing love, that was poured out from Heavens for us, that it may be revealed to us, in the sacrifice of our Lord and Savior Jesus Christ, the Way, the Truth and the Life, that was, that is, and it is to come, to bring Salvation, Redemption, Healing, and Deliverance, for our eternal soul, and our mortal body.

I am talking, though, about the opportunity that people may have come their way if they neglect the absolute Truth and open themselves up to the temptation of being manipulated and influenced by the Spirit of deception, and by doing so, starting to elevate their testimonies, their convictions, their own experiences to a level of nothing short of idolatry, looking for other fellow's approval and admiration, clothing themselves up in a false humility for personal triumph, thus forgetting about the revelation received from the Word of God in Truth. So how is it possible that being exposed to the Truth of God, receiving the disclosure and the testimony of the Truth, within our Consciousness of the Mind, we are still dangerously opening ourselves to the influences and movements that are opposite and contrary to the Truth received, and contrary to the living Word of God, that it is Yes and Amen? If we bring our input and slowly insert our futile thinking into the revelation received in Truth, we bypass the will and the purpose of the Word of God that came to us so that we may have life and have it abundantly.

Our relative truths that we and everyone else experience in life are part of the expressions that contour and shape us as living beings and who we are, and we understand that these truths are true to us. We will live in denial if we say otherwise, but to be able to reject the daily attacks we face at the level of our Complete Consciousness and not expose ourselves to the dangerous manipulation of powerful and deception spirits, we do need to ground our testimonies, our experiences and our relative truths, firm into the Absolute Truth of God, that is the source of life, the source of everything that has the breath of life, movement, and motion in all the creation and all form of existence, that came forward from and by the power of Word of God, the Creator of Heavens and Earth.

I used the word 'Complete Consciousness' because we need to reflect on the many levels of our Consciousness that exist within each other, and everyone who has the breath of God in them will experience it.

As a rapid point of introduction on 'Complete Consciousness' and for a better understanding of its functions within its very existence and purpose, sending and receiving information, processing them, and disseminating them, keeping them in a clean, uncontaminated format, that will flow throughout the entire Mind, from the source of revelation received, till the information it is reaching its destination and purpose, let's cover this topic in few paragraphs.

At what level of our 'Complete Consciousness' we are processing and releasing the information received from the Absolute, and what is the relationship of the Consciousness to our own heart, and are there any sending and receiving information signals between our Consciousness and our nature that can affect or even manipulate our behavior?

Is there also a relationship and a connection between our Consciousness and our Spirit, and are there any sending and receiving information signals between our Consciousness and our own Spirit that can affect and even manipulate our own Spirit behavior? What is the relationship and the communication of our Self Consciousness within our very own Sub Consciousness and the built structure and frame of our very human complex Complete Consciousness?

Can our own Sub Consciousness bypass the filter and levels of our logical mechanism built inside the Mind and within the Complete Consciousness schematics to send and receive signals and information directly, in and out, to and from our heart, Spirit, and soul?

Can the heart bypass and use the complexity of the Consciousness to send its information or even desires, using the Sub Consciousness level of influence, to manipulate the Spirit and affect the soul? Can the Spirit bypass and use the complexity of the Consciousness to send its information or even desires, using the same level of Sub Consciousness influence to manipulate the heart and affect the soul? These are legit questions that we need to be able to address to understand that we are created and formed by the Almighty God, in a very complex nature, we are designed and developed by the hands of God in His image and likeness, and we need to submit our Complete Consciousness to the will and the absolute Truth of our Creator, which will guide us. It will help us to understand how we process the information, the revelation, and the acceptance of His Truth in our lives. It will, without doubt, directly affect our very life and existence on this Earth leading into our eternity.

Let's go to the scriptures and see what the Word of the Lord brings to light and teaches us about the relationship, if there is any direct connection between the heart and the Mind, and if the heart and the Mind can team up to fulfill their desires, for or against their physical nature or their spiritual nature.

In Psalm 64: vs. 5-6, the scripture says: "They encourage each other in evil plans, they talk about hiding their snares," they say, "Who will see it? They plot injustice and speak. We have devised a perfect plan! "Surely the Human Mind and Heart are Cunning. The Word of God brings forth knowledge and understanding and tells us that there is a connection and relationship between the Mind and the heart.

In the Oxford dictionary's definition of "cunning, "the adjective means "Having or showing skills in achieving one's end by deceit or evasion.

"Then, in the Merriam-Webster dictionary's definition for the word "cunning," the adjective meaning goes further, "dexterous or crafty in the use of special resources like skills and knowledge or in attaining an end."

What comes into focus when we cover the ability of the heart and Mind in their properties and attributes of the power to deceit and manipulate their resources and information that they receive from either realm of manifestation, being a physical realm of existence or a spiritual realm of reality, is that the scriptures tell us about the first entity character having a cunning and a deceiver attribute, that was from the very beginning around humanity, to deceive, to doubt and to bring forth a separation and to put a divider between the Almighty Creator and His Creation, and we all know who he is. Genesis 3:1," Now the serpent was craftier (cunning) than any of the wild animals the Lord God had made."

This revelation is a compelling truth, and we need to understand that for the heart, the Mind, and the serpent, all three entities, to have the same ability to be cunning and crafty is so very dangerous as this kind of trait and exposure is the gateway and, the open the door to manipulation, deception, and infiltration of outside powerful forces of darkness and waives of winds that are bringing nothing else, only destructions for themselves and those around. For someone to be able with knowledge, or without knowledge and understanding about it, to deceive others, that person, that entity, is the prey to their deception first, then they will try to deceive others.

Just a thought for later subjects and argument points: was the serpent, that old deceiver, because of his strong cunningness and craftiness ability that he possessed as a trait of characteristics attributes, the reason for his own falling into its deception?

Before he deceived Eve in the Garden of Eden, had the serpent have been himself deceived due to its exposure and cunningness?

Let's read together one more passage from the scriptures, 1 Corinthians 11:3, "But I am afraid that just as the serpent's cunning deceived Eve, your minds may somehow be led astray from your sincere and pure devotion to Christ." Based on the Living Word of God, we covered the subject of the heart and mind relationship and the dangerous openings for deception they both possess based on their attributes and character traits, and that the heart and the Mind itself can fall prey to their very own internal fraud from within or the danger of being exposed to an outside deception due to their willingness to open themselves to praise, pride, and greed based on their ability and based on their received revelations.

Let's go forward and discover together if there is also a relationship and a connection between our Mind, our Consciousness, and our Spirit, and if yes, is this connection between the Spirit and the Mind a strong link like the connection between the Heart and the Mind, only processed at another higher level of manifestation and expression within their powerful mechanism established, for transferring their information and revelation to and from directly between our complete Consciousness and our Spirit?

Reading the Word of God, we can see a connection between our Spirit and our Mind, the majestic complex processor wired to disseminate the information and data received from various communication planes within the physical and the spiritual worlds.

In 1 Corinthians 2: verse 11, "For who knows a person's thoughts except their Spirit within them? It looks like the only entity that can penetrate the complexity of the Mind in all its levels of Consciousness and look deep inside the information and revelation that the Mind is processing daily, including its own generated thoughts, besides the thousands of ideas it's receiving daily, that find their way inside people's minds from the visible and invisible forces around them, is their very own Spirit.

Is our Spirit directly accessing the thoughts and the information with our minds to know and control our thoughts by bypassing the heart, or does the Spirit connect to our Consciousness using the same connection already established between the heart and the Mind?

The Spirit has direct access, and I will write about this powerful topic later. Still, we need to know that the Spirit can bypass the heart and have direct access to profound inner revelations and information, including the very active and expressed thoughts that are processed and released outward from within our Complete Consciousness.

Considering the human's heart cunningness and its power to deceive and mislead, if the Spirit connects with the heart before accessing the Mind's thoughts, the Spirit can also be fooled by the heart's very own nature, thus not being able to differentiate any longer if the revelation and the information, the thoughts that it is accessing within the Mind's functions, are released from the absolute Truth or a relative truth or even from a deceitful heart or an evil thought from within its foundation.

Let's protect ourselves against deception by submitting our minds, hearts, and spirits to the authority and Truth of the Word of God. I mentioned in the book the levels that exist in our Complete Consciousness and their powerful connections between our heart and Mind and between our Spirit and Mind to help us understand their strong living interconnectivity.

In the following few paragraphs, I would like to dive a little deeper into this topic and see if any other connections can directly affect our Complete Consciousness and if outside powers and forces, regardless of their purpose of influence and origins, are continually active and working within us. Does our heart send its desires and impulses and its live signal expressions to fulfill them at the level of our Self Consciousness within the functions of our Complete Consciousness? Does our Self-consciousness start implementing the active desires of the heart's fulfillment impulses when the Mind's information-capturing apparatus is receiving the waves of information and signals coming from the heart by trying to bypass the Spirit?

Does our Complete Consciousness it is the location and place of the battlefield, where both the Spirit and the heart are actively fighting to establish and claim their territorial influences to bring the implementation and the fulfillment of their agenda and their active expressions of their manifested desires from within?

One significant point I want to make before going further is that we do need to understand and take seriously the influences and the powers that are at war with each other and against our survival in this physical realm and the spiritual realm, which are both dimensions expressed in the body and the soul. So far, we have covered together the magnitude and complexity within our network of existence as living beings between our hearts, our Spirit, and our Consciousness, which is strongly activated and expressed at the level of the Body, the Mind, and the Soul.

Going further in a few more thoughts in this chapter, we want to explore the function and exposure of our comprehensive Mind, which is also able to process and disseminate the information and revelation received, not only from within our internal structure of purpose, but also from outside powers and forces and their influence, that can access the Mind directly, at any level within the frame of our complete Consciousness, being at the self-consciousness, or subconsciousness levels of its functions.

According to the scriptures, the Word of the Lord spoke and revealed to the prophet this powerful message in Jeremiah 31:33," This is the covenant I will make with the people of Israel after that time," declares the Lord." I will put my law In Their Minds and write it on their hearts. I will be their God, and they will be my people. Our Almighty God, the Creator of Heavens and Earth, the Majestic and Marvelous Master that formed with His own hands and shaped our existence and our complete Consciousness within the Mind,

He can tap into and access directly into what He created to release and reveal His laws of life for salvation.

God, in His grace and mercy, not only puts His laws in our minds but also writes them on our hearts so that we may be able to remember within our hearts what was installed and revealed into our minds. The Word of the Lord teaches us, and it brings us to the understanding that God has the authority and direct access to put His laws, information, and revelation inside our minds. One more short point about who can access the complexity and vast network structure of our minds directly or indirectly: let's look at one more scripture from the Word of God together.

Matthew 16:23," Jesus turned and said to Peter." Get behind me, Satan! You are a stumbling block to me: you do not have in mind the concerns of God, but merely human concerns."

Looking at the previous paragraphs' study, we covered this subject together, showing and revealing the unique complexity and networking power within the Mind. At all its levels of Complete Consciousness, the human Mind can receive information, revelation, and data, but using the power of thoughts to perceive them all within the ability to classify them accordingly within their very origins and forms from all their realms of existence that surround it; it has to be submitted entirely to the guidance and the protection that comes from the authority of the Word of God and in His Absolute Truth.

I pray that the anointing of the Holy Spirit and the revelation of His Word will help us to understand that at this robust level of information and trafficking of data that we, mere humans, are being exposed daily to receive, we need entirely to surrender and submit ourselves to the power of God that can and will indeed protect us, guide us and bless us on this Earth and forever into His eternity.

In Philippians 4:6-7, the scriptures bring forward a powerful and true statement, "Do not be anxious about anything, but in every situation, by prayer and petition, with thanksgiving, present your request to God." And the peace of God, which transcends all understanding, will guard your hearts and minds, in Christ Jesus."

Chapter Four:
Projective Truth

Isaiah 59:14:" Justice is turned back, and righteousness stands at a distance, for truth stumbles in the public square and uprightness cannot enter."

Now that we covered together a few chapters on the subject and topic of understanding the Truth, about unchangeable absolute Truth that is revealed by and from inside the Word of God, and the relative Truth that can be part of our life experiences, let's go forward on covering in the following few paragraphs the subject and topic of the projected truth subject, that many times takes priority in our life, exposing ourselves to our internal desires that take hold of our heart, that we may be able and try to influence people and even systems around us, by projecting and applying projective truths, based on our own belief, our thoughts, and our own experiences and testimonies, that takes part within, and even outside of our own life living experiences.

People will not be able to project and use projective thoughts using the absolute Truth as a foundation, as the Truth of God, the Word of God, is not subject to any relative truth that may become true, even if it pulled its relativity and existence from the absolute. In Matthew 24: 34-36, our Lord and Savior Jesus Christ said, "Heaven and Earth will pass away, by my words will never pass away."

The absolute Truth that is the Word of God has been

indeed revealed to our humanity in the person of Christ, the Logos of God, the Truth of God, and our relative projections will never be able to shake it, change it, or distorted, by our very human's thoughts and imaginations, that many times takes hold of our minds, using its executive power functions to bring forward their revelations, movements, and ideologies of constant change by projecting their humanistic and temporary truths even when they originated from the wellspring of God's absolute and unchangeable Truth.

But this is not the case of the relative truth that becomes true in people's lives due to their own experiences, manifestation, and revelations that once originated from the absolute, took a stronghold of their heart desires and pride for their very own self-edification and exaltation, by starting to pass around their teachings, rules, and regulation that have been all based on the results of their experiences and not based on the absolute truth's divine revelation and its source, thus using their projective reality to bring followers into their own living experiences and outcomes, based on their temporary trues, and not based on the absolute truth. I said temporary trues because trues are not by default ready to satisfy the whole truth's criteria, and even on a physical or even deep within the ever-evolutionary circles of today's humanitarian search for truth, our yesterday's authentic experiences, may not be realistic and an accurate true for today, and what to many people, movements, manifestation within the churches or outside the churches, and what may be ringing in their ears as an authentic and a realistic experience of today expressions, it may not be ringing authentic as a true expression of tomorrow's humans experiences.

The more we get the knowledge of a proper divine understanding to be able to process and make the difference between our relative truths and trues, the more we will be able to shield ourselves within the Word of God, that we may not be exposed to other people's relative solid truths and trues, that will deceive us and influence us, that we may turn away from the Truth of God, to be caught into their philosophical expression and ability to bring forth a temporary truth and an image of a God, not based on the True Living Word's revelation, but based on their very own humanistic interpretation of the Living Word, influenced by their very own understanding of who they think God is, based on their experiences.

After observing for years the patterns and the human reactions and interactions on many different platforms of operation systems of life's manifestation, being in business settings, religious settings, or any other activity settings, including denominational or non-denominational organizations, it is my sincere opinion, that the humanity fabric, has graved deep marks and channels into, and within its plane of existence, the desire to pull into their center of gravity and revolving action, the emotions, the reactions and the approvals of others, thus feeding on their impulses of expression and manifestation responses, their internal self-induced form of acceptance within their understanding and belief.

Many times, we are exposed to fall when people are asking us different questions regarding the Word of the Living God, and some questions may sound like this: "I was reading the Bible, and there was this verse, it caught my attention, can you tell me what you think about it?"

I want to illustrate an example of the dangerous and slippery opening channel when many are falling prey to their pride and their heart desires, taking the question in as an opportunity to elevate themselves up to a higher level of comprehensive interpretation thought within their own " self-ability," by trying to explain it without understanding it, and by doing that, they will start to project on others their very own thinking and their very own thoughts, and their interpretation and meaning of the Bible verse, which has been based on their own experiences or firm convictions rather than the Word of God.

I love this passage from the Bible that is revealed to us in Proverbs 3: 5-6," Trust in the Lord with all your heart, and lean not on your understanding; in all your ways submit to Him, and He will make your paths straight.

Based on what we just read together in the above paragraph, we need to acknowledge that we can be tempted and led, into involving our own understanding and thoughts, when processing within our own minds the information and the revelation that comes from the Word of God, and also from dreams, visions and prophecies, and exposing ourselves by explaining them and communicate them outward to others, by the means of projective methods, that may benefit temporary our own agenda, our own self personification, and the desire of controlling others, by pulling them into our own understanding of thought processing expressions, and by doing so, not realizing the dangerous opening that will trap people in a state of confusion, making them vulnerable to false movements, teachings and other forms of manifestation, away from the Truth and from the revelation of God and His Salvation, that is still available for those seeking and searching, for a true revelation that can and will feed their hunger and quench their thirst, in the name of our Lord and Savior Jesus Christ, the absolute Truth. We need to know that the deception and manipulation of spiritual forces originated and released from the pits of darkness in their waves of influence to corrupt and to keep humanity bound and chained in their grip of destruction, causing separation and death, even spiritual death, has no borders or limitations, that will limit their quest to influence and corrupt the Consciousness, the heart and the spirit, even of all of those that are today firm and deep grounded and planted into the Word of God's roots.

These are genuinely tough times we live in today as a society and community. We do see, and we are witnessing mighty winds of turbulent influenced manifestations within all realms of our existence, being them earthly or even heavenly realms, that are continually blowing all over the world, with new revelations, innovations, and new information that are trying to change the identity of humanity, even to change the things that are surrounding us, affecting the thinking and even trying to affect the worship and the entire core belief of humankind in the Almighty God. Returning to God's Living Word, we can read together what our Lord Jesus Christ prophesied by releasing this Truth to humanity.

Matthew 24 in verses 23-25." At that time, if anyone says to you,' Look, here is the Messiah!' or, there he is! 'Do not believe it. False messiahs and false prophets will appear and perform great signs and wonders to deceive, even the very few that are elect.

See, I have told you ahead of time. I pray that the power of God, the love of our Lord Jesus Christ, and the anointing of the Holy Spirit will keep us shielded and protected from any outside forces or influences that are trying to crawl inside our hearts and minds to deceive us, and forcing us to start believing in our self-ability to process and to interpret God's Word, and not by the power of His revelation, and not by the power of His Spirit of Truth. When we are using our ability to send and transmit for the reason to influence other people, the information processed by our internal thought mechanism, what is the safety module that will start blinking red signals when we begin applying our human input to a spiritual revelation, within our complete Consciousness, that at times may fall prey to its influence of hidden thoughts, and if there are any such safety modules build inside our Consciousness, how they are calibrated and connected in the Truth?

Are we trying to understand the spiritual revelation received from within the Word of God, processed by our logical thought process?

Who will benefit most if we speak the Word of God in Truth, unprocessed by our projective thoughts? Ourselves, or those around us who are exposed to receive and capture it within their minds, hearts, and souls? Making all these points emphasizes the opportunity that will arise in our life, and that will enable us to start to project the Truth received for our benefit and our self-personification, thus exposing our Consciousness to become corrupted in its desire to achieve a fulfillment of earthly positions and statues, admiration, and approvals from others and doing so disregarding the Truth and the revelation received from the Word of God. How often do we hear preachers and pastors telling others in small groups? I wish I could say this word in church on Sunday. Still, if I do, many will leave, others will judge, and others will stop giving tithes to the church, affecting my attendance and salary or even causing me to get fired.

Receiving the Truth from within the Word of God, then exchanging the Truth and the revelation received with a projected truth processed within the ability of their mind for financial security, a future at the pulpit, and the approval and admiration of others, in other words, exchanging the Truth of God for personal gain and self-elevation within the realm of a corrupt identification society, that becomes so detached from the absolute Truth, that even if the safety module build in its Consciousness sends red signals of warning, their self-motives and pride will bypass the sign.

They will continue to feed themselves with their affection for the things fueling their deepest desires to have control over the emotions and feelings of others.

The scriptures revealed the Word of God that Jesus Christ spoke in Matthew 23:13, "Woe to you, teachers of the law and Pharisees, you hypocrites! You shut the door of the kingdom of heaven in people's faces.

You do not enter in, nor will you let in those trying to." We live in these challenging times with so much pain and suffering.

People seek relief, comfort, and salvation from their brokenness and affliction. In their search for amelioration, humans are being all over the world exposed to false teachings and movements that are powered and influenced from the depths of darkness to keep them away from the Truth and from the salvation that comes only from God, and that has been revealed for all the humanity in the image of our Lord and Savior Jesus Christ, the Word, the Truth of the Almighty God. Looking at the projective truth's ability to mask itself under the pretext of an absolute truth reveals the power of the confusing spirit that crawls onto and upon those exposed to it.

The Word of God is guiding us to pray and to ask our Father God to receive the Spirit of Discernment so that we may be able to recognize and shield ourselves from the confusion and the winds of deception powers that are counterfeit to itself but also so close to the absolute Truth, that if not being grounded and firmly anchored into the foundation of the Truth ourselves, we will be prone to failure and error. To make another analogy on this subject of projective Truth that will only benefit the ones that practice projective manipulation for their own gain and recognition status, let's analyze this topic a little further.

The possibility of using my relative Truth, which can become a temporary truth to me, based on my experience and results of my life experiment on matters, then, for my benefit or my financial gain, I am projecting my temporary actual results to those around me, that are searching and looking for options to also have experiences in their life, or to improve their relationship with God for their salvation, that based on the Word of God, it is free and offered to all, by grace and mercy of the Almighty, made possible by the sacrifice of our Lord and Savior Jesus Christ, that humanity may be able to receive salvation and redemption, will significantly increase, if my self-personification starts to take shape into its own identity and brand, offering its touches and spinner interpretations, away from the Word of God and His Truth.

We are all quoting the scriptures when John testified about Jesus Christ. In John 3:29-30, "The bride belongs to the bridegroom. The friend who attends the bridegroom waits and listens to him and is joyful when he hears the bridegroom's voice.

That joy is mine, and it is now complete. He must become greater; I must become less."

The sad situation is that from the starting process point of quoting the scriptures and their Truth to power to the process point that will allow the scriptures to bring forth authentic life-transforming results within our hearts, minds, and souls, it is an undeniable gap that based on the events and based on their progressive agenda of today's living standards that are leading the Christians preachers, pastors, prophets, on the pathway of becoming a "self-identification brand and persona," in these deceptive times we all live in, it does look like that this vast and dangerous deep gap it is tough to be connected and bridged. John the Baptist, in his ministry times when he encountered and received the revelation of Jesus Christ, announced and declared that his joy had been made complete; when he heard the voice of the bridegroom, he understood that he must become less, so He, The Christ, the bridegroom must increase and must become more significant.

    How can we calibrate our mind consciousness in the Truth of God, which will enable us to realize and recognize the influences of the deceptions of the world, if our mindset is turned away from the Word of God and is continually feeding itself towards achievements that are being based on the world standard of living information, and their propaganda platforms of deception and manipulations, for their self-imposed status of being accepted and approved by others, to a higher standard of recognition as being revealer's and protectors of the Truth, while themselves and those that receive them, are ignoring the Word of God, for their own enticed benefit, and I used the word enticed because it is the reflection of the manipulation that produces a special kind of pride induced attitude, to attract followers into their circles of a projective truth, with no sense of remorse, for themselves or for those that are being caught up in their grip of power, influence, and deception.

    I am closing the chapter with this scripture paragraph from 2 Corinthians 4:2," Rather, we have renounced secret and shameful ways; we do not use deception, nor do we distort the word of God. On the contrary, by setting forth the Truth, we commend ourselves to everyone's conscience in the sight of God."

    I pray that the Holy Spirit will guide us to start a process to calibrate our Consciousness by setting our mind in the presence of God, and may His Truth be revealed by the power of His Living Word deep inside our very own souls and own hearts, that will protect us, against deceiving ourselves first, then deceiving all those that are being exposed to our very own influences and corrupt teachings.

Chapter Five:
Truth vs. Realities

Jude 1:12-13" These are blemishes on your love-feast, while they feast with you without fear, feeding themselves. They are waterless clouds carried by the winds; autumn trees without fruit, twice dead, uprooted; wild waves of the sea, casting up the foam of their shame; wandering stars, for whom the deepest darkness has been reserved forever."

In the future, covering this topic, we need to consider the subject that will help us to understand that in our own life and our search and pursuit of the Truth, we will encounter many teachings and influences in the name of powerful realities that will affect us and confuse us with their robust ideologies, that will try to entangle our minds and corrupt our consciousness with their very temporary facts and views, to keep us away from the Truth of God.

I am naming this chapter Truth vs. Realities because there is only one Absolute Truth. The Absolute Truth is not subject to any outside waves of influence. It stands on its very own expressed authority from before the first created existence that we know to be the Creation of the Heavens and the Earth, even long before there was a beginning. We cannot say so about our temporary humanistic realities that can constantly be exposed to change because our facts cannot and will not stand and exist by themselves without the power of our inner or external expressions and their influences molded and shaped by our surroundings. Moreover, by default, it did not mention the word, reality, because reality does not apply itself and is not subject to temporary facts.

Even if the realities are proven to have within themselves a temporary form of Truth in their short existence, they do not elevate themselves to the level of the Absolute Truth and the Oneness of the reality of the Truth.

Absolute Truth in its fundamental reality cannot and will not be influenced by any temporary facts and temporary trues that will stay activated in their existence until a change occurs in either realm of our physical matter or our spiritual body; then, by default, when change does occur within their factual environment then their temporary experiences and also their realities must also change to be able to accommodate themselves into the frames and templates of another brief experience and produced realities.

Trying to make this analogy to reflect the difference between reality and the realities, between the absolute Truth and all other truths that may be surrounding us by their philosophies, like relative truths, projected truths, and even sometimes alternative truths or lies, and to bring forward the information that makes us understand that the reality and the Truth, will never change and be influenced by realities, even if they are pulling forth their existence from the absolute Truth and its reality that are truly divine and unchangeable in their omniscient capability, the energy of life, the power of Creation, the expression of everything visible and invisible, being within the frames our own earthly surrounding or being within the boundaries of heavenly realms of God's divine firm power and manifestation.

The reason I want to cover this subject in more detail

is to bring forward the level of ignorance of the manipulative processes and applications used by those who are considering themselves and see and believe in their own eyes that they are the guardians of the Truth of God, but are neglecting the very notion and the very core foundation of the absolute Truth in its fundamental reality and its unlimited power, to bring forth its result and resolve, that it is not changing due to any outside influence, or third party manifestation or their expressions, but strictly in its divine nature and holiness, flowing down from within the source and nucleus of life, the Almighty God's very own eternity. Life as we know it today, or as we sometimes do not know it, came forth into existence from its true core and divine holiness source that has no beginning. Because of life's expression roots, the power of the absolute Truth and its absolute reality became imprinted into the hands of God and then released and revealed forward into the entire realms of Creation, that all expressions of life, regardless of their created shapes and forms from Heavens above and Earth below may be able to experience it and to be guided from the very beginning by God's very own expression fueled by His steadfast love and His everlasting power, and because of the magnitude of Almighty God's very own expressed manifestation, willpower, and desire for an actual proper function and order for the Heavens above and Earth below, every expression of life, every living spirit, and every living organism, nucleus, atoms, elements of energy powers, and all the blocks of life's DNA's expressed existence, are subjects to God's absolute Truth and to God's absolute reality.

Some of them, so-called "guardians of the truth," got so comfortable with their ability to maneuver their expressions for self-benefit in order to achieve the fulfillment of their desire for self-personification that are starting to project not only their very own relative truths that are being fueled and based on their temporary trues, but they go even further deeper inside their very own and corrupt consciousness and pull out from their dark pits, thoughts that are processed then brought forward, by their deep imaginations and offer and present them, to all of their followers as an alternative truth (lies), that are being wholly based and produced by their futile realms of imaginations and their fiction expression of their own internal though mechanism for processing various desires, to be able to achieve control and power over all of their followers, that live and exists within their firm grip of power now, or that may be held captives to their waves of influence and deception later.

The existence of these people in our present times who are practicing and using these techniques of manipulation, offering alternative truths that are "lies," is nothing new to humanity.

From the beginning of the Creation of the Heavens and the Earth, the spiritual powers of darkness offered their deception to influence and to deceit those exposed to the absolute Truth, to the Truth of the Almighty God. In the scriptures, the Word of God reveals the first case of an alternative truth or a lie released to humanity.

Let us go and read together the word in Genesis chapter 3, verse 4: "You will not surely die," the serpent said to the women. Here is the first example of an alternative truth, "lie," offered as Truth to humanity. Here, we can see the active power of deception and manipulation that started to work against humankind from the beginning of its existence.

The Almighty God, the Creator of all life, the source of all expressions of life, is releasing His Word, His Truth, the Word of God is Truth, to the first man created and formed, Adam, and He commands man and says, in Genesis chapter 2 and verses 16 and 17, "And the Lord God commanded the man, You are free to eat from every tree in the garden, but you must not eat from the tree of the knowledge of good and evil, for when you eat of it, you will surely die." Not discussing here the doubt, the entrance, and the opening statement that the serpent exposed the woman to; we will cover and discuss these expressions and manipulative techniques later in the book. I wanted to briefly make this point that when God speaks, He only speaks the Truth because He is the Truth. When the Almighty God released His Truth to the first humankind, Adam, He said, "For when you eat of its fruit, you will surely die," and there was no room for compromise.

That was the actual reality and the true Absolute Truth revealed to Adam, created as the first humankind by the power of God's spoken Word. Here comes the example of the first alternative Truth revealed by the serpent to the exposed and tempted women. "You will not surely die ." I wanted to be able to briefly bring forth this point for the later chapters when we dive deep into the deception and manipulation that are happening today all over the world, to suppress the Truth of God and to replace it with its alternative options, new revelations, and new expressions, that are manifested within their corrupt ideologies, to have control and dominion over others, regardless the many and various operation platforms where they are being actively implemented and exercised, being them, economic, political or religious atmospheres of existence.

Because the actual fight and war, that it is still very active on all fronts of the battlefield realms, that started from the very first opening salvo, when the deception and manipulation that was fueled by its own desires of pride, greed and to have its own control, made a declaration of war, against the absolute Truth and against the revelation of God, that started in the heavenly and spiritual territories of their own existence, and expanded into the physical and material parts of their own reality, is for controlling the destiny of the soul of humanity, I will discuss in more depth the manipulation and deception from a spiritual, and a religious view, praying that the peace, and love of God will protect us and keep us rooted into the Truth of God, to be able to discern and realize the times we are living today, are dangerous times, and the levels of manipulation and deception are on a very high ground level of its own manifestation, expressed on many different surrounding planes and dimensions of life, crawling even into the hearts and minds of those that are considered by many people, that are elect and are grounded into the Truth of God, but are opening themselves up to alternatives truths, and or other relatives truths, that are being projected into their own self-consciousness, not based on the absolute Truth of God, but based on their own lifestyle and standard of living.

Due to a self-imposed level and character of a strong personification attitude and acceptance by their surroundings of existence in life, instead of bringing their lifestyle and heart desires and checking it into, and against the parameters of the absolute Truth established by God, they are trying to bring down and dilute the Truth of God to fit their very own lifestyle templates for achievement and success in life.

Now we do know that the absolute Truth of God is not influenced or changed by any desires and expressions of our hearts and minds, and will never be altered or manipulated by outside winds and waves of new revelations, no matter how powerful they may blow throughout the Earth, thus making impossible the process of our thought mechanism system, to mold and to alter the absolute Truth of God, that may fit our lifestyle and manifestations that are arising from within our complete consciousness by exposing us to the deception and the corruption of our very own internal thought mechanism, that will then define us and will bring us on a new pathway of life, that will identify in itself as a prerogative ideology that will make us corrupt in our very own teachings, and that will lead us and our followers that are exposed to our false teachings, to believe that there is a pathway for self-salvation and self-edification, contrary and wholly opposed to the Word and the revelation of God that needs to be actively received in Truth. Because of the world's lifestyle and the world's atmosphere power and control, dealing with its very own spiritual high-temperature fever that is causing heavy spiritual migraines in the hearts and minds of the people that are trying for ages to alter and mold the Truth of God, into a template frame for life's standard living encapsulated by today's current social and cultural events, to be able to fit in, and to be in the sync so to speak with the world's expressions and with the world's manifestations that are daily surrounding all of us, we do need to ask God for the true gift of spiritual discernment, that we may be protected and shielded by the love and by the power of God in His Truth, away from any deceitful influences and approaches and their manipulative solid skills of the world's energy and control surrounding us.

    Here is a compelling message revealed by the Word of God, and this Word rings so powerfully today that it encapsulates the true power of the Word and the revelation of God that never changes. The spoken Truth for humans existed thousands of years ago. It is also the spoken Truth for all generations of our current and existing living times.

    Let us go together and read the scriptures and the Word revealed in Two Kings chapter 17, verse 15: " And reject His statues and The covenant that he made with their fathers, and His testimonies that He testified against them, and go after the vain thing, and become vain, and after the nations that are round about them, of whom Jehovah commanded them not to do like them." and verse 16 first part," And they forsake all the commands of Jehovah their God, and make them a molten image." (YLT*)

What strikes here in the above message of the scripture that we just read is the undeniable power of deception and its manipulative spirit that if it is left to operate unchecked and if it is not submitting to the absolute Truth of God, it will influence the deepest places of the heart's foundation to bring forth its desires by starting to process their thoughts and intentions, that will begin to produce within its chambers of pulse, the waves and the vibrations signal that will start taking shape and a form into building a molten image completely contrary of the commands and revelations received in Truth from God, strictly a product and an image released forward by its own mind's imagination and desire and then passing it around to other people as realities.

In the previous chapters I did mention the word phrase "False Truth", and the subject covered in this chapter brings forth its own action directives, when false truths become realities to people if they are deceived and influenced by their own power of their complete consciousness to create and to build complexed images and systems of manifestation within its own confused and corrupt realm of existence, where they will be able to express their own false teachings and narratives, contrary and opposed to the Truth of God, thus enable them to become their own realities when released from their own corrupt consciousness, to their outside surroundings and outside realms, using the communication and the expression of their realities thoughts to capture and to influence others that they may be brought in into their own circles of false realities operation, that are not going to bring salvation, only a delusion of a feeling good experience, based not on the Truth of God, but based on their own false realities.

Going back to the first example that we covered in the above paragraphs on this subject, when by the power of deception and the manipulation used against the first human, the serpent managed to shift away from the Truth of God when he passed as Truth to Eve, its altered Truth (Lie), right in the very presence of the Almighty God environment, created and designed with the intent of complete harmony between heavenly hosts and the rest of the entire Creation and its surroundings.

Based on this event that was presented to us, that it did happen right from the beginning of time, it warns us and makes us aware that the closer we are to living in the Truth revealed from God to us by the power of His Word, the more exposed we will be, to the powerful dark forces of deceptions and manipulations that will never cease or stop flowing, as long this world will survive in its structural existence allowed by God, with the intent to try to take us out from the presence of God, luring us into alternatives or lies offered to us, by tempting us to reject the Truth of God for a vain thing, that temporary may be pleasant to the eyes and may bring a fake good feeling about it, but as soon they can capture us it will reveal its original intent to control, overpower and destroy us and our relationship with our own Creator, that we ourselves will become vain in our own existence and purpose of life, and doing so, that we may slip away from the presence of the Truth of God, and to start living into a realm of destruction and death, not realizing that we became victims to deceptions and manipulation of our own expressed desires, emotions and feelings, making us to reject the Truth of God for a lie, that will become realities in our life and then we will expose it to those around us, our own facts based on our own emotions, feelings and experiences and what the desires of our hearts hold, disregarding the Truth of God.

Reading back and forth the Word of the Living God in regards to the messages of this event that took place in the presence and the dwelling of the Almighty God, I did realize that the serpent did not tell, ask, or force Eve to take any action and to do anything against her will, besides having a conversation routed deep into the foundation of its manipulative skills and cunningness that reached its goal to bring forth, Eve's very own desires and emotions from the depths of her own heart, that put her in a direct collision between her newfound and awakened desires and the spoken Truth of God, and in a direct clash between her new very own realities and the reality of spoken by God.

In the scriptures in Genesis chapter 3 and verse 6, the Bible says: "When the woman saw that the fruit of the tree was good for food and pleasing to the eye, and also desirable for gaining wisdom, she took and ate it ."Can our desires and the intent of our hearts expose us to our very own realities and our own experiences of life to a level of a solid corrupt self-consciousness that will enable us to walk on our very own path of destruction and separation from God and that the "good food we may eat it may poison us, and the good things pleasing to the eyes it may blind us, and the desire to become wise will make us fools"? The first short point I want to address is about the communication between God, who was walking in the cool of the day in the garden when He called on Adam, who was already hiding with Eve amid the trees in the garden. When God asked Adam what happened and if he ate from the tree that was forbidden to eat from, the man excused himself by blaming the woman that God put there in the garden to be with him and to be a helper to him and that she gave him to eat the forbidden fruit.

The second point I wanted to make was that God did not ask the woman if she ate, but asked her," What is this you have done?" and the woman blamed and pivoted the question towards the serpent, saying that the serpent deceived her, but based on the event that happened the sole decision to eat from the forbidden fruit was hers and hers alone that aroused from her internal heart desires, and that moment when she was exposed to the serpent's powerful manipulation and deceit.

The third point I want to address is that God did not ask the serpent" what you had done and went directly into the punishment curse by decreeing," Because you have done this," "Cursed are you above all livestock and wild animals! Moreover, you will be crawling on your belly and eating dust all the days of your life. Furthermore, said God, will put enmity between you and the woman, and between your offspring and the woman's offspring, he will crush your head, and you will strike his heel.

Here, we see that the serpent did not pivot or try to blame other influences or forces that he was exposed and opened to due to his craftiness and cunning abilities because there was no one to blame. Because of that, he had no excuse and no escape route when he took upon himself the authority to offer its alternative Truth that was a lie and its own expressed desires and realities by bypassing the Truth of God to feed a deceptive influence deep into Eve's very own heart that she may be able to awaken her very own heart desires and emotions based on false feelings produced by powerful and deceptive control expressions, that have been fueled into existence by the signals of temporary pleasure, of being in control of her very own actions and decisions, even if it caused a painful separation and punishment, deep sorrows and even death.

As I mentioned and covered in the previous chapters of this book, our very own hearts and minds have been deep-rooted inside the human core, within their very own frames and foundations that are holding on their structural blocks that same powerful craftiness and cunningness characteristic abilities as the serpent had in the garden of Eden, and if we expose ourselves to the influences and structures of the firm deceiving expressions and movements of the surroundings of this world, to be opened and tempted into starting to awaken our very own heart desires to achieve power and control at any cost, and by doing so disregarding the Truth of God, when we will be all held to account one day, there will be no one else we will be able to pivot or to blame too, for feeding our realities established and rooted into deceptive wellsprings of waters, that will never quench the thirst and never feed the hunger of the soul and the expressions of its spirit of life. We can see and also we can hear all around us the movements and the expressed manifestations, of many teachers and preachers and pastors that are being very agile in their ability that sprinted forward from the depths of their own heart craftiness and cunningness of their inner self, to be able to bring to people a message that is based, more on the foundation of their own desires for success and achievement of a dominative control over the people that are exposed to their messages, to keep them enslaved to their own made rules and their regulations and realities, that has nothing to do with the Truth of God, is just an approached and a mixer of the processed information released from an expressed driven agenda to deceit and to manipulate others, and in doing so they try to maximize their own power of a corrupt influence flow of self-ambitions and dreams, while trying and working hard to minimizing the power and the Truth and the influence of God, in their own life and in the lives of those around them, not realizing that their consciousness got perverted and manipulated in itself due to its own exposure to pride, greed and control, that has its own origin into the darkness and pits of a deceitful heart, supported by its own evil intent.

Does the unconsciousness has the influence and the power of producing its own thoughts, if is receiving information and data at its own level of operation mechanism, from the spiritual realms and other forces of dark influences, that will have an easy access to download it into an unconsciousness state of mind, allowing the production of deceptive seeds deep into the unconsciousness level, build into packets of complexed signals and movements of their own expressions, that will be then allowed, or forced to transfer its own influenced corrupt thoughts into the depths of the subconsciousness active level of its own complete consciousness system of data and information processor, that will then be picked up by the consciousness operational system from within, and doing so bypassing the safety functional module and logical comprehensive thought of action, without being able to discerned and to disseminate the originality of the corrupt influence thoughts, then sending and output data by starting to release their own influenced and deceived thoughts as realities, without realizing that their sources and their inputs were manipulated and installed in their unconsciousness by winds and deceptions of influence that are trying to contradict and oppose the reality and the Truth of the Almighty God.

Opening themselves up to express their own realities based on their own process thought established under the influence of a seeded doubt that was planted into their unconsciousness state of mind by the deceptive winds with manipulative skills, with the intent to corrupt and to alter the Truth of God, at the receiver's consciousness state of mind level, their unchecked and unbalanced expressions, will bring forward the error to release outside and outward to their surrounding their own information and their own realities, that were already processed and dressed as a produce of their own thought system that fell prey to a potent infused seed of doubt that was planted into their very own unprotected and their unconscious state of mind, and thus giving birth to myriads of various thoughts completely opposed and utterly contrary to the living Word of God, but in their own view and in their own sight of their comprehensive understanding of releasing their information, they do firmly believe that their realities are not altered in any ways, shapes or forms, and their very own temporary and expressed facts are as accurate and as good as the absolute Truth and the reality of God's own.

The Word of God released by the Prophet Isaiah brings to a living light a compelling statement that we do need to absorb deep inside our minds and our hearts with a severe intent that will help us to understand that our very own thought process system can produce its express thoughts from the very information received from any external and outside sources and any other inner forms from within own self sources that our very own minds are actively exposed to interact and communicate with on a daily bases, being their sources from a spiritual realm and expression or being their sources from a physical realm of manifestation, or from within their individualistic plans and dimensions of their existence.

Isaiah 55: 8-9 "For my thoughts are not your thoughts, neither are your ways my ways," declares the Lord." As the heavens are higher than the Earth, so are my ways higher than your ways, and my thoughts than your thoughts."

Furthermore, this is a prime example that our very inner thought process system mechanism can generate its very own active thoughts and then release them into existence based on the information and the data that it is being exposed in receiving signals from any outside sources or even in the processing activity of receiving information from their very own self-interact live streams as a result of their eyesight's and visions, established by the robust traffic information and receive data inside their inner core processor and systematic chambers, being capable and wired with the ability to produce and generate thoughts, that will be transmitted to the human consciousness state of mind level, to start the command control action of their application, by beginning to implement the realization and the realities of those active thoughts, as a result of their very own processing understanding and signals that can be actively produced by the power of their very own sense abilities of sight, sound, smell, taste, and touch.

Because of this very powerful thought system mechanism build inside our own consciousness to generate and to bring to life realities from within their each and own profound rooted experiences of manifest expressions that happened in our lives due to our humanistic own way to understand and perceive the influences and the signals that are transmitting, their own information inside our unconscious state of mind, that will be than picked up, transferred, and allocated into the operational system command in its consciousness, to minimize the error of thought manipulation due to its fundamental limitations of the originality of its revelation, we need to bring every thought that we are processing within our consciousnesses before releasing it to our outside surroundings, into the frame and the parameters established by the Word of God and His Truth, that will guard us against the danger of using our very own imaginative produced thought internally by our own exposed and influenced, and sometimes corrupt consciousness due to our capability to express it and to process it, through the internal senses and ability mechanism system, that can be easily affected and also infected by our own emotions and feelings, that it is based not on the Truth of God, but it is being based on the outside corrupt tunnel visions and impressions, a product that has its foundation build and anchored in the structure of its many different waves and winds of false teachings, that our humanity it is exposed to, and it is also on a daily base influenced and deceived by it.

How can we be protected and shielded within our own sense of functionality sight of the power of interpretation and translation of the data received as information from the different realms of influence, if we are not able to identify its sources and who planted the seeds of doubts, or sometimes already fully grown produces of the deceptive thoughts implanted deep, into the subconsciousness level that will come up at a later time to surface with the intent to influence us or even forcing us to move by acting to implement their desires, masked as signals of righteousness expression of a deep belief already established as own realities, that was based on a physical expressed own life experience, but completely opposite and utterly contrary to the absolute Truth and to the fundamental fact of God, that was released from the eternity and from the heavens above, safeguarded by the spiritual wisdom and the spiritual knowledge of the Creation, and given to humanity within the scope and the revelation by its own expressed manifestation that was fully encapsulated within the authority and within the power of His Word.

Because of these multiple levels of their establishments that are true in their realities but with entirely different views on the interpretation of the information and data received internally, the questions that are arising strongly and reasonable to ask is: If there is only one source that it has been revealed by the absolute Truth and the reality of the Almighty God and if the same revelation and authority of information apply to all humanity as a whole, why and what causes the powerful outward release of the one unchangeable absolute Truth, that it is sustained in its reality, once processed within the internal mental power of the one's consciousness, to be then released to our very surroundings on our different living levels of express manifestation, and their translation and their interpretations, to end up opposite and contrary to the data and to the information that it has been received initially under the power and control of the Truth and its potent revelation from within the authority of the Word of God?

The answer to this question comes across as the possibility of this false expressions and release interpretations from a consciousness state of mind, as being the end result of the multiple levels of the internal malfunction of the inner consciousness processors of information and data, that it is being influenced by its own networking and synergies connections that operates within its own frame of structure and existence as part of a complex and a complete consciousness system mechanism, that it is than being exposed to the hidden signals that are continually beeping corrupt information received into the unconsciousness level, or at the higher subconsciousness level, from the outside influences of deceiving powers that have access to the inner and most deeper levels of a complete consciousness, by bypassing the already established and normal route of how the consciousness is receiving information and data, to than be able to start the implementation of their thoughts by acting of fulfilling their own desires, without realizing that the absolute truth was suppressed by its own and one's consciousness as it was being received at the very entry level within the state of mind, that was exposed and already influenced by winds and powers of deceptions at their deepest levels of their own existence and expression and of their own manifestation that is exposed and visible and also accessed by darkness waves of rebellion against God, but invisible to us, and not controlled by our own ability to understand what motivates us and what moves us or even what guides us, in giving us the ability to be able to suppress the absolute truth of God, that after we are receiving His reality and His truth internally and also after His revelation being fully captured by our own internal senses, to start to release to our surroundings that are around us, including also to other people by affecting their own beliefs and thoughts, our own realities and then passing them as a reality of God, based on what may seem good in our own eyes, and what will make more sense to us, disregarding the fact that we were influenced and infected by the seeds of doubts and their sources of influences due to our own pride, that comes to life from the bottom of the hidden and corrupt files of the unguarded and unprotected platforms and their chambers of its operational thought system mechanism, that it is exposed to its own craftiness and cunningness of its mindset that was infected by the traditional and cultural manifestation of the expressed ideologies that were released from the realms of their spiritual existence, not based on the reality and the absolute truth of God, but based on their winds of deception whirlpools, battering the humanity for the control of its soul, from the beginning of time, creating and manipulating their lifestyle by a structure of a belief system, that will take away the reality and the truth of God, and replace it and exchange it with their own realities that will be in their own sight more easy and more able to conform to, based on own understanding of perceived interpretation of their senses of touch, sight, hearing, taste and smell, and considering that each one has the capability to process and to release its own thoughts, we do need to bring them all senses and submit them to the authority and to the reality of God and His Word that will guard and protect us against our own realities.

Chapter Six:
Truth vs. Thoughts

Isaiah 55:8-9" For my thoughts are not your thoughts, nor are your ways my ways, says the Lord. For as heavens are higher than the earth, so are my ways higher than your ways and my thoughts than your thoughts.

We embarked together on this journey of discovering the multiple levels of our internal ability and functions to start to produce, perceive, and project thoughts that will be then released to our outside surroundings based on our interpretations and translations of the received information and data from the multiple realms of their existence based on their dimensions of influence, being the material, physical, spiritual, and even biological platforms.

I finished the previous chapter of this book with the pledge and prayer that God will protect us and guard us within His reality and absolute truth against our realities that will put us on the wrong pathway of life if we do not submit them and their information that we are to receiving in, under the authority that comes by the revelation of God's expressed and living word and in its absolute truth.

In the future, in this chapter, we will cover the dangerous ability of our internal process mechanism system that can produce and bring forth thoughts to life. If these inner thoughts spring forward from within each and their very own place location and are established to create new ideas of life's expressions that are all designed and powered to interpret and translate the information received at their very own individual level of expression and perceptions of their understanding of who are their sources, and if these new revelatory ideas and their very own expressions of life are not being sincerely and genuinely submitted to the reality and the truth of God, under the genuine released power of knowledge and understanding of the Word of God's true revelation, it will negatively affect our pathway and our journey in this life and also the end destination of our souls which is the forever location of our eternal life.

We humans are a very complex, built creation. Our multidimensional apparatus can operate and adapt on many different planes of expressed manifestation within our existence of life because our maker and our designer, the Almighty God, installed inside our beings the capacity and capability to create and to bring forth from within our channels of direct connect communication skills, the results of our own processed thoughts regardless the sources of its information and their powers of influence and origins.

I believe that Adam, the first man created in the image and likeness of God, was the only creation within the heaven realm and the earthly realm, besides God Elohim, who created and formed him, to have the ability and capability to express his thoughts having the root of its influence received from the earthly realm, and to release and act on them forward into the heavenly kingdom, and also to be able to express thoughts having the root of its influence received from the angelic realm, and to release and act on them into the earthly realm, thus making the first man created, Adam, a potent and complexed being within the original purpose of its creation and expressed existence of manifestation, to act and to operate as a channel of direct connect communication between the heavenly and the earthly realms within their very own planes and dimensional platforms of the processed information and data released from their sources and establishments, with the authority to rule and have dominion over the earth by tapping into and accessing the knowledge and the instruction data, available in heavens and its sources, that also pulls their own existence from the information and data that flows continually, and this information and data, it has and it is being continuously released from within the flowing wellspring of God Elohim, directly establishing the heavens and the earth as the foundation upon He himself build the expressions of life and their entire existences as a valid and divine creation that it was, it is now, and it will be always sustained by the authority and the power of God's word and the power of its truth, as longer He will allow its creation to exist as we know it today in the creation's own different platforms of dimensional forms of their very own expressed manifestations of life in a continual movement on earth as an earthly expressed existences of life's dimensional plane, and in a constant expression in heavens as a heavenly expressed existences of life's dimensional plane encapsulated by their original purpose and intent.

    The sources of every energy plane of existence establish their footprints deep into the foundation of the building blocks of life in life's many different forms of forward-expressed manifestations and their movements that are rooted and anchored deep inside the spring of a flowing river of complex and uncontained magnitude energy of the creation that it is being continually released from within the central depths of the Almighty God's absolute truth and His majestic love to sustain in and to keep its creation and its existence active and in a full motion of express and manifest design and intent, that sprung forth from within the Creator's very own centralized energy nucleus and His will of eternal inner and everlasting desires, manifested and brought forward by the power of Logos, the absolute truth that powered into existence all the visible and invisible elements of creation, being the aspects of the formed elements of design in the earthly realms and all their expressed and manifested shapes and forms or being them elements of formed creation in the heavenly realms and their very own expressed and manifested shapes and forms.

Adam, the first man created in the image and likeness of God Jehovah, with the intent and the ability to be the channel of direct contact communication between the earthly creation of God and the heavenly creation of God, was empowered and allowed to produce and bring forward its action of thought understanding that was acknowledged and accepted by the Creator as a truth and as a reality for the ages that followed. Let's see what the Scripture says about this. Genesis 2:19:" And Jehovah God formed from the ground every beast of the field, and every fowl of the heavens, and bring in unto the man (Adam), to see what he (Adam) doth call it; and whatever the man calleth a living creature, that (is) its name. (YLT*).

God, the Creator of all, created the beast of the field (earth) and the fowls of heavens and brought them all before Adam that he will name them, and He wanted to see how Adam would call them. He allowed Adam to bring forth from the depths of his own bestowed and complex mechanism of the thought processability that was installed and created by God within and inside Adam's depths, in its originality and in its uncorrupted stage of expressed functions, to bring forward thoughts produced revelations by calling upon them names, that God then accepted, and because He took the terms and the words that Adam called ahead for each beast and each fowl, then, it means at that point of time, the man's thoughts were God's thoughts, because the source and the revelations of calling something new forward, as names, were not being influenced by any corrupted stages of existence and deceptions that later on, crawled into and took hold by manipulation and by deceit, the humankind, someone that was once pure and innocent, the man Adam the first creation, molded and formed in God Jehovah's image and likeness, as Adam was intended and created to be, a channel of active direct communication in the creation of the Almighty God, that will be able to have dominion, and to rule, and to exercise its very own power of revelation for active producing thoughts, that will bring forward platforms of expression in their manifested works and ideas, that at one point in time were accepted by the Creator as being pure and without the interference of the influences and manipulations, that later on appeared on all of the levels of the creation's stage landscaping, due to the corruption and the alteration that caused a virus of rebellion to be released into the depths of the humankind's self-consciousness, due to the exposure of their desires that they wanted to be able to fulfill by the ability of a craftiness and cunningness operational spirit that took over their dominion.

As I mentioned in the previous chapters of this book, the serpent being open and manipulated by the Satan, had the same ability as the human mind and as the human heart to be able to operate at a higher level of craftiness and cunningness expressions of their own works of the process thought mechanism, above and behind any other beings created or called into existence by Jehovah God, and equipped with more attitude and understanding of its own reality of life and their complexed designed, due to the close proximity and communication it had with the Creator, more than any other created beings in heavens or on earth, and were allowed to have and to activate within their depths, their own expressed form of manifested thought produced and brought forward into existences, from within their own consciousness to a living life's signals expressions, that in the beginning it was pleasant and accepted by God, because it was in an excellent operational and uncorrupted mode, free of outside influences or winds of deception.

He was designed and intended to be a ruler with an inherited dominion over all God's creation, no matter where their realms of operation and existence were allowed to be expressed and were all allowed to be manifested.

In order the capture as much possible information on the thought process mechanism application system evolved within the deepest root at the core and foundation of our complete consciousness stage, we need to understand what feeds into the hidden channeling chambers of the consciousness and if the sources feeding the information and its data, can expose, alter, influence and even manipulate the foundation of its own thought, that by the time the thought will come forward for expressing its revelation, at the innermost stage of the logical understanding of its consciousness level, to move on it and to activate it by its applications to act on it, by passing it to its surroundings and also to its own internal system of action process ability, as a thought that was to be believed that it originated in truth with no error, and thus considering to be a thought of God, but in the reality of its core foundation, it is nothing more than a thought that was influenced, manipulated and then infected with raw false data information received deep into its foundation chamber location of its operational functions, even before it was activated by the human body system processing ability, to came forward as a reality and as an truth of a thought, that will be implemented as a true revelation, considered and accepted that it was based and originated on the Word of God, but came forward as an active implemented thought in action, completely opposite to God's truth and its authority purpose, due to the exposure and error in its own ability to be open to deceit by the influences and powerful winds of rebellion, that have gained access within the deepest levels of human unconsciousness stages of its hidden expressions, thus creating an understanding of God's revelation received from above, but it is understood and processed from within their own foundation of application system, under its own cunningness power of ability, and also many times it is being understood through the influences and the manipulations of the powers from below, with an undercover access into the human direct complex channel of communication, with the plan and desire to interfere between the revelation received from the Word of God for humanity, thus causing a corrupt reaction and a confused response of our humanity self-desires, towards the Creator released information and data, due to the processing of His will and acceptance of His true revelation, under the suppressed waves of misunderstandings, and flows of misconceptions that are activated at the lowest and deepest chambers of the self-communication levels of our own human existence within the structure of our manifest and expressed capability functions, encapsulated into the definition and the authority of our own free will, a complexed systematic mechanism and a powerful force that is localized within our own complete consciousness operational and executive chamber, established to empowered and to bring forward into existence the action and the revelations of the innermost thoughts, regardless from where they originated or where they came into existence from, and if their sources were influenced or corrupted.

The reason I am emphasizing this point is to start looking into and studying the depth and the high realms of the unchecked influences that can affect our utmost and sacred ability that was gifted and implanted into the foundation of our executive branch authority location within our complete consciousness by the Almighty God, that it is the free will, in each one of us humans that we may be able to manifest it, and to express it, followed by the action and the impulses of our thoughts, that are produce of our biological senses, our physical surroundings, or our spiritual exposure, that is, establishing their levels of operation and influence by capturing into their waves and winds of powers the function of our entire humanity manifestation and humanity expression of life, regardless of their religious, political, or economic belief systems, building its core and its focal nucleus, as the center point of its existence, as the activator pulse processor, that without its signals and its output sensors of relying on the information and data received within its system, to its close surroundings and the receptor senses of its entire human body operational function mechanism, there will never be an active movement, expression, belief or even our existence as a society, as we know it today, at least at our level of understanding our design and complex perceived thought propulsion system within each and all of us, and its internal operational activator power and control it is holding.

    I like to bring forward this example released from the Word of God for a better understanding and a better view into the dangerous influences and powers of rebellion and destruction, fighting against the truth of the almighty God and also fighting against the people of God, using its power of deception under the scheme of a cunningness ability to gain access into the deepest chambers of humanity's internal system mechanism thought process, that is actively exposed to the outside winds and their infiltration, to release raw and unfiltered information and data, from different sources and their manifest realms of existence, by expression their desires to achieve a result by planting a seed of deception by manipulative means, into the deepest chambers of the unconsciousness foundation location, and then when it is picked up by the senses of the consciousness logical thinking application mechanism that can and will produce and bring forward thoughts, to be activated and sent on into the executive dimensional Mind's plane for implementation.

Let's go to the scriptures and see what the Word of God teaches us about this subject and the influences that can affect our thoughts. 1 Chronicles 21: 1-8 (HCSB) * Satan stood up against Israel and incited David to count the people of Israel. So, David said to Joab and the commanders of the troops," Go and count Israel from Beer-Sheba to Dan and bring a report to me so I can know their numbers."

Joab replied," May the Lord multiply the number of His people a hundred times! My lord the king, aren't they all my lord's servants? Why does my lord want to do this? Why should he bring guild over Israel?"   )" But he did not include Levi and Benjamin in the count because the king's command was detestable to him….7)" This command was also evil in God's sight, so He afflicted Israel."

When it comes to King David, the man of God, who experienced the power of God, the grace and the mercy of God, and His mighty Salvation and Revelation, it is my sincere belief that only a handful of people from the beginning of the ages that were living and breathing life on this earth's expressions have experienced the power encounters and the relationship that has been firmly established between the Almighty God and a mere mortal human. David's growth into the understanding of God's Word, received by the power of revelation and the love of God showed to him from when he was just a child, was at a level of trust that, as I mentioned above, only a few had the blessings to experience it in its truth. I am covering this powerful example to bring into evidence the bond, the relationship, and the connection that King David had with the Almighty God and the grace, mercy, and blessings that,

God had shown to David from his youth. Even though we can see from the passage of the Scripture we read above that the power of deception and the winds of influences of the forces fighting against the truth of God that there are real and active powers and principalities, and they can gain and have access, deposit their seed of manipulation and deceit, to affect and bring forward a negative outcome, by entering into the lowest levels of the unconsciousness chamber of operation stage, then when it is activated, it will be then picked up by the human's consciousness operation system and processed by using its logical thinking ability, by producing its own desired thoughts that it will be then followed by the action and the implementation that will create a dangerous and a destructive result.

When King David that he knew the Word of God, he knew the authority and the revelation of God, he knew what to do and what not to do under the strict instructions received from God, and considering that he had access to God's information, first hand so to speak when he called Joab and the commanders of the troops, ordering them to act and to implement his order, did he brought forth from the depths of his innermost consciousness operational mechanism system, a thought to life, that was processed in his logical ability that was understood and molded by the word of the Lord, an active idea to existence that was processed with his very own ability to understand his heart senses and desires, or brought a thought to reality, that has been planted into the depths chambers of his very own thought's foundation mechanism by Satan himself, to incite and to provoke God, that He may act against king David, and may act against the people of Israel, and punish them?

This example of King David teaches us and also cautions us that in our life's existence and the experience of its manifestation, we can be exposed to the fundamental dangerous influences of darkness that can tap deep into the lower levels of our thought's foundation-building blocks, without us knowing or realizing that their planted seeds of destruction are hidden inside our mechanism thoughts processor, to manipulate us and to deceive us by enabling us to produce and bring forth from within our consciousness complex systems, ideas that when activated and acted upon, will have a result entirely different from what was intended by God's word and His will in our lives, causing destruction, and many times pain and suffering, and even death.

I mentioned in the previous paragraphs the term and the power phrase "chambers of humanity's internal system mechanism thought processor." I want to elaborate a few moments in regards to our realistic ability that was designed, built, and activated in the innermost parts of our consciousness by our Creator to be able to pursue and to bring to fruition and to bring to life actions that are following the disseminated and processed information received internally, through the chambers of our internal system mechanism thought ability, after had obtained or after it was exposed to various information and other raw data. I also mentioned the hidden chamber locations that are genuinely in existence and are all encapsulated deep inside our very own built communication chamber channels, and just because they are hidden from us, this doesn't mean that they are hidden or cannot be accessed and interfered with, from many influences and powers that exists even outside of our realms of manifestations, that will want nothing more than to be able to control our humanistic senses, our creative abilities, and our very own beliefs.

Did King David, the man of God, when he acted and provoked the Almighty, to turn against him and the people of Israel by ordering Joab to count the people, did he know that Satan planted that thought and that desire into his hidden chambers that he later picked up on, and brought it up from the secret and unconsciousness chamber of his innermost depths? I am positive that if Satan was going to plant that seed of destruction into the active consciousness of David, using and tapping into the chambers of he's internal mechanism thought process system, revealing that he is the source of that information and that he has the desires to produce and bring the punishment of God, upon his life and his people, David knowing the word of God and having a heart after God's own heart, a declaration of the Lord about David, he was not going to act on a thought planted, deep into his inner system processing information, by Satan himself, that later on will be the cause of a devastating and a painful, destructive result.

This powerful example that was brought forward by the action and the implementation of a thought implanted into the lower chambers of the unconsciousness of King David by Satan himself reveals the vulnerability and the dangerous opening that exposes us, as humans, to powerful influences behind our self-control and logical ability, to process them and to identify them and their incoming sources of information blocks of revelation, that once penetrating the lower level of an unconscious mind, produces the desire of bringing forward into the consciousness operative system, thoughts, that are being manipulated by masking their point of origin and their authentic sources, and in the same time using its ability to influence humanity, by reaching its desires to bring a rupture into the direct communication system that God established between himself and its creation.

For humanity to protect itself against the daily nonstop attacks from the binding spiritual influences running wild upon the earth, that is, rebelling against God, by manipulating God's Creation into rejecting the truth and its original released intent for humanity's existence and expressions that have been established from the very beginning between the Almighty God and His Creation by the implementation of a purpose and expressed function of its divine and created order, the humans need to come to the understanding power and protection, that it is released inside the depths of humanity's complex consciousness system, by the will and the truth of God, in an unaltered and an uninfluenced state, and without any outside interferences that may try to affect or infect the direct communication channels established between humanity and God.

Knowing and coming to the understanding of reality, that the complex and powerful thought system of humanity structure, has the foundation of its processor build into the depths of the unconscious level of the complete mechanism block of the consciousness, that is the executive power for the action control and expressions, to pick them up and to bring those thoughts forward into the motion of existence, we need to have the desire, the search for, and the discernment module, activated and calibrated, by the will and by the Word of God, that will help us to navigate through the continues waves of information and influences, that we are exposed to daily, and comes against us with its desires to damage us, or for us and its desires to bless us, from the opposite and completely different powerful winds of realities or deceptions, from the outside surrounding and their realms of existence, and also from within our internal capability of producing a systematic thought or thoughts that will benefit us, or it will not help us, when we act on those thoughts to fulfill the desires and the plans, of their manipulative seed of existence, that was planted into the depths of our own nucleus platform that brings forward and activates our internal mechanism system processor, that is able to receive information and raw data, that is than analyzed and disseminated, based on our own feelings, our own emotions and our own desires.

One quick point I want to address in this paragraph is about the robust fundamental and original properties of our internal abilities and the powerful integration system between the feelings of the body, the emotions of the mind, and the heart's desires.

The synergy and networking links that keep us together into the original intent form of creation enable us to operate and to move about in our existence and manifest progress in the original intent form as longer we submit ourselves to the Will and the Living Word of our Creator, and that will help us to be able to bypass the powers and the influences, that from the beginning and starting point of our creation never stopped trying to influence and to change humanity status and its original intent form of manifestation and expression that has been bestowed on and upon the first man created, Adam, to be in the image and likeness of the Creator.

The original intent form of our creation and our existence was brought forward by the powerful and expressed love of our Creator, Jehovah God, that was revealed and released in Adam when He proposed and declared, let's make man in our very own image and likeness when it had been established and connected by a direct communication channel in a pure and divine relationship level, without any interferences from any other outside surrounding and other created forms of expressed elements of life, that sprung forward from the depths and from within the Creator of heavens and earth, the source of everything that moves and has life, and everything that is visible or invisible in heavenly realms and their expression form of existence, or on the earthly realm and its temporal expression form of existence.

In our daily living and activities, we tend to believe that everything that we push forward into the executive action module of our consciousness chambers, for the manifestation and implementation towards the fulfillment of our very own expressed desires, has to be started by the power of thoughts, that comes to life, inside of our inner core system, due to our very own understanding of perceiving the signals that we are exposed to, based on our way to interpret and to translate the feelings, the emotions and the desires of our frames and structures, that from the very first day a human comes alive into the earthly realm, until the day that human leaves this earthly realm to pass on through the threshold that leads into the eternity realm, it will always be activated and will permanently be wired ready to receive signals of information from outside or from within their very own power of influences and end desires.

The reason I want to cover this powerful point and its explanation, is to be able to express the reality, and the existence, of very real and powerful influences, that are already rooted into the inner core system of humanity, and those powers and their waves of effects that can be activated, into the lower chambers of our human thought producing system location, and when activated, they can mold an opinion, shape an idea, and create a vision, to influence the end result they are looking for, towards reaching their own fulfillment that exists within their own form of expression and manifestation, thus bypassing humanity's own feelings, emotions and desires of life, but in the same time using and manipulating humanity's own feelings, emotions and desires of life, and by doing so, society is exposed to acts and to actions, by bringing forward into the consciousness levels of executive powers, thoughts that were planned, and planted into the inner core system and into the foundation of its expression of life, long before even it was formed and long before was taking the shape of a thought as we know it to be, coming to life in the upper executive chambers, based on the information and raw data it was exposed to, without realizing that we are releasing thoughts through our humanity channels of expression to life, that are not our own built and processed thoughts, and we released those thoughts to our surrounding as they are our own, because our own feelings, emotions, and desires that were manipulated and influenced at the inner lower levels and into the depths and foundation of our system processor that is fueling the manifestation, and the operation and the expression prints of life, that from the beginning of its existence never stop fueling its desires for own control and own power, away from, and many times against the design and the purpose that have been created and deep seeded in the humanity behavior by its own Creator and God.

To be able to understand, at least at a minimum, the differences of the opposite waves of information that could be captivated into the inner lower levels of our very own systematic thought process foundation and its mechanism system, we need to be able to receive help and allow to be enlightened, by the power of the living Word of God, that will help us to a certain degree, to be able to distinguish between and discern between the many sources and powers and influences that never stop trying to use humanity's very own ability to create and to bring forth thoughts to action, for their own end goal pursues of their result that will be than manifested into the earthly realm, knowing that without humanity's ability to produce and act on their thoughts and under their deceit and influence, these powerful dark forces will not be able to be transferred from their very spiritual forms and realms of their existence into earthly forms and domains of their search of manifested presence.

In closing of this chapter, Truth versus Thought, I am praying that the will and the purpose of our Lord God Almighty will help us and guide us and cover us with His protection power that we may be able to realize, that in our pathway of life and in its journey of existence, we humanity, will be exposed to opportunities that will come to influence and to manipulate us with all kind of sources of influences, and also all kind of spiritual powers from outside of our own realm of express existence, and also from within our own sphere of express existence, and both express realms of their spiritual and their physical presence can, and have the power to, connect and to seed their influences and their desires, in the same time and at the exact moment, into the lower chambers of our foundation of our complex thought mechanism system, that will then be activated and expose, to start producing many creative thoughts that later will be send and activated into the upper chamber of the executive level of humanity's conscious for implementation towards the fulfillment and achievement of their own desires.

To be able to understand the thought subject and its purpose in life, we do need the gift of humbleness to come before our Creator, the Highest God, the Creator of heaven and earth, and everything in the heavens and everything on earth, and pray that He will enable us by the power of His Spirit to be able to receive knowledge and understanding that will keep us safe and will allow us to discern when we are exposed to the forces of the spiritual or the powers of the physical realms and their released information and raw data into the very depths of our very own consciousness or unconsciousness levels within the parameters of our very own complete consciousness mechanism systems.

The Living Word of God will help us and will guide us on the pathway and on the journey of life that we are embarked on if we will call upon His name and if we genuinely acknowledge His guidance, if we will start searching and seeking His will and His precepts for us and our life, with a sincere and a willing heart and with a renewed mind by the power of His Spirit, that today still transforms and still helps humanity and its existence.

1 Chronicles 28:9

"And thou, Solomon, my son, know the God of thy father, and serve Him with a perfect heart, and with a willing mind, for all hearts is Jehovah seeking, and every imagination of the thoughts and He understands it; if thou dost seek Him, He is found of thee, and if thou dost forsake Him, He cast thee off forever. (YLT)

He, Jehovah God, understands every power of human imagination and the power of every thought produced by the very human mind.

And He can and will help us humans know all the relevant sources and all their firm influences that are tapping into our very own thought process mechanism systems if we will sincerely submit ourselves to Him who has the power, the grace, and the mercy to protect and to guide us, and to lead us in our pathway of life and in the temporary express journey of our existence to be able to start producing and act on the thoughts that are being grounded, seeded in rooted into our inner beings core foundation by the Spirit of God and his Living Word.

Chapter Seven:
Shifting Shadows

Romans 1:22-23" Claiming to be wise, they became fools; and they exchanged the glory of the immortal God for images resembling a mortal human being or birds or four-footed animals or reptiles."

Along the passages of the previous chapters, we covered in some details and extends, the real and the dangerous paths, that we are continually exposed to, and are influenced to walk on them and on their own made signals and signs along its streets, to bring humanity, the guidance and the assistance, established by their own point of origin as an alternative and or as projected trues, that once they will be able to take the shape and the frame and the structure of an alternative existence, will try to replace and to alter the Truth of God, and it will be able to position itself under an alternative and fake projection of a self-made image of a light created and sophistically used to release and project its light, before its own subjects, that will be then able to reflect its own shadow on humanity realm of existence and purpose, with the desire to control and to have power over the creation of God, that was from the beginning established and brought into existence by the power of the Word of God the Logos, the true spoken expression of God's love in Heavens and also confirmed by the power of the Word of God, the Logos, the true vocal manifestation of God's love on the Earth for its inhabitants regardless of their forms of life and ways of their expressions and manifest existences, that covers all shapes and forms of life's living and breathing created entities from the humankind race, to plants, trees, animals, birds, and everything else that moves and breaths their very existences from the wellspring of God.

The Absolute Truth of God will never be moved, and any outside push of interference will never change it and will never influence its divine existence because God does not change; his Truth and Word will not change, and because He is Eternal without a beginning and with no end, the Truth, the Absolute Truth of God, also it has no beginning, it will always exist, and it will never end.

Let's go for a moment and read together a passage from the Word of God brought forward by the apostle James in his writings.

James 1:16-18" Be not led astray, my brethren beloved; Every good giving and every perfect gift is from above, coming down from the Father of the Lights, with whom is no variation, or Shadow of Turning; having counseled, He did beget us with a Word of Truth, for our being to be a particular first fruit of His creation. (YLT*)

Some translations mention the phrases: "who does not change like Shifting Shadows" and:" to give us birth through the Word of Truth.

The sad part is, that a vast majority of humanity in its actual existence and expression of its own life's desires, what was at first once a beautiful creation of God, that was brought into a divine presence, as in the image and the likeness of God, that was birthed by the love of God through the Word of Truth, is living under the curse of deception and the manipulation of the power of darkness and its influence, that has the ability and the power to surround all that are opening themselves up to exchange the

Word of Truth of God with any alternatives and or any projected trues that will originate their influences, from a different point and a different source, that continually its changing its origin and its foundation, bringing forward shadows and shapes formed by their own made substitute lights, that will always continue to change and to move and to turn, with the purpose to keep up humanity busy, continually looking for, and searching for, the next big thing, the next big revelation, the next significant movement, that they will be able somehow, and to some levels and some degrees, to bring forward and to release upon humanity, its own revelation and its own light, that is masking its own source and its own end desires, with the promises to satisfy their hunger and quince their thirst, that it is and will always be rooted deep into the Soul of humanity and in their search for enlightenment, and for an eternal result, but in truth, it will never be able to fully satisfy it, because their temporary shifting shadows and their temporary revelations that bring forth temporary manifestation and express emotions based on their temporary feelings will never be able to complete and to fulfill a desire and a search that came forward, by being rooted into the humanity's Soul an expressions from the beginning of times, when it was founded, created and also sourced in the eternity.

Considering that something and anything temporary cannot satisfy and cannot fulfill the eternal desires and voids and emptiness that are alive and awake in the depths of our Souls, we have to be made aware that the influences and the powers that are arising against us, and in doing so, to influence us, trying to fill in and bridge the gap between the spiritual realm and the physical realm with substitutes and also impressions of their manifest revelations, that can be very real at times and will stop at nothing if given the opportunity and the access into the lower levels of our complete consciousness system processor, to use us and our existence received from our Creator and the Highest God, as paws for their very own rebellion and their disobedience against the Almighty.

The reason I am making this point is to bring forward and in focus, the dangerous pathway and journey of life we are embark to walk on, when there will be opportunities and influences that will offer us their answers and their guidance towards the eternity and towards the salvation for our Soul, by masking their original sources of deception and manipulation by releasing and by bringing forward a temporary light on our pathway of life, that will shine upon its subjects, and upon those accepting it as a revelation light, causing the reflection and the projection forward of shadows, that will always turn, and will always move, producing waves of many different variations, to be able to keep up with a constantly shifting and a continually changing world, that is surrounded and encapsulated by its own temporary existence and time, and its short lived desires, by trying to satisfy their hunger and their thirst that will never stop burning deep inside its Soul, that is confined by the physical barrier and contained to a physical realm and plain of its existence, with a substitute and a temporary enlighten that can be formed, manifested and expressed in the flesh and its physical body, but without being able and will be never be able to satisfied the Soul and its spiritual body.

But this does not stop the manipulation, and they continue to be the shifting shadows of potent influences of darkness that are using their powers to pass their schemes and their artificial lighting on humans, thus causing severe damage to humanity's expression of life and its belief system, by forcing them to shift with knowledge, or without knowledge and understanding, towards the false teachings and their false revelations coming forward from their reflected shadows, causing them to act and believe that a prosperous physical and a temporary stage of existence, by default, will be passed into and as a triumphant and eternal spiritual stage of its Soul and its living reality.

Let's go together and read the words that our Lord and Savior Jesus Christ had spoken to His disciples when they were with Him by revealing them the Word of Truth and His actual teachings for life, and for salvation, in regards our physical realm and its form of existence, and in regards our spiritual realm and its state of existence, that will help us also to meditate and will help us to be able to resist the influences and the powers and waves of destruction, that will bring upon us its confusion and its error, by making us to build a false structure and a false belief system deep into our very own soul foundation and its movement of expression, that if our flesh and its physical form of existence is satisfied by its achievements and results of a temporary life goals, by default the flesh's fleeting desires and its temporary satisfaction and purpose achievements and its element status, will automatically be moved, shifted and transferred into a, and passing by, as a satisfaction and goal achievements of and for the Soul and its eternal divine desires, and without the power to discern and to distinct that the physical realm of our existence and the spiritual realm of our reality are two different and two very opposite realms, we will be prone to error, and this was not the case in the beginning as a default, and it was not the case in its original stage of creation as it was not intended to be separated, but became separated due to the corruption and its powerful influences of deception that arose from within the wellsprings of two completely different desires having completely two distinct goals for their living existence and expression of their own manifested activity and search for fulfillment, and the only way to have them both engage with each other once again into a synergy and a divine networking form of expressions, it will be made possible only if both living expressions the physical and the spiritual are sincerely submitted to the power of the Living Word of God and His Absolute Truth.

Luke 12:15-21" And He said to them, "Take heed, and beware of all covetousness; for a man's life does not consist in the abundance of his possessions. "And he told them a parable, saying," The land of a rich man brought forth plentifully; and he thought to himself, 'What shall I do, for I have nowhere to store the crops?' And he said," I will do this: I will pull down my barns and build larger ones, and there I will store all my grain and my goods. And I will say to my Soul, you have ample goods laid up for many years; take you to ease, eat, drink, and be merry.

But God said to him, 'Fool! Tonight, your Soul, it is required from you, and the things you have prepared, whose will they be?

Reading the first words of the parable spoken by our Lord and Savior Jesus Christ, we get an understanding and clarity about an accurate definition of life and its purpose of existence, that our life is part and molded in a physical realm of its express movement. Also, it is pulling its energy and focal purpose from a spiritual realm that will guide it and lead it to a higher level of understanding, meaning towards its achievements and end desires.

To be able to comprehend and understand what life is, and what can complete its purpose and its expressing existence and movement, we do need to come to the Word of the living God for the instruction that was revealed by the power of its Spirit and by the words of our Lord and Savior Jesus Christ, by bringing forward the information released into humanity's express movement to shape its behavior, in the knowledge and understanding of what life isn't.

As an example of words and phrases, before we discuss

this powerful topic in this chapter, Shifting Shadows, let's meditate together in the following paragraph's words.

To be able to receive the understanding and the discernment that will help us build deep inside our mechanism thought process system and its foundation, the wisdom and the knowledge of understanding life and its purpose of existence on a temporary journey while aspiring and searching for a fulfillment that is rooted in the eternity and its desires for an everlasting transformation through the enlightenment of the Soul, and its salvation and redemption, we need to come to the source and to the revelation that only the Word of the living God can bring forth.

Suppose we are willing to receive instructions and the revelations from heaven above to teach and help us along the pathway journey of our life's expressions. In that case, we can reach and grow into a positive understanding and maturity. The understanding stages of life and its purpose fueled and sprinted forward from the Word of God; it will help us to start to perceive and look at our life and our lives surroundings through an entirely new perspective and understanding of who we are and why we are here, and how long we will be here, on this temporary journey of life and its expression, while we are constantly searching the meaning and the foundation of an eternal and everlasting existence that is rooted and anchored into the depths of our Souls, yet that is still contained and encapsulated by our physical and temporary realms and forms of this earth, its powers, and its robust influences.

The three big W's questions: Who are we in this physical realm of existence? Why are we here in this physical realm of reality? How long will this physical realm of existence last for us?

Searching for answers that will enable us to get a glimpse of what life is and who we are, those answers are what fuels our living life, and if we understand them, it will guide us towards the reality and truth that only comes from the Absolute Truth's foundation that established life and all its forms of existence regardless of their forms and expressions.

To realize and understand what life is, we must focus and learn what life is not. To recognize and understand what life consists of, we need to focus and know what life consists of not. And to understand what humanity is, we need to focus and learn what our humanity classification is not.

The reason I am addressing this point is to bring forward the teaching and the instruction that comes from the Word of God, revealed to humanity by other than the Lord Jesus Christ the Word of God, the Logos, the spoken expression of the Almighty God, through which everything came into existence as an expression of life and its movement and its formation.

He addresses the disciples by teaching them about the foundation of life, in our way of formed expression, movement, and action by revealing to them what life is not, and what life consists of not, by saying first and foremost the warning:" Take heed and beware of all covetousness; For a man's life does not consist in the abundance of his possessions. Humanity has shifted this teaching over the years. During the millennial ages, people's very own lights and desires caused the reflection and shadows of powerful influences and manipulative actions, enabling them to achieve power and control over other people based on the abundance of their very own possessions to achieve a desired status no matter the cost due to their very own powerful corrupt intention and corrupt desires.

If life does not consist in the abundance of someone's or anyone's possessions, regardless of what the form and express manifestations of that possession that is being manifested are, being that a material possession or being that a physical possession, or even being a spiritual possession, what do our own life and existence on this earth consist of?

Reading forward into the parable that Jesus Christ spoke of in the first part of the story right after the warning and caution that He released to the people that were following Him and listened to His teaching, we can, to a certain degree of understanding to comprehend and made to believe that there is nothing out of ordinary and nothing is wrong with the actions that this rich man took, and by doing so, this is what life and its journey on this earth it is all about, from the time we come into existence to the time of leaving this physical and mortal realm of reality, part of the actions of who we are, and part of the actions of what we do, to establish ourselves a foundation and a structure that will sustain us and our temporary existence on this earthly realm, until we expire it.

I mentioned previously in one of my sermons that we, as humanity, from the very first time and from the very first moment we are taking in our first breath of life on this earthly and mortal physical realm, are bounded by our birth, by our growth, by our desires, by our planning, by our actions, by our achievements and by our death that will culminate our existence and our passing through this life and its journey, searching for an eternal stop but being bound and exposed to a temporary physical and mortal stage, on the pathway towards our final destination and forever dwelling place.

If this is what bounds us as humans living on this physical and our mortal stages as part of our temporary existence, and if we are bound by these stages and levels of our life's forms and expressions that are manifested into its growth, desires, planning, action, and achievements, and bounded by anything else that may happen and takes shape and a form and a structure in our life, from the moment of our birth into this earth until the moment we leave this earth, what are the stages of energy that can influence us, what is the level of our understanding that can deceive us, and why is there a warning from the Master, making us aware of taking heed and of being mindful that someone's life does not consist in the abundance of his possessions when this is what life it is all about right?

From the very first time when humans came into existence in this physical and mortal realm, humanity's daily struggles and fights for their very own survival have been deeply enclosed within their temporary phase of existence, defined by passing through a time-bound and controlled stage of expression and the manifestation of how they understand life, by bringing forward their own actions and forms and describes them as norms, in their own comprehending of what consist life of it, and in doing so they are exposing and opening themselves up to very powerful shifting shadows of deceptions, that will keep them grounded into an mislead belief system, thinking and assuming that their temporary achievements and fulfillments of their own brief life's goals and desires will be added by default and transferred automatically into the internal and eternity desires and fulfillment of the Spirit and its Soul, that will never be and cannot be satisfied or fulfilled by the actions and achievements of the flesh and the flesh's temporary actions and impressions of it, no matter how much, and no matter how intense the manipulative schemes of the dark powers and their influences will try to convince humanity's Soul, to exchange its internal Soul's search of its eternal desires and its spiritual fulfillment, with a temporary achievement of a standard life journey and its own classified definition of success and achievements, based on what may seems good and what may make sense in its own control ability of understanding it, while and in the same time being mis-guided, by being chained by its own self impressions and manifestation into the stages of its life classification and status in what may be seen and deemed as a life's success and as a life's purpose for its existence.

As I mentioned in the paragraphs above, if this is what life is all about, and if we exist in this physical temporary and mortal stage of an impression of life's designation, fueled by the life's expression and its manifestation into a realization and its achievement that is culminated in what may be established and classified as a human success, that will be than by default transferred and implemented, as a stepping stone towards an elevate eternity for their followers in their search for enlightenment and fulfillment, then why our Lord and Savior Jesus Christ brought forth the teaching and the warning cautioning us to take heed and to be careful that we may not be deceived into believing that life may consist in its possessions and its ability to produce them, thus bypassing every so seemed normality of an established life and its purpose as we may all try to implement and to live by its indeed revealed actions and works from the very first day we were born into it?

It may mean, then, that our purpose and our existence in this temporary and mortal realm of a physical expression and manifest action towards understanding life and what life truly is all about has to be understood and has to be connected at the core of its spiritual pulsation of its end desires and fulfillment of its search for eternity, by the revelation that comes forward by the power of the truth of the Almighty God, using the connection and the guidance of the Spirit of the Living God, that will help us humans in the temporary journey of our existence to bypass the influences of our mortal desires, that is reflecting its power for control over life, with its impact and ability to disguise itself in its temporary achievements of life behind its possessions and its characteristic attributes and functions.

By doing so, it is using its shadows that come forward into the humanity-influenced and corrupt understanding of its purpose and its life's desires from a continued substitute and manipulative light that comes and emanates forward from various and different locations without an original created foundation, constantly shifting and always moving, causing people not to be able to identify their sources and their influences correctly while being exposed to their waves of raw information and data released upon humanity by bypassing the foundation and the location of the truth of God that will never move and that will never change its source and its original location and its foundation, that was established by the Almighty God when He brought forward from within Himself, all the existence of life forms, all the expressions of life's conditions, and all the movement of life's forms, regardless where they are placed by God in the Order of His Creation, that they may be able to live it and to manifest it, by expressing their very own existence fueled by God's unchanged truth.

Because of humanity's ability to express their own manifestation of its life form in the order of creation, and because their build in operational system for survival and adoption, that was designed by God himself and gifted to all the life forms that we may know of, or life forms that we do not know yet that they may exist around us, because we are limited and we are contained into a realm of a physical and mortal reality, where we are planted and where we are allow to express ourselves within its borders of established laws by the Creator, until our expiration from it, due to the date of our transplantation that will happen sooner or later because of the process of transformation from this very temporary life's form expressions that no one will escape from it, and no one will be able to bypass it, into the another realm life form of existence that it is planted and rooted into the eternity, and sprinted further by its revelation, from its divine and its complete source of movement and presence from the Almighty God, that holds all dimensions and planes of manifest life in existence, know or unknown to us, in Himself, but humanity from the beginning of ages, wanted to bypass the truth of God and His order already established in the creation and by doing so to start acting on its own fueled desires and achievements, towards establishing themselves, due to their survival skills and ability that were gifted in breathed into them by God the Creator, as a form of expression and the manifestation of life existence, that they will benefit of, and that they may be able to, and will achieve the transplantation from a mortal stage of its physical realm of existence, into the eternal and its eternity realm of life form and its existence, by bypassing the process established by the laws and rules of its transformation and its requirements, that was revealed and brought forward by the Word of God and by His Absolute Truth.

    When God installed into the deepest parts of the structure of the Soul, the desire of its manifest express eternity that it was rooted and planted into it, and the desire to spend and live its existence in the presence of its Creator, also installed in the roots of the Soul and in its deep structural foundation, the blueprint and the instruction that came forward and were revealed by the power of His Word, to show and to help the first man created Adam, how to remain and how to live in the active manifestation of its existence and its expression's begotten life, into its Maker and its Creator's presence and its everlasting living light, but also to show and to instruct and to help its existence that is propelled and fueled by its eternal existence and desires, to be able to find its way back into the presence and the living light of its Maker and its God, if he will default or will fall away, from its Creator's active presence and its everlasting living light, by being cast and sent out into the darkness and into the sea of deep sorrows, riding the waves of eternal regrets, due to the influenced powers of deception that can take control over when will be exposed to, tempted, and or tested with, or even being cast away due to its very own grown actions and expressed revelations, that came forward from within own self inner foundation, due to its very own abilities, but then it started to take shapes and forms due to the mighty and emotional stages of its express existence and manifest behavior, by producing and birthing its very own self desires for power and control, over or above or behind, of what was allowed to express and to control, or permitted to manifest and have dominion over it.

Let's go together and read a few passages from the Word of the Living God, the scriptures from Deuteronomy 30:10-14" If you obey the voice of the Lord your God, to keep his commandments and his statutes which are writing in this book of law, if you turn to the Lord your God with all your heart and with all your Soul." This commandment I command you this day is easy for you, and it is far off. "It is not in heaven that you should say,' Who will go up for us to heaven, and bring it to us, that we may hear it and do it?' Neither it is behind the sea that you should say,' Who will go over the sea for us, and bring it to us, that we may hear it and do it?

But the Word is very near you; it is in your mouth and heart, so you can do it. See, I have set before you this day, Life and Good, Death and Evil." (RSV*)

These are compelling words revealed by the Almighty God to its people after He delivered them from the hands of the enemies. Here, we can see a pattern of God's grace and mercy that was revealed by God's everlasting love for His people on earth, following the exact instructions and the same protocols established and originated in the fabric of the heavens when the actual teachings of the commandments were brought forward and revealed to the first man in creation, Adam.

What comes as a striking and decisive revelation of God's truth and its everlasting love for His creation is that He does not change, He does not move, and in Himself is not any variation or any shifting shadows, as the way Apostle James writes in the scriptures.

In James 1:18," Of His own will, he brought us forth by The Word of Truth." (RSV*), and this is the same revelation, it is the same truth and they are the same instructions, that were established and were originated from the beginning of time, that were given to His established creation in the original stage of Adam's existence, from the very beginning of the millennial ages, when its existence was activated and it was manifested, as the creation of God in an uncorrupted stage of expressed existence in heavens above, and also it is the same revelation, it is the same truth, and they are the same instructions, that are given to His established creation in the image of the fallen Adam's existence, that it is now activated and it is manifested, as the creation of God in its very corruptible stage of its expressed existence on the earth below, due to the acts of its disobedience and the acts of its very rebellion against its Creator and He's commandments, and now, even now in this very present age, the fallen Adam's existence it is being continually moved and shifted, it is being continually harassed and manipulated, by the dark influences and rebellion waves that are rooted into the depths of darkness, fighting against the living light, holding the fallen Adam hostage to its very own influenced stage of its fueled desires and its own manifest fulfillment goals, that it may be able to remain in the perpetuity, on the same stage and on the same field of its expressed form of corruption and disobedience, by the very powerful and by the very dangerous influences and waves of deception, that are running across the face of the earth in a nonstop assault against God's creation, that they will may be able to keep the fallen Soul captured, away from the truth of God, to keep the fallen Soul, away from the Word of God, and to keep the fallen Soul, away from the instructions and the guidance of God's love, that were installed and deposited in the very fabric of the structural foundation of the Soul's salvation and restoration mechanism system, that it is actively expressing its search for eternity, and it is very actively expressing its desires for everlasting life, hoping for and dreaming for, that it may be one day transformed, completely liberated and transplanted successfully, back into the heavenly realms of its original form and expressed existence, that once the Soul experienced, to be refreshed and restored into the very sound and the very presence of its Maker and Creator, its Father and Almighty God forever and ever again.

  Going back to the parable spoken by our Lord and Savior Jesus Christ in His teachings about the things that life consists of not, we can see the influences of the powerful shifting shadows revelations, that even in our own very living days, and in our own very present times, are being very active at work, by releasing its manipulative influences and its deceptive information, to create havoc and to create confusion, by capturing humanity's lost and its crying Soul, in their desires of rebellion against the Father of the heavenly lights, that once they will be able to manipulate it, and if they will be able to capture its Soul in their schemes and networks of its deception labyrinths that now are under their active control and allowed to operate for a period of a temporary time, it will be cast away and bound away from his Creator's forever living light, into the cold and the darkness places of its forever regrets and forever sorrows and tears, working and established in the both realms of the Soul's existence, while living under the laws and under the limits it is now exposed to come alive and to exist, while surrounded and encapsulated by this present physical and mortal realm of its expressed manifest existence, that it was established from the beginning of the millennial ages in the Order of Creation, by God's unlimited unleashed power and love, and also when the Soul it will be called and transplanted from this physical and mortal realm of existence, into the transformed and the renewed spiritual and eternal kingdom of its expressed existence, at the appointed time, that it was also set and established from the very beginning of the millennial ages in the Order of Creation by God's unlimited expressed power and love, and no one that had, and has the breath of life, had fueled, and it is fueling their desires and their existence from it, it was ever able, or it will be ever able to avoid it, or it will be ever able to cancel their own transformation and transplantation between those two already established realms of existence, the temporary realm of a physical and a mortal expression that it is being manifested below within the earthly existence, and the eternal kingdom of a spiritual expression and its never ended manifestation and presence in heavens above, and sooner or later, being young or being old, being rich or being poor, believing or non-believing, rooted into, or not rooted into the systems of their own lives and into the designs of their own establishments and in their own structural foundations of living and learning how to express its manifestation, that came about when they were activated into their own existence, based on what they classified it or based on how they understood it, that a successful and established life may consist of, based on their very own learned abilities and learned self-reliance, that was brought forth by their corrupt, or their incorrupt way of understand it, they all, we all, will be one day face to face with our own established appointed time of transformation and transplantation between our own exist physical realm and its temporary mortal stage location on earth, and our own spiritual and its forever and eternal realm stage of its existence in its place in heavens.

'In the very own words of Paul's writing in Hebrews 9: 27-38"

And just as it is appointed for men to die once, and after that comes judgments, Christ, having been offered once to bear the sins of many, will appear a second time, not to deal with sin but to save those who eagerly are waiting for him (RSV*)

For the rich man in Christ's parable teaching example to His disciples, and where God has called that wealthy man and has been addressed by God as being a fool, his appointed time of expiration and also his appointed time of transformation and transplantation from this physical and mortal realm of his existence came at that very moment and point in time when he wanted to transfer and pass his life's possessions and his life's abundance and successes that were accumulated on this physical and mortal realm of living under its natural laws of expression and manifestation by its allowed abilities to be able to grow, to learn and to work for its temporary living and its temporary survival, as eternal life's possessions and successes to its inner Soul's existence, that it will never be satisfied and will never be feed and its Soul thirst will never be quenched, by anything that has a physical and a mortal expression of a manifestation or success, and their influenced surroundings that manifest their activities and their actions around a Soul's temporary dwelling place.

Luke 12:19-21" And I will say to my Soul, Soul, you have ample goods laid up for many years; take you to ease, eat, drink, be merry." But God said to him,' Fool! This night, your Soul is required of you, and the things you have prepared, whose they will be?' So is he who lays up treasure for himself and is not rich towards God." (RSV*)

Here, we can see a real contrast of actions and words that came forward from the mouth of the rich man and the mouth of God regarding how humanity perceives what life consists of and what the Word of the Living God reveals to humanity the truth about what life consists of not, in the eyes of the Soul and the Soul's cry for redemption, the Soul's cry for restoration and the Soul's cry for salvation.

What we experience as a humanity living in this dangerous time of our place and in our stage of express existence we are exposed to today, is witnessing how the manipulative powers of the dark forces and influences that are rebelling against the Soul's redemption, are using their classification levels and their technicals schemes of various deceptions, to confuse and to bind humanity in their always new, and in their constantly changing belief systems that do not, and are not originated from the Living Word and from the instruction of God for, and towards humanity, but are brought forward from the powers of their substitute lights that once hits its exposed subjects are producing and emanating ahead shifting shadows, holding those that are exposed to, captives and prisoners to their own corrupt understanding, and to their own perceived life's attributes that will later enable them, to develop it, by taking a form and a shape into a foundation that will be able to hold together, upon and on it, the structures, the framings and the buildings of deceit, housing their own and powerful false and corrupt influences, thus bypassing the Word of God, by offering to humanity, their own temporary substitutes and resolves that are bound, kneed and build into the fabric and structure of its temporary stage of existence in its physical and its material realm where it is allowed to manifest and express its quick achievements, as something that will benefit the restoration and the salvation and the eternity of its Soul.

When these artificial and substitute lights of corruption and manipulation take hold of humanity's perceived understanding of what life consists of, based on their own released sources of information, bypassing and reflecting their constantly shifting shadows upon its controlled subjects, it will stop at nothing to maintain and to sustain it as active, their own brought forward as alternative views of what life consists of, as a life form and its own expressed understanding that was being projected into the minds, and into the mind's ability to produce thoughts leading to their implementation and actions, at the lower levels and chambers of the consciousness existence in humanity's functions as primal, and in all of them subjects that were being exposed to their schemes and powerful influences and deceit for their results and their desires for the resolve and the destination of the eternal Soul.

As I mentioned in the previous chapter when we talked about truth versus thought, the real fight between the spiritual realm of what is good, versus what may appear and present itself as good, or the actual battle between the spiritual realm of the absolute truth, versus what may appear and present itself as truth, and their own alternative powers to capture and to influence those exposed to its information, it is not at the level of the consciousness in its logical activated system of executive actions that follows the instructions, the orders and the signals that are powered and are propulsion forward by its own thought processor system and its abilities, but the real fight for the restoration, the salvation and the eternal destination of the Soul, it is actively taking place in the lower chambers of our comprehensive understanding of our own consciousness functions, or in the plain expressed words, at the much more deeper and more profound levels than human eyes can see, or at the much more deeper and lower levels than our own human mind and our own human understanding can be able to perceive it.

I believe, and this is strictly my own belief, and this is not a theological or a doctrinal opinion or an argument point I will address at this time, but we will cover this subject in a more detailed approach in the later chapters of this book, that if we are exposed and influenced and manipulated at the lower levels of our unconsciousness stage in its own place and location, that it is playing a very real and powerful expressed vital part, and also a very essential role in what makes and completes our humanity's total consciousness design and system application, that also can act on its own build expressions and on its own very powerful and very real creating abilities for their purpose and functions, that were been released into, and also bestowed into its innermost accessed parts of its deeper consciousness, and that are also been activated by the Creator, to be the central nucleus hub station that it is acting as an active center of its own power processor and transfer of all its information received into it, and that also it is being exposed to be able to capture multiple signals and their individual raw data, in an instant, and can and will be capable of working with them, and for them, or against them, and actively using its frames and structures, and also its active established form that has is foundation build into the capability and also into the capacity, that is classified as the only active and expressed connectivity integrated power system allowed, and also by designed build to be able to operate in the very vast area of their multiple networking's and crossed realms and their living and active movements, and expressions, that are powered by their own synergy portals of their existence, to be able to receive and to send, and also to move and to act on the information that it is being exposed, to and from all of the very expressions of lives that can tap into it, being them of a spiritual, a psychological, a physical, or a biological inputs in their own powerful origins and forms, designed to bring forth their own interests and their own end desires for their own established mode of survival on their very own platforms of their active existences, that are being actively very strong acting on their temporary desires of their own physiological, physical and biological forms, or being and acting on their eternal desires of their very own spiritual forms of expressions for the humanity's eternity and its salvation, including our own human restoration of our own Soul's existence that it will be made possible and able to reach back its original created purpose form, only if our sincere and most profound and lower levels of our expressed and active existence, and also the foundation of our complete consciousness structure and its operational platform, it will be ultimately surrender and yielded back under the will, and into the hands of our maker and creator, Jehovah God, that will mold us, protect us, and guide us by the power of his Absolute Truth and by the power of his Living Word that can and it is being activated inside humanity's Soul, by the power of the Spirit of Life and by the control and the movement of his Holy Spirit.

In closing of this chapter, Shifting Shadows, I am praying that the Spirit of the Living God's power and the anointing and the clear discernment that comes forward from it, that never end flowing river of life, released from the very heavenly holy sit and the throne of God's holiness, to soak in our Soul, and our Heart, and our Mind, that we may be protected and shielded from the influences and from the revelations that are continually released upon the humanity by their artificial sources and their constantly shifting and blinking lights, that are being activated and are being propelled forward from their multiple sources that are established in the many spiritual realms that are surrounding us, searching for their own desires to be fulfilled, and these spiritual realms are continually expressing their own and powerful abilities, using their ways of active manifestations to be able to capture the humanity in their nets of control by passive deceptions, or activated and propelled forward from the physical existence realms and their own human made expressions and desires, by manifesting in their own search and their own end desires and fulfillment, by being able of capturing and controlling other peers that are, and more or less will always be exposed to their own power of corruption and deceit, build in by their own human understanding and their own manifestation of moving the sources of their own lights, that will never stop producing confusions and also many deceptions that are being brought forward by their always shifting shadows to be able to produce a temporary influence, and also to be able to produce and to achieve the results of their own plans, by design founded in the depths of their own self certified righteousness status, but behind the scenes they are nothing more than an open and an engaged competition, within the limits and bounds of time and within the many crossed realms of existence and their own desires for having and achieving a complete control over humanity and its expression of life, thus using any schemes and techniques available to them that are sourced and breathed into a manipulative existence from all realms of expressions and their movements surrounding us, and also from all the realms of expressions and movements that are real and very active within us.

Chapter Eight:
Transcendental Realm

Genesis 1:4:" These are the generations of the heavens Genesis 1:4:" These are the generations of the heavens and the earth when they were created."

To be able to dive deeper and forward and further into the subject of the eighth chapter of this book, Transcendental Realm, for a better understanding of all of our surroundings and establishments that are all around us, that we may be made well aware of them or not, and that is continually manifesting and are frequently expressing their active influences for helping humanity or being against the humanity's life expression and purpose, we will travel back into time, and take a look at the foundation of the Creation that was established and brought into existence by the power and the Word of the Living God, the Most High God, the Creator of Heavens and Earth, Glory be to His Holy and Most Majestic Name, Jehovah God.

Let's go together for a few moments and read what the Word of God is revealing, and it teaches us as a ground start on this subject.

Genesis 2: 1-4: "Thus the heavens and the Earth were finished, and all their multitude. And on the seventh day, God finished the work that he had done, and he rested on the seventh day from all the work he had done. So, God blessed the seventh day and hallowed it because God rested on it from all his work in creation. These are the Heavens and Earth generations when they were created. (NRSV*)

Also, one more read from the Word of God from Genesis 1:31:" God saw everything that he had made, and indeed, it was perfect. (NRSV*)

Based on the Word of God, we can learn that at the end of every single day during the first five days in the Order of the Creation, the phrase that God saw it, and it was good, and after that He made the declaration after the six day of the creation that everything He had made it was indeed good, after that He blessed it and hallowed it the seventh day in the Order of the Creation, the day when God rested from all his works which he had done in the creation, emphasizing and proclaiming that definitely the expression of His love and the manifestation of His power through which He brought forward into an active existence all the life elements of His Creation, that were expressed and manifested by the authority of the spoken Logos the Christ, established a perfect and a magnificent realm of multiple forms of existences and their moving expressions, where everything and all that God created, were to be able within this original and perfect realm to be manifested and to be actively connected with each other, in a complex but bonded together into its unison synergy frames, propelled forward in their movements and actions, by the source and the spark of life that was released upon it from within the Creator himself' s unlimited wisdom and knowledge, a realm formed and molded from nothingness into a perfect expression of God's love and manifest power, that brought into the existence the reality of a divine holiness innocents, having its deep foundation created of an incorruptible and pure desires, that allowed in the beginning, for all them established forms and their own active existences, and their life's expressions and their continue movements, to be bonded and also sourced to be able to work together with each other as a one single manifested entity, compressed into a realm, by being expressed, build and connected by the power of love and its perfect harmony and its entire and created atmosphere, made possible and also being able to be released forward, upon and within, and also into everything that Jehovah God brought to life, by the power of the Word and by the power of His revealed will, including the heavens and the earth, and all their created, all formed, and all activated movements of their life-expressions, within their own powerful elements that were being created and manifested, allowed and also activated and authorized by the Most High God, to be part of the original and the fundamental rock foundation in the Order of its Creation's divine purpose, its divine existence, and its active and divine manifestation, and in conclusion as the Word of God says" These are the generations of the heavens and the earth when they were created. (Genesis 2:4).

I want to emphasize this strong point that will help us develop a better understanding for the following chapters of this book, when we will address the intensity and the reality of hostility between the powers of the elements of the creation that were established in one unison, in a perfect and a single realm, united and combined by the spiritual and the physical existences and their living expression and in their manifest powers.

The point is that in the first phase of the Creation's existence, there was not any enmity or disagreements or rebellion, or disobedience in the Order of the Creation between the living express manifestations of their spiritual or physical powers of the Creation until there started to be a rift and an envy that was fueled and was driven by the pride of their own self- identities and powered egos, because of the Order, the establishment, and the authority the Almighty God had placed and ordained by appointing for the Order of the Creation, the rules and the decrees, to fuel and to sustain the Order in the Creation, its purpose and function, to become a divine natural synergy environment, built in a wholly perfected holiness structure and connectivity by its robust ray networking, to be able to keep all the powers and all the elements of the creation in a completely perfect movement on their own living expressions, as the Creator wanted them to be when he brought them all forward to existence, from within himself and his own fueled and sourced wisdom, knowledge, and energetic understanding flow, which is the foundation and the complexed fundamental block of the Creation, in its entirety and in its vast unlimited and majestically operation and control function and abilities.

By having the Order in the Creation established as a fundamental, vital, and operational system of expressed connectivity mechanism to exist between the powerful elements of the creation brought forward to Life by the power of the spoken Word of God and by the craftsmanship of His hands, the Order of the Creation needed to be able to function and to act as one perfect and united realm created and manifested and expressed by the powers of Heavens and by the forces of the Earth, by the authority of the spirit and by the capabilities of all of their created spiritual and physical expressions and movements, under the rules and the laws and the regulation that were put forward and ordained by the Almighty God, for and within their own established identities, but also united into a single operational system and function, as a complete and also as complex and as a perfect realm, created and built into self-continuing sustainment for its existence, that was activated, and was empowered to be allowed to exist and to be expressed in its movements by an incorruptible connectivity network system, between the original elements and the original powers of the creation, their functions, and their purposes, while being encapsulated in the frame and structure of the time, its developed space and its accumulated matter, as one expression and as one true manifestation of God's divine and everlasting love.

His unlimited power and unsearchable deep knowledge have been released from the depths of His pure and eternal wisdom foundations. God's wisdom and knowledge have been revealed forward from within the parameters and scopes of His divine and perfect ethereal realm, and the structural frames of His entire spoken into existence all of the original elements of life and all of the actual manifested powers, that all came to be actively expressing their substance within the Creation's transcendental realm.

Going back to the first chapter in Genesis, the Word of God teaches us that there was a beginning that started and took a form and shape as a new location for the manifestations of new revealed forms of life and as a temporary stop in the midst of the everlasting, where the notion of the time and the space and the matter did not use to exist and before anything that and everything that came into existence as an outside expression and manifestation of the Almighty Creator's wisdom and knowledge, it was God, the True One, without a beginning and an end.

Then we learned that when God's unlimited power, wisdom, and proper knowledge started to manifest and to be expressed from the inner depths of its own everlasting, sending forward the outburst flames of their majestic movements, released ahead from God's very own core and by God's very own authority, the stop amid the everlasting eternity, as we know it today as The Creation, being encapsulated and molded by the newly expressions of time and the space and the matter, it happened and exploded into a manifested face of Life's expressed living, through the process of transplantation into their very own existence, from the deep wellsprings of God's own and eternal substance of life.

Under the authority of God's power and wisdom, there came forth into existence the powerful and original elements expressed movements designed by God to be the fundamental and structural blocks in the Order of the Creation as He intended to be.

Therefore, there were many original elements of life, and their life expressions brought into existence by the Creator. Some of the aspects of life were Created into their living existences, some were formed into their living realities, some were made into their living existences, some were spoken into their living existences, and some were breathed into their living existences, but no matter how these powerful elements and these powerful fundamental blocks of Life and their Life's expressions came about when they were released forward and appointed into the Order of the Creation, they were all connected into the same source that released and activated them from the depths of God's majestic and unlimited wisdom and power to be able to interact with each other, and together to be able to operate as One Connection, to be able to be connected into the establishment of God's holy and perfect unison realm, existed to fulfill the purpose and the functions that were revealed and authorized by the Creator for their very own expressions, and their very own movements, as one perfect Connection, bonded together by the power and the majesty of God's wisdom and its holy revelation, into the foundation and the structure of God's manifestation of His love for the Creation, to be able to express their very own authority, their very own powers and their very own responsibilities that have been appointed to them all, by God's wisdom and knowledge, revealed in the commandments and decrees put forward and assigned to them to follow and obey, all along, and across God's Creation paramount, activated by His Will within the Life and the expression of His entire Created Transcendental Realm.

I want to be able to address this point before going forward in this chapter that according to the revelation received from the Word of God and revealed to humanity in the first book of the Bible known to us, Genesis, we can also learn that there at the very beginning foundation of God's Creation expressed and manifest structure of Life's existence, were ever-present, also the very powerful and also the solid unimaginable magnitude of the defined movement of the Spirit of God, The Wind that was hovering over The Waters, and The Darkness that was hovering over the surface of The Deep.

From this information revealed to us by the Scriptures, we learn that these four unlimited and unsearchable entities, and their very own powerful expressions of God's majestic divinity within His own-self manifestation and movement, The Spirit, and The Waters, the Darkness, and The Deep, were actively part of God's Wisdom and Knowledge that blasted forward from within the Almighty's very own innermost holiness and his divine and righteousness desire, without being ever created or called or formed into existence, as all of the other fundamental elements and powers of the creation that were brought forward were, but these four absolute and original existences, The Spirit and The Waters, The Darkness and The Deep were very active in their own very strong movements and their very own expressions and their powerful own manifestations, even long before God's Order of the Creation came forward to Life as we all know it to be today, release to us from the Word of God's revelation, and this point concludes that their existences were deep-rooted in the everlasting, they had no beginning and were part of God's own solid expression and part of God's powerful own manifestation even long before there was a beginning and a Creation as we know it, and they still are today, as God's Absolute never changes, He is the same yesterday, He is the same today, and He is the same eternal and forevermore .

All created, formed and manifested entities known as the original elements of the creation's powers, that God brought forward into the existence after the " In The Beginning God" , the words and the exclamation sounds from Genesis's first chapter, were founded and structured in the foundation of the, " Without The Beginning", and it is going to be one Day coming, when all created, formed and manifested entities, that are expressing their own Life's existences, in heavens above and on Earth below, that are part of " The Creation", as we are allowed to know it and to experience it today, by living in its manifested time and expression, will end, and all the Creation, it will be transplanted by the action of breaking through the threshold of the eternity, into the place and the location of the, " Without The End", in the presence of The Almighty God forever, the One that it is the Creator of all, when He will restore the corruptible and the incorruptible, the mortals and the immortals, the heavens and the Earth, in that majestic, and in that holy and marvelous Day, when the Creator will return us and our living and breathing expressions, and also when He will return the entire' s creation living and breathing life expressions, back into Himself, back into the original innocence holiness of what was once a perfect and a majestically and glorious Transcendental Realm of God's everlasting existence expressed and manifested from the spring of his infinite wisdom and steadfast love.

Reading the powerful prayer of Moses from Psalms 90, we can see that the man of God, the one that was chosen by the Almighty to bring the message and was chosen to be the guide and the leader used and anointed for the deliverance of God's people from slavery, how he acknowledges in verses one and two the powerful truth of the Everlasting.

"Lord, you have been our dwelling place throughout all generations. Before the mountains were born, or you brought forth the whole world, from Everlasting to Everlasting, you are God".

This compelling truth that God had revealed to Moses helps us to realize and allows us to come to the understanding that amid the Everlasting Presence of God's wisdom, power, and knowledge, a sudden stop occurred due to His unlimited expressed grace and love that was uncontainable, and exploded forward from within the Deep of God's Presence, and this stop in the midst of the Everlasting it is called The Creation.

What seemed to be just a dot and just a pinhead size exclamation point and design is formed and encapsulated by the Everlasting Presence of the Almighty Creator and embraced and surrounded by God's unlimited grace and infinite love in a holy, majestic expression of His divine wisdom, it is the glorious crown jewel of His magnificent Creation, that had been framed and structured by the passing of time, by the windows of space, and by the manifestation of their element produced and manifested matter, all that was created, and were formed, and were called and were breathed into the existence of Life, within their moving expressions, by the Righteous One by the Holy One, by the Just One, the One that declared and announced by the power of His Word in the Scriptures, as it is written in the book of Revelation 22:13 " I am the Alpha and the Omega, the First and the Last, the Beginning and the End."

What a blessing, and really what an incredible revelation received from above, to come to the understanding and the proper knowledge that the Creator, the only One without a beginning and with no end, amid His powerful and infinite Everlasting Presence, chose to reveal Himself outward, by manifesting His actual and His infinite wisdom, by the proclamation of His Word, and by the Works of His hands, and in His knowledge, and own power, and love, establishing and forming in perfect unison the synergetic and networking movements of all life element powers, released forward into their very own active purposes and functions of their existence, fueled by God's purity and holiness, within the bounds and the limits of what once was, an accurate perfect and an incorruptible Transcendental Realm, called The Creation, the manifold works of His own powerful hands.

As I wrote in the previous pages of this chapter, about the perfect Order of the Creation, which was brought forward into its manifested existence by God's wisdom and will by establishing, at the beginning and foremost, the creation of the Heavens and the Earth, and I am calling the Heavens and the Earth, the very first fundamental and majestic powers and living elements of the creation schematics and structures, that started to take shapes and forms, by being connected directly into the foundation of the Everlasting Presence of God's unsealed Eternity, and together being anchored and imprinted into the Almighty God's very own works, and also in his very masterful crafting designs that He had produced and brought forward to Life as a result of the myriads of living expressions that His very infinite and divine powerful hands crafted.

The pillar foundation that was holding the first elements of Life and their very own expression as an active manifest creation, holding together the Heavens and the Earth, was the pillar formation of the uncreated manifest powers of the Almighty, revealed by the Word of God back in Genesis chapter one, verse two" the Earth was a formless void and Darkness covered the face of The Deep. And at the same time, a Wind from God swept over the face of The Waters. Other living translations of the Word of God mention the phrase, '(Spirit of God).'

Suppose God will allow us to comprehend the unlimited magnitude and the power of these revealing words to a small degree of understanding. In that case, it will help us to realize that everything He had created in the Order of the Creation had their beginning anchored and held together by their original and divine Connection that God brought forward into existence as a direct communication portal between all the constructed expressions of life and their very own activated movements.

At the same time, the four uncreated and powerful eternal living elements of life and their power movements were revealed from God's infinite wisdom and power within the Transcendental Realm Landscape that encapsulated within its frames the entire Heavens and Earth's complex foundations, known to us to be the Darkness and The Deep, The Spirit of the Living God and The Waters, as the fundamental and the foundation structure that holds within their infinite built the entire Order of the Creation and its divine Connection.

We can learn from the Scriptures, that before there was the first spoken Word of the Living God expressed in an outward sound of His's infinite and divine wisdom, by calling to come forward the Light in the accordance with the book of Genesis 1:3 where it is written" Then God said,' let there be Light; and there was light", long before the sound of the Almighty God's voice broke the barriers of time, space and their matter expressions and movements, that there was already a divine inner core established Connection, made by the Creator, to facilitate as a balanced focus and purpose, between Heavens and Earth, between the Covering of the Darkness and the face of the Deep, between the Spirit of the Living God and the front of the Waters, that will allow them all to be activated into, and as to be known that they were called to be the first elements of the creation blocks of existence, outsourced from the Everlasting into the framing and the structure of the Order of the Creation, by the power, the grace and the love of the Almighty God, the Creator of all things, seen and unseen.

With the Light being spoken into existence by the power of the Living Word of God, the Order of the Creation started to take the first steps into being shaped and structured to be formed by the masterfully designed plan released forward from within the unlimited and unsearchable depths of God's true own wisdom and knowledge.

God saw that the Light that came forward into existence at the sound of His Word when its name called it that it was good, and He separated the Light from the Darkness, not because the Darkness was terrible, per se, but because He wanted to make a distinguished statement, that He desired to establish in the Order of the Creation, the First Order in The Creation, the Day and the Night, and also God in His divine wisdom, released forward from within their very owned manifest expressions, what it is revealed by the writers of the Scriptures, as a revelation from God to humanity, as it is known to be for all the coming in, and going out generations of the Creation, as The Evening, and also as The Morning.

The Evening was established by God to come forward and to exist in the Order, as a buffer time zone, between the Light of the Day and the Darkness of the Night, and The Morning, that had been established by God to come forward, as a buffer time zone between the Darkness of the Night and the Light of the Day, thus made them to be and to exist and to be known to all creation, as the first set of appointed rules and regulatory structures of God's divine purpose and function, through which

He brought forward and established, the movement and the existence of Time, as a compass, and as a guide build into the very foundation and fabric structure of Creation.

As it is written in the Scriptures, in Genesis 1:5," God called the Light Day and the darkness he called Night. And there was an evening and a morning, The First Day.

We want to be able to distinguish between the powerful elements of life creation's block fundamental and structural existence that God's Order of the Creation established, and their essential and structural functions bestowed and appointed upon them and for them when it was established by God's Order in the Creation, for their continuing operations and their purposes of their own sourced existence released and revealed forward from God's divine planned will, for the creation's functional, operational and structural complex of its Life and also its expressed sustainment.

The Order of the Creation, as we learned from the Scripture's information revealed to humanity, is based on and also consists of the seven days of the creation and, in their very own chronological Order, of being called forward, created, formed, or spoken into existence, to their very own life manifestation and expressed movements, starting with the first known Day and finished with the last Day in the Order of the Creation that it is known to us as the seventh Day, the Day of rest, the Sabbath.

As a side note, I want to mention that the period in the creation, from the complexity of the words that are encapsulated in themselves as being the most known and popular phrase words in the history of humanity's life form, within the phrase that starts with, "In the beginning, God created the heavens and the earth," the very beginning that moved forward from its everlasting foundation springboard of eternity to that period in time when the Word of God declares that "there was an evening and there was a morning," the First Day. It is all a vast span of duration and process; it is part of the hidden and untapped mysteries of the Almighty God's imprint into the majestic structure and fabric formed Crown of His Creation.

For each day that came forward into the Order of the Creation, by the authority and by the fulfillment power of the master designed plan established by the Almighty God's infinite wisdom and knowledge, came forward also from within the depths of God's unlimited understanding, the expressions and the authorized manifestations of creation's fulfillment and its sustainability immense powers, established by appointment, by the rules and by the decrees of the regulatory mechanism system of creation's functions in the creation's lasting expressed operations and movements, that are to be known as the Ordained and the Established Order in the Creation, by the Creator.

As I mentioned in the above paragraphs from this chapter, the First Order In the Creation was the Separation of the Light from the Darkness, that it is, as we know it today, the separation of the Day from the Night, using the buffered time zones of the Evening and of the morning, as a standard and unique ground effect of their own exist manifestations, between these two very magnificent and original elements of the creation powers, that were ordained by God, to bring forward and to introduce to an expressed life and existence, the Order to facilitate the records and the recorded time, for all the coming generations of the creation from Heavens above and from the Earth below, that at one point in the original stage of their existence, were both part of the one true majestic, perfect and divine transcendental realm.

The Second Order in the Creation was the establishment of the Dome, which we also know today as the Sky, amid the mighty waters, to facilitate, hold, and sustain the separation that was authorized and ordered by God to exist as a buffered zone, and also as a live connecting field of its existence and its complexed build structure that was activated between the waters, thus allowing the movement of the waters that were expressing their presence above the Dome, and allowing the activities of the mighty waters to define their existence below the Dome, the mighty waters, the one original element of creation sourced directly from eternity from the very everlasting expression and foundation, part of God's very own substance, that God himself separated and divided to bring Life and to sustain the existence of the heaven above in heaven's own expressed form and manifestation, and to bring Life and to sustain the Earth existence below on the Earth's self-expressions, conditions, and representations.

One quick point I want to make by addressing in a few words the clear distinguishes and the differences between the first Day of the separation process that was established by the Order in the Creation, when God separated the Light from the darkness, and the second Day of the separation process that was found in the Order in the Creation, when God separated the waters from the waters.

On the first Day of the separation process that was between the original elements of the creation and their fundamental blocks of existence both the Light and the darkness, were opposite to each other's expression and manifest functions, and while the Light was called forward into existence by the spoken Word of the living God, and the Light came and presented itself before the Lord and was declared good, the darkness already was busy and actively moving upon the surface of the deep, long before there was The Light, thus their completely different matrixes of expressions and their fundamental purposes that were established by the masterful design and perfect executed planning from the inner depths of

God's wisdom, are acknowledged as being the first living elements and powers in the creation, that were separated for their very own specific functions and their very own manifestation purposes, but also both powerful forces of the creation's life elements were being together rooted and anchored into the same fundamental structure and foundation of God's Creation to maintain the Order and the decree that God established by his own authority and by His own powerful spoken commands.

On the second Day of the separation process for the Order in the Creation, which was established by God's Word spoken by decree, when He called forth the Dome, the Sky, that immense field of controlled designed system separator with its unimaginable powers, ordained and bestowed upon its unsearchable and vast span of manifestation, by God's himself in his intent appointment, and assigned authority for the Dome, also known in our terminology as the Sky, to be able to split in two, and also to be able to hold it apart and separated in two very similar expressions and manifestations, the only one in its very own unique form of an uncreated element existing divine substance, the Waters, that were released from within God to facilitate the creation's existence, from the very vast depths of the Almighty God's deep and majestic divine wisdom, as One single entity power enabled to sustain the Life in the whole entire frame's structure of the creation, with its streams of living waters, flowing continually in the Heavens above the firmament, and on the Earth below the sky, by supplying and fueling the entire vast creation with God's expressed power in the Heavens above, and also with God's express and manifested divine and steadfast love on the vast Earth below the firmament.

In the future, discussing the Order of the Creation in its chronological steps revealed by the Scriptures, we are going to address the Order in the Creation that God established by the authority of the Word of the Living God for the third Day, that Day when Life and matter came forward into the existence as we know it and as we experience it today, and because the Almighty God the Creator is the True Absolute Life, in purpose I did mention in the above statement, that Life came forward into existence as we know it today from the depths of God's Spirit because Life is from the everlasting and has no beginning and has no end.

Like the Waters, Life was brought forward from God's inner expression and manifestation by God's revelation so that the entire creation will be allowed and blessed to experience life and live.

Let's go to the Scriptures and read together what the Word says in Genesis 1, verses 9-11," And God said: Let the waters under the Sky (the Dome, the firmament, space), be gathered into one place, and let the dry land (matter) appear. And it was so. God called the dry land Earth, and the waters gathered he called Seas.

And God saw that it was good. Then God said, " Let the Earth put forth vegetation: plants yielding seed, and fruit trees of every kind on Earth that bear fruit with the seed in it. And it was so. And Genesis 1:11" And there was evening, and there was morning, The Third Day.

Sailing into the journey of studying the Word of God and the Scriptures, and finding and discovering along the historical time frame expressions and their many and real powerful events and resolves that are associated with the "Third Day's end results and their manifestations, it rings in very accurate, and also it is carry on its very own and actual reality, that we may be able to proclaim it, and to witness it, and without a doubt to agree that indeed the powerful Third Day in the creation, is the Day of Life, when the seed of Life was revealed and also was planted into God's original and magnificent creation, and also being deep seeded, rooted and grown into the midst of the earth's ground platform systems, and its own build manifest structure that was already being established from its very young beginnings for the sake and the resolve of the creation's future restoration and regeneration stages of its existence by the power of Life in the resurrection to come at the very and real appointed time, already set in motion by the Almighty God's own divine and unlimited wisdom and power in His unsearchable inner core depths, for all the elements of Life, for their own expressions and their very real and powerful own manifestations, that are being actively encapsulated by their existence and their movements, in the Heavens above the firmament, or on the Earth below the firmament, the Dome or the Sky, like we are to know it today as in the terminology of our own spoken words and languages.

Mentioning the sky and the vast space that God had created and brought forward into existence on the second Day of the Order of the Creation to separate The Waters from the above, from The Waters from the below, it brings us to the fourth Day in its very own, powerful and unfathomable divine Order in the creation by the Almighty God, when He spoke the fourth Day's dominion and assignment by decree, by what the Scriptures reveals to us in the Genesis 1:14-19", And God said,' Let there be lights in the Dome of the Sky to separate the Day from the Night; and let them be for signs and be for the seasons and be for days and years, and let them be lights in the Dome of the Sky to give Light upon the Earth. And it was so. God made the two great lights- The Greater Light to Rule the Day and The Lesser Light to Rule the Night and the Stars. God set them in the Dome of the Sky to give Light upon the Earth, to rule over the Day and the Night, and to separate the Light from the Darkness. And God saw that it was good. And there was evening and morning, The Fourth Day".

One quick note I want to be able to bring forth in attention to the readers of this book, that we may be able to understand and may be able to make a clear distinguish between the first called and established decree word of separation between the Light and the Darkness that was established by God in the very first Day in the Order of the His Creation, when God called the Light forward into the existence and saw that it was good, and separated it from the Darkness, and between the second called and established decree word of separation between the Light and the Darkness that God purposely found, and set in the Order of the Creation on that powerful Fourth Day.

As a teaser for future references on this powerful actual subject, let's consider for a moment that the first separation between the Light and the darkness established by God on the very first day of its Order was a separation between the Light and the Darkness, for the whole creation's spiritual and physical existence in its beginning form and expressed manifestation, covering the entire and all its perfected transcendental realm, that was brought forward into the reality by God's divine power and wisdom, a complete separation between Light and darkness in every single nucleus and atom formed, expressed or not expressed, manifested or not manifested, moving or not moving, in the entire and the unlimited vast and perfect creation, covered by the Creator's established Order for all the heavens and all expressions of heavens, and for all the Earth and all the manifestations on the Earth.

But in the second separation process that was established and decreed by the Word of the Living God, on the Fourth Day, the separation of these powerful elements of purposes and functions for His called and formed creation, between the Light and the darkness of the fourth Day, was a separation that was called forward and established strictly for all the expressions and all the manifestations of Life's forms, that already existed or were to come later in existence by being created, formed, and also sometimes called by the Almighty God in the Order of the Creation, to exist, and to express and to manifest, below the firmament, the Dome and the Sky, a separation between Light and Darkness, between Day and Night, that were established in their own physical levels and structured stages by God for their works and functions in the Order, to be able to move and operate in their very own visible and living expressed forms and beings powered by the manifestation of their systemic energetic matter.

On the fourth Day, established by God in the chronological Order of the creation, when the visible lights were spoken into existence by the Creator, to separate the Day from the Night and to give and to provide and to be the lights into the Dome of the Sky, that will also give Light upon the Earth, God also made the two great lights, The Greater Light to rule the Day, and The Lesser Light to oversee the Night and the stars.

We learned this from the Scripture's revelation from Genesis 1:16" where the man of God writes the following: "God made the Two Great Lights, the Greater Light (the Sun), to rule the Day, and The Lesser Light (the Moon), to rule the Night and the stars. (NRSVACE*)

The lights that were called into the existence by the power of the spoken Word of the Living God, the Logos, and the two great lights that were made and formed into their existence by the divine planning and wisdom from the Creator's own everlasting expressed presence, that came forward into the fourth Day, were given the authority within their own very powerful and established assignments, sourced directly from the Almighty God's energetic inner core, for their own functions and for their own expressed purposes for the Order in the Creation, to release and to provide Light and also to sustain Life, and to be the original and also the fundamental and the structural frame of its mechanism's live focus, for all the generations of the creation and for all the generations in the Creation, the ages of the past, the generations of the present time, and for the generations of the future time, and for how long God will regenerate, and sustain, and maintain His majestic creation active, to be the established map in its operational and accurate blueprint design form, for the signs, and for the seasons and for the days and for the years, and also being appointed to them to continually release forward their lights and reflection in the Dome, and also to produce and to provide and to give Light upon the Earth and to all Earth's habitants, regardless their Life's form and their expressed manifestation.

God, in his masterful design planning for the Order in his Creation, already prepared and established the foundation of Life that will be sustained in the Order as He intended, to take shape and the forms for the Life in itself to be able to function and also to be able to be manifested, by the multitudes of created beings and their molded life expressions within the frames of their very own numerous life forms, that were called forward by the power of God, to be ordained and also to recognized as the actual original life forms and element blocks in the creation. And God saw that it was good. And there was evening, and there was morning—the Fourth Day.

Then God said,' Let the waters bring forth swarms of living creatures and let birds fly above the Earth across the Dome in the Sky. So, God created the great sea monsters and every living creature that moves, of every kind, which the waters swarm, and every winged bird of every kind.

This powerful revelation brought to us forward by the Scripture, in accordance with what it is written in Genesis 1:20-21", it is helping us to at least at a minimum, to understand that in the original intent of God's planning of his divine creation, was that all the created, and all the formed, and all the called or made structural and fundamental powerful sourced elements of their own Life's expressions, were to be integrated together into a single synergetic structure and source networking mechanism location point, being part of the original purpose and function of their own express manifestations, within the core foundation of God's divine creation in its own magnificent and majestic unlimited movement of Life, as one heavenly and perfect in-transcendental realm, that was to be defined by the multitudes of their many different forms and their many other expressions and manifestation of Life's movements, but also being very actively knitted together by a very powerful energetic proclamation under an holy and unmoved eternal declaration, that was revealed forward to all the elements of Life, that there it is only One Creator, that brought into existence by His own will only One Creation, and established by His own decree only One Order in the Creation, that it is to be authorized and also it is to be appointed and incorporated to be able to continually be sustained and operative in its functions, from within the depths of God's own perfect and divine holiness and wisdom, which is the absolute proper and fundamental foundation of all the living elements and organisms of all living and breathing Life's expressed forms that are encapsulated in His creation.

The fifth Day was the Day when God, in His unlimited divine wisdom and knowledge, by His decree and will, called forth the first integration mechanism system of the manifest and expressed Life between the powerful original elements and living blocks of its fundamental structure by his proclamation for the creation, to be able to manifest their very own different functions and their different purposes, within the One Divine Unison Platform structure within the Creation, and together with all their appointed and decreed positions by God, to be involved in, and together to be part in the awesome, and in the masterful, and the majestic complexed design expressions of the Almighty God's own will and for His manifold purposes and works assigned by decrees to his creation.

Using the power of his word, the Creator commanded and ordered the waters to bring forth swarms of living creatures, and commanded the birds to fly above the earth across the dome of the sky, also known as the firmament, by establishing his Order in the creation for the original elements and their active powers created and formed, that from the very beginning stage of being shaped into a created living structure, were fundamental to the foundation's block of moving expression of life itself reflected forward by their many different shapes and forms of their own kind, to be able to coordinate with each other, and also to be able to connect with each other's functional and designated purpose, that were to be authorized, and delegated, and ordered by God himself for them to be able to exist and to operate properly, and also to allow their immense and powerful own structural functions, to be an active location placed within God's perfect and divine in-transcendental realm, where their own free movement and also their own sourced and active existence of the manifestations of life's unlimited expressions, that already existed within God's own knowledge, planning and design, even long before they were created, and called and activated, but will come into the known existence later on in the creation's manifestation, so they will be then activated into their own expressed existences at their very appointed time within the creation's realm, to be maintained and also to be all together sustained in a continually movement of life, but in truth and in its power, way behind our own limited human comprehension of thought, in the very unimaginable vast and glorious untapped wisdom of God, all these powerful and magnificent carriers of life's expressions and their movements, were already being activated in the inner depths of the Creator's own masterful design plan, even long before they were released from the depths of God into a forwarded existence, as an outward movement within their own and very powerful life's expressions, that were being ordained and that were being activated into the realm of the Creation, when the beginning was called into the existence, when the time appeared as a guide structured and formed from within God's own energetic substance and source, in that very real, and in that very true and powerful moment when they were being transplanted from the place within God's inner expression of love, and being activated and called forward to their existence, to be masterfully revealed in God's creation, that it is the ultimate paramount movement of its very powerful outward manifestation of God's divine expression of His everlasting and eternal love that was sourced and produced from within His own will, wisdom and knowledge.

We can see how by the divine God's wisdom from everlasting, long before heavenly wisdom started to be manifested, on the fifth Day of the creation, it was established in the Order, the interaction and systemic approached communication synergy portal between the very powerful and the original elements expressed and manifested in the fundamental blocks of Life in the creation, between the waters and their swarms of living creatures that the waters brought forth at the Order and the commandment of God, and between the firmament across the Sky, the Dome and every winged bird of every kind, created by God, to fly above the

Earth, thus making the right environment for the sustainment and the movement of their life and forth expressions, including in their corporate and complexed networking of active communication and control for its Order; also God's created great monsters, together with every other living creature ordained to move, to swim or to fly.

Here, on the creation's fifth Day in the Order, for the first time, we can read about God's first proclamation, followed by a blessing and also followed by a commandment after the statement that the Scriptures reveal to us by its declaration of the spoken words and its acceptance criteria, that was" And God saw that it was good," at the end of all the previous days established in the creation. Genesis 1:22-23 "God blessed them, saying,' Be fruitful and multiply and fill the waters in the seas and let the birds breed on the Earth. And there was evening, and there was morning, The Fifth Day.

The Fifth Day when the Almighty God brought forward for its creation and the creation's expressions of its manifested, and decreed and appointed Life, the first known Word of proclamation that was to be encapsulated in God's very own unlimited love, released upon the creation, the powerful word 'blessed,' when God blessed them, all that the waters brought forward, and all that God created in the Order in that special fifth Day, when their life expression started to be manifested on a different platform, in different shapes and different movements, different from all the previous created forms that were also called forward, in their own and very powerful expressions of Life. And God saw that it was good. And there was evening, and there was morning, The Fifth Day.

On the sixth Day of God's Creation, God also established by the decree of His Word and by the power of His divine wisdom, another compelling fundamental and structural foundation for God's Order in the Creation when He commanded the Earth to bring forth living creatures of every kind, cattle and creeping things and wild animals of the Earth of every kind. And it was so; we know this from the Scriptures and from the living Word of God that was revealed to us according to Genesis 1:24-25, where it is written, "Then God said,' Let the Earth bring forth living creatures of every kind: cattle and creeping things and wild animals of the Earth of every kind. 'And it was so.

God made the wild animals of the Earth of every kind, cattle of every kind, and everything that creeps upon the ground of every kind. And God saw that it was good".

If we start looking into the powerful depths of these words from God's living scriptures that describes for us the humanity, and it is bringing forward the revelation of the entire creation, we can see clearly the relationship and the communication that the Almighty Creator, initiated directly with one of the original and fundamental element for his Creation, the waters, that were released and activated forward from the everlasting depths of God himself, that were established in The Fifth Day, when He commanded and ordered the waters to bring forth swarms of all kind of leaving creatures, and the relationship and the communication that the Creator initiated directly with a powerful and majestic created element as a fundamental and functional and as a living block manifestation for His divined and purposed creation, the Earth, when He commanded the Earth to put forth vegetation, plants, trees of every kind that bear fruit with the seed in it, in the Third Day, and also when He ordered and clearly commanded the Earth, to bring forth living creatures of every kind, cattle and creeping things and wild animals of the Earth of every kind, in the Six Day.

The reason I do want to make and bring this point forward

to an active thought of a meditation phase in our life, is because by reading the Word of the Living God, we can learn and we can see how from the very beginning in the Order of the Creation, our Lord God Almighty by His will that was degreed, that was ordered, and also that was commanded, He by His own unlimited wisdom and power, established a genuine and a unique relationship designed by its active functions, a communication divine system encapsulated by their build sensors of their own moving expressions, by a powerful sourced and forwarded release of a dynamic energy integration capability force, to help synchronize and to help to facilitate and to help to coordinate all life existences, between Himself and all the Creation, and also to simplify and coordinate all life existences and all life expressed forms or shapes or active manifestations, between all the powerful and fundamental elements of God creation for their own life functional expressions, their own dynamic movements, and their own active participation within the vast limits of the created ethereal realm, and also to be activated by a single source point in the creation, sourced and fueled from the Creator, by being allowed to freely expressed their own delegated functions and purposes within God's created in-transcendental realm borders and limits.

What comes clearly into focus attention is all the vegetation, plants, and trees that the Earth put forth on the third Day, and all the living creatures, and all the creeping things, and all the wild animals that the Earth brought forth in the Sixth Day, and also all the swarms of the living creatures that have brought forward by the waters, and all the winged birds that were flying above the Earth, across the Dome, the firmament, the Sky, in the Fifth Day, they were all created and also were being made by God, as it is written in the scriptures that it is by the revelation from the Word of God that says" So God created them, and God made them."

In analyzing these two powerful phrases of, the Earth's "put forth", and the Earth's" brought forth" actions, we come to the understanding that these two mighty called and active expressions of Life's existence in the creation, are two very similar purposed activated manifest functions, for creating and birthing Life into the Creation' paramount landscape of its existence, by the direct decreed Order from God, for all life expressions and forms, and movements of their own kind and for their own kind, but in their reality purposed called functions, these two active expressions in the creation, are acting very entirely and wildly different, in their own structural forms and fundamental approaches for their own end results in their processed and authorized way of producing the activated the much needed elements that were desired by the Creator and called forwards from the depths of the unlimited and unsearchable Earth's depths, that was established and empowered with the capacity and with the ability to produce forth and bring forward, the atomic and the nucleus foundation of its particle matter of all physical life elements, that God use it to create and to made with His own hands, all the living and moving expressions of Life's forms, that were put forth and that were brought forth from the depths of the Earth's own deep core.

We clearly can see the correlation and the fundamental integration in the God's majestic creation, between the living expressions of their new life forms, that were activated by the "put forth" and by the "brought forth" bestowed capabilities of the immense powers of the waters, and of the unlimited magnitude powers of the Earth, received and ordained by the Creator into the depths of their own immovable foundations of their deep, the Water's foundation deep, and the Earth's foundation deep, and that were being actively delegated and appointed to them, to be able to release forward from within themselves and from their own foundation's deep, the powerful elements required in their own divine and masterfully designed and molded particle of God's will and desire encapsulated by its matter and revelation functions, the life block's element and its sparks of synchronized nucleus structure, that He alone, the Creator will use later on to create, and to make, and to plant, every single living expression of Life's forms, beings and shapes, that even today are very active manifesting their existences, and their movements, and their presence, all within their complexed water environmental limits, and also within the expressed Earth's ecological limits, and also within the firmament and across the vast skies environmental limits, where they were been activated, and also where they are today connected, being all allowed to be exposed to, and to be all manifested by their own created majestic abilities that were being adopted within their very own existence and movements of the their breathing life, to be able to swim, and to be able to walk, and to be able to fly.

One quick point I want to address and write before moving forward on this beautiful, but complexed subject in regards these very powerful blocks of life's elements and their nucleus structure released forward into the hands of the creator by the waters and by the earth, and by the firmament's atmosphere, at the voice of His powerful word, and at the authority of his commandments, is that no matter where their fundamental and their foundational original point of activation came from to be released forward, if their element of life foundation originated from within the depths of the water's fountains, or if their element of life foundation originated from within the depths of the earth's core, or if their element of life foundation originated from within the Hight of the Firmament's living atmosphere, they were all actively expressing their forms, and their movements and their presence in many different ways of breathing their existence of life, but also in the same time, and for their own different purposes and functions, all these different fundamental and foundational elements of life in the creation, were then, and are still now, bounded by its unique and common mechanism atomic sourced dominator force, by being all together connected and plugged into a single point source of its signal atomic structure and molecule frame into an unimaginable and unlimited and powerful massive synergetic complexed and living pulse, known to us as the only One true life activator for all elements of the creation's existence and movement, and the expressions of all life's living forms and living beings, located into the depths of God's own divine wisdom, and God's own divine understanding, and God's own divine knowledge, from where all the life fountains of the deep waters, all the life's untapped depths of the earth's core, and all the majestically but unsearchable heights of the vast firmament's multiply dimensions, even all the highest heavens that reigns above them all, are all together and in the same time joined in a nonstop synchronized movement for their allowed and for their continuous sustainment and expressions of their delegated and raw appointed living orders of the creation's purposed function, are pulling forward their active life's energy, to continually sustain and maintain their own expressed existences and their own manifestations for their breathing and living forms.

    When God by His decreed Word, ordered the waters and the Earth, to put forth and to bring along all the active living creatures that are swimming, that are swarming, that are flying and crawling, and walking all around the vast paramount of God's creation's transcendental realm of active expressions of their own robust kneed connectivity at the hands of His own masterfully designs plans for them all living creatures that will be exposed to

Life in the creation, established the contained structural atom's functions within the deep and active fundamental sustainment environment for the foundations of the Water's fountains, and for the foundations of the Earth's deep, and for the immovable foundations of the Dome, also known as the Sky, and the firmament above it, that has its own powerful and its magnificent structural nucleus frames built and then anchored into the Earth's living core, proclaimed and told to all them living and powerful original elements of Life in the creation, to accommodate and to maintain and to sustain all the living forms, beings and shapes that he is about to bring forth, that he is about to create and to make, and that he is about to ordain, for all the living and the breathing life's creatures, for their own kind and for their own purpose in God's living and actively sustained and maintained breathing, of all them masterfully created, in his wisdom made, and also being called forward by the power of the Creator, to manifest and to express the movement of all the Life in the creation, regardless what forms, what shapes, and what beings they were designed to be, that are still very active in the existence today.

At the end of the Sixth Day of Creation, when everything that God created thus far was all synchronized in a single point of synergetic nucleus active structure powered by his total divine and expressed motions established by the will, by the power, and by his heavenly revelatory desires that God himself propelled them into a forward and into an outward existence, from within His own depths of His infinite wisdom and uncontained love, and unlimited knowledge, when all the original elements and fundamental blocks of Life in the creation were set and were ordained to function together as one unison to maintain and to sustain and to create within themselves the decreed environmental and also the necessary platforms for the living creation, when all the completed forms of all life beings, and shapes, and all of their expression, were designed to be able to communicate and to collaborate and to understand each other's functions and their ordained and bestowed purposes assigned to them by the Almighty Creator, at the very end of this majestic sixth Day of the creation, God in his grace and his mercy choose to revealed and to introduce to his entire original elements and powers in the vast created realm, and to all that he called, and to all that he formed and to all that he made, to all the powers of life, and to all their moving expressions within the entire and vast in-transcendental realm, the majestic treasure of His creation, the masterfully designed and planned created life, contained and totally encapsulated by the manifold and mighty works of His own hands and by the breath of his own release fountains springs of activated and sustained life from within himself, the one and the only one, known to all forms, movements and shapes and manifestations, to all from above and to all from below and to all from the center's balance stage of living and breathing life, the Human, the first Human created in God's own image and likeness, the humankind after God's unique kind.

    The revelation brought forward by the works of God's own hands in the front of all of the creation's original and elemental powers that were in a completed operational and active structural form of their own assigned and delegated purposes to them by God for their own functional and own manifest existence, the majestic humankind, the Adam Creation, revealed to the creation, and for the design to maintain and to sustain the Order in the Creation, was created entirely different from all of the other previous created and brought forward life expressions and their manifestations, and their majestic beings, and their forms and shapes within their own established and allowed living expressions to exist and to operate within the perfect realm of God's magnificent creation.

When God created all the swarms of living creatures and all the great sea monsters, and all of the other live animals that were ones of the first brought forth and original elements in the creation, the Mighty Waters that has its own powerful root and origin anchored into the everlasting Depths of God, the Waters brought forth the substance and the products of its atomic submatter used for the creation, functions and purpose of all the swarms living creatures, at the powerful decreed Word and at the commandment of the Creator, and all of them that were created by God to be the living creatures of every kind after the property elements of the Water's very own style, and all the winged live birds that are flying above the Earth across all the firmament's Dome and Sky's atmosphere created by God, to be the living creatures of every kind after the waters and after the atmosphere and the firmament's own kind elements and structural forms from within their own, but at the very same time, connected within their own fundamental combinations of their powerful living impressions and imprints elements of Life in the creation's design of God's divine and revealed wisdom, and all of the live creatures that God created, all the creeping things and all of the wild animals in the existence, when one of the first created original and fundamental elements in the creation, the Earth, had brought forth from within its own core's deep foundation, the elements and the atomic forms and structure matter, at the decreed Word and the commandment of God, they were all created to be the living expressed creatures of every kind after the living fundamental elements of Life and their functions, after the Earth's own's DNA and own nucleus matter of its expressed and manifest kind.

But when God created the humankind, the Adam, the majestically jewel of his creation, the only one that will be able to integrate and to contain within his own depths and within his own structural designed for Life and living build capacity system mechanism, many other signals and many other expressions together with their different manifestations and movements of Life in the creation that were already being created and expressed even long before Adam will come into the creation's own breathing existence and in its own's fingerprint identification and authority of a living being, when he was created, and when he was molded and when he was formed by the hands of the Almighty God, from within the substance and the identity of the powerful elements and their created and revealed subatomic matter and their DNA, brought forth by the Earth in the Creation and for the Creation at the commandment of God, and from within the infinite substance and the identity of the powerful elements and their subatomic matter and their DNA, brought forth by the waters in the creation, and from within the substance and the essence of their powerful features and their subatomic forms of its own DNA, brought on by the firmament's sky and atmosphere in the creation, and being together added and integrated within the vast depths of the immense structural and the complexed and fundamental foundation of the first human cell and expression created and named Adam, that were all allowed to bring forth into the creation's paramount landscape, their own individual forms and existences, to be able to move and to express themselves in the accordance with their own and each individual created kinds, under the will and the wisdom, and the divine guidance of the Creator, and we can learn from this powerful revelation received forward from the written Word of God, and from the scriptures where in the book of the Genesis, that the Almighty Creator it is communicating, his will and his desire to bring forth and to create a true dominator ruler for his creation, and an authentic living being expression of its manifestation for the Order of Life, in his own divine image, and also in the accordance with his own divine likeness, to rule and to have complete dominion over God's creation, and to fulfill and to be able to maintain and to be able to uphold by God's own decreed and spoken authorization and powers bestowed upon him, with the very necessary and powerful divine capabilities and abilities to maintain and to sustain and to have dominion and control over all God's Order in the Creation, and for the creation.

Genesis 1: 26-27: "Then God said, 'Let us make humankind in our image, according to our likeness; and let them have dominion over the fish of the sea and the birds of the air, and the cattle, and all the wild animals of the earth, and every creeping thing that creeps upon the earth.' So, God created humankind in his image, in the image of God he created them, male and female he created them."

Based on this powerful and true revelation from the Word of the Living God, that after millennial ages reached even us, a distance but not forgotten fruit of what was once a majestically created seed in the human form's robust structure within the foundation of God's creation, we can see that for the very first time, He the Creator himself, the unlimited and the powerful spring of living waters, the wisdom's source of every expression and manifestation of their moving energy within the vast paramount of God's perfect realm, He is pouring himself out into the creation, by creating the first Human in his own image and in his own likeness, by taking the substance and the elements of the Earth's ordained and produced matter of its own kind life, by molding it and also by forming it within the Human's subatomic and atomic expressed nucleus system activator, the place and the chamber capacitor where he will add and also will combine the substance and the elements of the waters ordained and their produced matter of its own kind life, and their own importance and characteristics of the firmament's untapped atmosphere and sky that was ordained to make living matter of its own kind, creating the unique and the perfect and the divine location chambers of Life, where all these different and powerful expressions and manifestations of the fundamental and original elements of God's creation will be able together to co-exist and move in a unison complexed shape and divine form, propelled and activated in the creation's transcendental realm of existence, by God's own unlimited and powerful Breath of Life.

Going back to the Scriptures, we can see from the description of the event that was revealed to us in Genesis 2: 7, Then the Lord God formed man from the dust of the ground and breathed into his nostrils the Breath of Life, and the man became a living being, unquote," and many other translations are referring to this event also, that the man became a living soul, became a human, The Human, when the Creator pours out from the depths of his own infinite vast and deep energetic atomic and particle matter, his breath of Life into the innermost and deep chamber of expression and existence of this majestic jewel of his new creation, designed and created, molded and formed by God's own hands, to be able to contain and to sustain within the fundamental and structural chamber of his existence, God's very true own breath of Life and God's very own DNA released in the creation for the continued maintenance and sustainment of His Creation.

I have always been fascinated by this robust process of inhaling and exhaling life's breathing air. I will not debate it or expand on this subject at this time. Still, maybe in the future, God will allow me and help me to develop it in a more detailed format, but what fascinates me is how we take the first breath of Life coming into this realm of Life's existence through the functions of the nostrils, and how we are releasing it out, or return it to God from the depths of our very own living expressions, at that very moment when we are exiting this realm of Life's truly experiences and their living expression, the last breath of our lived Life on this Earth through the functions of the mouth.

It is purely astounding to be able to understand the masterfully designed and planned map structure of God's breath of Life from the point when it enters to activate the living soul's existence in this earthly realm through the Human nostrils and when it is exiting at the expiration of the soul's living expression from this earthly realm of its manifestation through the human's mouth. In the anatomy of the human body, the nostrils and the mouth are next to one another and are deeply connected. Yet the traveling of God's very own breath of Life from the moment when it enters the human chamber of Life's expressions through the nostrils to the moment when it exits out from the human's living chamber of its life's motion and expression through the mouth, it is called the Human's Overall Lifespan of its existence on this earthly realm of its temporary active motions, living expressions, and complex manifestations.

It takes as long as God the Creator allows his breath of Life to sustain the human's existence as a breathing living soul on his created and expressed journey within God's magnificent build and majestically designed and perfect in-transcendental realm.

Considering that the creation of the Human, the masterfully planned and designed living being, by the own hands of the Almighty God, is at the end of the sixth Day of creation, also known as the last Day of Creation for all of the created expressions of life forms in existence in their active and their manifest movements complimenting the vast magnificent and majestic creation of God, I believe that the Human being it is the most intrigued crafted and masterfully ever created living being in this entire creation, designed to contain and to hold within its most resounding and within its unreached and unsearchable parts of its fundamental and structural foundation of its atomic and molecular chambers of its living expression, the mysteries of God's true wisdom, and God's genuine understanding and knowledge, that were ever to be released within the creation, for the creation's function, for the creation's purpose, and for the creation's Order.

Like a king in ancient times, who used to rule by the authority of his decreed words penned inside the canvas of a letter when he wanted to implement his Order within his kingdom or wished to announce rules and regulations for the wellbeing of his kingdom's Order for all of his subjects, at the end of his letter to give authority for the decreed law and announcement, the king used to seal it with his signet ring that will validate it and will establish it, following his power and authority, I believe that the Almighty God the Creator of Heavens and the Earth, and the Creator of everything in heavens and the Creator of everything on Earth, at the end of the sixth Day of the creation, at the end of the spoken, decreed, formed and molded "letter of the creation," announced and revealed to all of the living expressions of their manifest life, to all of the powers and all of the original elements of Life's fundamental and structural blocks of the creation, the Humankind, the genuine seal and the treasured signet ring jewel of his active creation after his image and after his likeness, the Humankind, the only created and majestically design living being in the entire overall creation that it is indeed the only carrier of God's breath of life.

With the announcement and the revelation that God brought forward into the creation and for the order of the creation at the end of the Sixth Day, as the last created expressed manifestation that God had brought forward, and also that God had brought up, to be introduced to all God's creation as a ruler with a vast dominion and appointed authority over God's creation, the human living soul is established in the Order of the Creation, as the most treasured and significant life and living expression and manifest movement after God's very own kind. " God saw everything he had made; indeed, it was perfect. And there was evening and morning, The Sixth Day." Genesis 1:31*

    Thus everything that was created by God, and called forward into their existences, by being formed and by being shaped and molded for their own expressed functions and purposes in the creation, from the very first moment when this truth and powerful statement from the everlasting eternity came forth with the proclamation " In the beginning God created the heavens and the earth", to the very last moment when this powerful and truth statement came forth reaching even us with the proclamation, " God saw everything that he had made, and indeed it was very good, "were released and were activated and were appointed with all the necessary abilities and bestowed complexed capabilities upon each and every single one of their expression of their own kind living and breathing manifestation of God's given Life, to be integrated as one creation, as one movement, as one expression, and together to be all sourced, and all maintained, and all sustained by the wisdom and the power of the Almighty God, within this perfect and this majestic in transcendental realm of God's own design, that was revealed in the creation, and to his all and entire vast creation by his own unlimited and absolute divine love expression.

    In Genesis 2:1-4" the Word of the Living God says," Thus the heavens and the Earth were finished, and all their multitudes. And on the Seventh Day, God finished the work that he had done, and he rested on the Seventh Day from all that he had done. So, God blessed the Seventh Day and hallowed it because, on it, God rested from all the work he had done in the creation. These are the generations of the Heavens and the Earth when they were created.

I want to address a few rapid points in the closing of this chapter, "The Transcendental Realm," before I write the following few chapters for the readers.

The first point I want to be able to address here is that God, in his divine creation, ordained and established by his decreed Word and authority multiple dominions with their rulers within the newly created realm, and blessed them and empowered them to be able to govern and to able to maintain and to sustain God's Order in the Creation. Going through the revelatory scriptures from the living Word of God, we clearly can learn and understand that for all the created and all the live expressions of life for their very own kind, shaped and forms that were called into existence expressions by the Creator in his perfect and majestic ethereal realm, he appointed three powerful rulers for the containment of his established and decreed Order in the creation.

The first one appointed as Ruler by the Creator himself to maintain and to sustain his established Order in the creation was the Great Luminator, known in our terminology as the Sun, created on the Fourth Day by God to rule and govern the Day, and the second one appointed as Ruler by the Creator himself to maintain and sustain his established Order in the creation was the Lesser Luminator known in our time terminology as the Moon, also created in the fourth Day by God to rule and to govern the Night and the stars. Also, both Luminators, the Greater Luminator of the

Day and the Lesser Luminator of the Night were appointed and jointly authorized by God to maintain and sustain the separation of Light from the darkness within the creation for all their generations and their created multitudes and hosts. The third one was appointed as Ruler by the Creator himself, to rule and have dominion over all the completed works of the Almighty God that were expressing their manifested existences within the authority of the waters and the waters living swarms and created creatures, or within the dominion of the Earth and the Earth own's created living creatures, or within the authority of the firmament's sky atmosphere and all of their own winged and flying live birds of the air, across the vast paramount of God's creation, was the Adam, the Human created, formed and molded after God's very own kind, that received God's true own breath of Life into his nostrils, known to be the last created living being and its ever-living soul, at the end of the sixth Day of God's divine and magnificent and completed works of his creation by his own hands.

The second quick point I want to address in the closing of this chapter of the book is the robust revelatory understanding that came forward from the living Word of God to reach us from the everlasting eternity of the Almighty God's depths of his divine and forever wisdom and infinite knowledge came forward and forth into the creation the fundamental and functional foundation of all blocks and structures to maintain and to sustain inside their true own original roots, all of the powerful elements and expressions of their manifest Life in the creation. These original roots from within God's powerful own depths of everlasting wisdom and infinite knowledge, without the beginning and with no end, that always it was, that always is, and that will always be, rooted and grounded into eternity by God is the Spoken Word, the Spirit of God, the Waters, the Deep, and the Darkness. These five everlasting powers combined into one powerful and divine original root sprung forth from the depths of God himself; it is the root foundation that holds on its structure and its single point mechanism existence, everything that God ever created, every single expression and manifestation of Life, their movements and their existences, regardless their space, their time and their matter, where were placed or allowed to live and be manifested, in the creation and for the creation existence, the creation functions and its divine purpose.

    The third quick point I want to address here is that based on the Word of God, we can understand and learn that at the end of the Sixth Day, after God had proclaimed that there was an evening and a morning that Day when God finished the creation of the Heavens and the Earth, and were completed and filled with all their multitudes and their living hosts, that were actively expressing their manifested and appointed life motions and functions, God brought for all of them that were called forward into the realm of his creation and existence, for all the creation's breathing and their living life, to witness the revelation of the Seventh Day, the Day of rest after he finished the work he had done when he rested on that Seventh Day from all the work he had done. So, God blessed the Seventh Day and hallowed it, because on it God rested from all the work that he had done in the Creation, but there was not any longer other evening and there was not any longer other morning, that makes me to sincerely believe that the majestic Seventh Day that was blessed and hallowed it by God, that powerful Seventh Day when God finished the work that he had done, that magnificent Seventh Day it never ended there, and it will never end there, because that Seventh Day from there it is not the seventh day from here, the way I like to say this phrase " that Holy Seven Day from that perfect and that majestic and incorruptible and vast in-transcendental realm of God's creation, that eternal Seventh Day when God finished the work that he had done, that Seventh Day blessed and hallowed it by God, because on it God rested, that Seventh Day, that forever and eternal Day of rest it is not bound by the limits and the threshold of the time that it is reflected within the appointed authority functions and purposes of the Evening and of the morning's fundamental and their masterfully design and activated schematics for their time tracing capabilities, for all the creation's breathing and living expressed and their manifest Life and existence's span, and I will just leave it here for now, but definitely this is a very powerful point that can be debated across the many denominational platforms and their many different religious belief systems and forum structures that are so many man made and are being founded and located deep within their own self and rational understand spectrums of their own applied and manifested pressures and influences of power for domination, with their birthed desires to be able to capture within their active and manipulative control, the consciousness and the behavior of the masses around them for their own established schemes to fit their own expressed benefits.

And as a last point I want to be able to address in this closing summary of this eighth chapter of this book is the point of the truth that the man revealed from the Word of the living Gin regards to what once was, what it is now, and what it will be once again, with the only Ruler in the Order of the Creation that was established and appointed by God, created in God's very own image and formed in God's very own likeness, the humankind, the one that lost his dominion and lost the place that was reserved just below God himself from the highest heavens, to be able to rule and to have authority over the elements and all the expressions of the living and breathing Life manifested, and being fundamentally established in the creation of God, that are the works of his own hands.

The Sun still rules, and it is still governing the Day, and the Moon still rules and it is still governing the Night and the stars, but the once magnificent and majestic creation of God, the Human, created in God's own image and formed in God's own likeness, the Human, the only active carrier of God's own breath of Life, was taken away from his owned and established place from where he once ruled, and from his owned dominion that was in its entire realm of living expressions gifted and appointed by the Almighty Creator to him, the Human, who lost it all when pride was found in him, and when disobedience took control of his actions, when he, the Human, opened himself up to the very massive and powerful influences and their fundamental expressions that were all surrounding the Human within the realm of the creation, without realizing that the root of their effects and their powerful manipulations, sprung forward against the Human, due to their own envy and their own destructive jealousy that they released against him, the Human, when all them very powerful influences of Life that were manifested within God's magnificent creation, did not understood and could not penetrate the robust bond seal established and created by God's true own DNA revelation released within the human's soul creation, being brought forward, then activated and multifold increased from the profound depths of God's own wisdom and untapped infinite knowledge, into the very deep and depths of the Human very own soul's dwelling of its breathing and living light fundamental foundation, through the divine and eternally, and everlasting spirit of Life, and through the unsearchable magnitude and the infinite power of God's breath of Life that sustain, and that enables the soul's very living expression and manifestation to exist.

Chapter Nine:
The Truth Shifters

Romans 1:25:" Because they exchanged the truth about God for a lie and worshiped and served the creature rather than the Creator, who is blessed forever! Amen."

Along the chapters and pages of this book, so far we covered in more details the subject of the very real and very dangerous waves of deceptions and their powerful and real living manipulations that are rooted and planted deep within the foundation of their own established stronghold union powers, from which they are released and sprinted forward as a fully functional scheme, fueled by the always shifting and operative shadows of their own process understood and molded alternatives of the truth, through which they are trying to captivate and they are trying to influence the humanity's exposed and molded behavior with their own influenced sounds and waves of information that it is being powered by their own build and activated mechanism product of their own thoughts system application, that are being activated forward from their own released signals and pulses of their very own controlled data and information platforms and structures, to be able to prepare, and to be able to plan, and to be able to implement their own manipulative schemes and actions towards achieving their own end purpose and their final end result search, that it is being fully organized and released and energized, by their very powerful and masterful desires to be able to replace the powerful Absolute Truth of the Almighty God, with their own influences and their own self-made alternatives and also self-made relatives fundamentals and sources, that are being activated from their always shifting shadows and their always powerful dark influences, by passing them to all of their own surroundings and to all of them that are exposed to, as being the true Absolute Truth of God, for the very end destination and its final location, and for the eternal Soul's captivation, that it may be hold and tight encapsulated within their own and very powerful structural schematic frames that will try to continually keep the soul away from the very presence and from the very blessings of the only One Absolute Truth, the Everlasting and the Almighty Creator and God, the Father of its forever and eternal life, the One that when He breathed into the human's nostrils, the human became a living Soul, created and formed in the image and likeness of the One True and Infinite God.

Up to this point in the book, we covered in a more detailed frame, the very real warfare that takes place continually, and the very dangerous waves of powerful influences of the humanity truth shifters that are being activated from within their very own stronghold made union of their manipulative and fundamental structures and schemes, that are all being actively manifested and continually moving and revolving around us, and by surrounding us with their very own presence and their own targeted released powers that are fueled and sustained by their own deceitful field of information, from the very first moment of living life, when we are taking in, our very first breath of air, until the very last moment of living life on this temporary realm of our existence on the earth's living form, when we are expiring from it, by the way of releasing from within the depths of our own manifest and expressed existence, our very last breath of air, also known to us, to be the application process of the powerful release of our own human Soul, from the bounds and the limits of this mortality and this corruption of our expressed and manifested living form on the earth, back into the magnificent and the powerful infinite and majestic paramount transcendental realm of expressions and its allowed and manifesting immortality in the heavens above and the very everlasting presence of our Almighty Creator and God, within His divine and precious eternity forever.

To be able to understand what it is the real fight for the eternal survival of the human Soul, to be able to know where it is the location and the place where this hard fight for survival is actively being fought non-stop, and to be able to realize why there is a fight for the end destination of our own Soul's existence, we do need to, and must allow ourselves to be captivated and moved forward by the unlimited protection of the Spirit of the Living God, and also we need to be continually guided by the power of the Word of the Living God, that will help us to discover the things that matter the most in our temporary and short journey of life on this earthly realm of our manifest and express living, and that it is the everlasting salvation of our human Soul.

The fight for the eternal destination and survival of humanity's Soul is a battle constantly taking place even at this present moment of our living expressed existence. It has been an active fight module that has always taken place from the very first moment when the human became a living soul when God breathed into his nostrils, God's breath of life, and it will continually be active. It will take place till that defining moment when the human soul-expressed existence and manifestations allotted for the human's soul dynamic and living expressions to be manifested on this earthly realm within the temporary form of its living and breathing and created time frame will expire and come to an end.

It is critical and imperative for us to be able to understand and to be able to comprehend what it entails and where this decisive fight and battle for the soul's survival are taking place.

To gain the structural understanding and the clarity of the robust released information data and its powerful signals towards our Soul's survival fight and its reality, we must allow ourselves to be guided and driven forward and to be helped by the unrestricted protection and comfort of the Spirit of the Living God, and we must allow ourselves to be led and to be guided on our human life's active battlefield location and place, by the power of the Word of the Living God, that will be with us all, and that will help us all, to protect and to guide us, and to lead us towards the victory of our Soul's survival stage, into the eternal final and majestic destination and the forever location prepared by the Almighty God for the eternity of our living souls.

The structural and the compelling fundamental pin-point focus understandings of our very own surroundings that are revealed to humanity by the Living Word of God will enable us to be able to sense and recognize why the very true struggles and the genuine fight for the end destination of our very own human Soul's existence and our very own human survival it is so crucial and vital.

In a true essence of its manifestation, the natural and actual fight for the survival of our Soul, takes place very deep within ourselves and very deep within our own continue daily activities and expressions and interactions we have within ourselves own built and strong fundamental complex feelings and emotions, and their powered actions, that are encapsulated by our very own thoughts and by our very own structural opinions that are released forward into existence by our own understandings and morals standards and their appearance as norms, or within the world structures that are manifesting all around us that are always surrounding us all humans, with their own molded and build fundamental complex fueled by their own feelings and by their own emotions or thoughts and opinions that are all encapsulated within the world's view of understanding the meaning of life and the meaning of the Soul's eternal destination and salvation that are based on the world and the world's own moral standards and their own belief system and fundamental mechanism of their own produced thought and influenced view for the masses.

It is and ongoing battle against the everything that it is negative, and the everything that it is under the negative's powerful deceptions and their manipulative schemes and views, that are continually threaten to corrupt and to constantly threaten to destroy the real hope that keeps the surviving Soul engaged fully in this fight, that it is the Word of God and His Holy Spirit Guidance, on the life's battlefield fight for its survival and for its eternal destination, but knowing and understanding that the Word of God it is Absolute and it cannot be subject to alteration, or to any other changes or to any other outside influences, that are the real dangerous and the natural manipulative schemes of the enemy of the Soul, that it is trying to destroy the Soul's hope, will try to affect and will try to blurry the mind processor and its entire consciousness structure and behavior, and it's very complete and constructive belief system, by corrupting its thought processor mechanism and functions of the Mind's powerful active expressions, within the depths of its deep that it is located within the Soul's consciousness roots, that will then allow them to bypass the Reality and the Absolute of the Word of God, by passing them to all their subjects and to all their surroundings that are exposing themselves and their existence to their influences, through their very own and very powerful filters of deceptions and their corrupt foundation of structural thought, and their masterfully designed forces that are trying daily to capture the Mind and its living Soul in their forever sorrows and death, alone and afraid, without a real hope, in a total and complete state of desolation and helpless stage of never ending confusion and regrets.

But the Spirit of the Living God provides us all that are trusting in him, with the needed protection and strength for our Soul and the needed comfort and peace in the midst of our brutal and turbulent battlefield and fight that it is happening for our final end destination of our Soul, and the powerful Word of the Living God will always guide us all that are part of the living Soul's expressed form and its designed manifestations, on this temporary but real fight and journey of our life survival, by teaching us all, and by releasing unto us it's deep and its unlimited outsourced wisdom and magnified light, that are called and propelled forward into the humanity's very own Soul, by God's own magnificent and majestic divine and infinite power and steadfast love, towards, and for our own Soul's forever existence and for our own Soul's forever living manifestation into the holy presence of our Lord God Almighty, our true One everlasting Father and Creator, that from the very first activated and brought forward into the existence this very powerful connectivity moment, that happened between God and Human, when He breathed into the nostrils of the human His own divine sourced DNA, that the human, the last created and formed expression in the Order of the Creation, may became a living soul in God's own image and likeness, and that the human the one true magnificent living Soul, it will be able to exist and to live for the eternity, and that the Soul it will be forever surrounded by God's own presence and God's own everlasting protection and blessings, and his forever comfort and its eternal peace.

I had a conversation one day with one of my own family

member, and as we were talking and covering the subject of the very powerful deceptions and their manipulative influences of the powerful enemy of our living Soul, that I mentioned about it also in few words even in this chapter, that it is working hard against us without ceasing, by using our very own abilities and capabilities that were bestowed by the Creator upon us and within the depths our own fundamental and structural complex system mechanism of our life activated living expressions and movements, that it is able to receive and to capture and also to disseminate information that are always beaming their signals non-stop all around humanity's entire paramount of its powerful living forms that are framed and encapsulated by their own expressed manifestations, and I was asked during our conversation how can the enemy of our Soul, and how the enemy of our Soul, will try, and will be able to confuse our minds and also how he will be able to even blurry the consciousness of our minds if given the opportunity to unleash his deceptive schemes and influences into our own deep fundamental thought structure, when we as humanity and our very own living Soul, are in true the last and also the most magnificent expression of God's Creation, formed and created in God's own image and likeness and the only living and breathing expressions of life that are the carriers of God's own breath of life and God's own magnificent and unlimited and unsearchable and powerful DNA that was breathed into the human's nostrils when the human became a living soul, part of God's own unmovable and unshakable foundation and its purposed released and formed expression in the Creation to sustain and to maintained forever the Soul's living and breathing expressions in his protection, and in his forever presence?

I will try to elaborate in a few words the vital importance and its imperative comprehension actions of the realities that are surrounding all of humanity in regards their very fluid in active motions and their actual appearances, but also the activities of the facts that are being very dangerously processed by a completely different build complexity of information and data combinations matrix, part of a very vast multipronged variety of their own powerful and influential and fundamental frames and structural networking labyrinths with their own multitudes of hidden passages and tunnels that are trying to mask and bypass the absolute truth of God with its smoke and mirrors produced and released mirage, and this enemy of the Soul will stop at nothing to be fulfill and to reach its purposed results and goal, that it is to be able to ultimately affect the state of the human Mind and its entire and complete consciousness schematics and its active roots, located within the foundation of the deep chambers of the consciousness's own living powers of processing and also acting on its desires by being able to fulfill the expressions of its own manifestation, that if it is achieved, it will ultimately lead and cause the complete destruction of the living Soul's eternal hope and its planned destination that was ordained and established by God from the beginning of times, or I will may say that was ordained and selected for the living Soul, even from the depths of the Creator's everlasting and eternally steadfast and unlimited love for his entire Creation.

As I mentioned previously in the chapters and paragraphs of this book, the human that became a living Soul, it is the last and also it is the most magnificent expression in the entire Creation, the only breathing and living life shape, that was formed in God's own very image and in his own likeness, and we as humans that are experiencing this very strong and powerful manifestation and its undeniable expressions of the living Soul's abilities and its rooted and anchored eternal functions, and the faster we realize that from the very beginning of our existence our Creator wanted to forever surround us with his everlasting and infinite comfort and his blessings, and his protection and his peace, the faster we will allow ourselves to be leaded and guided by the unshakable and unmovable foundation of the Rock of Ages, that will bring deep into our consciousness's fundamental structure and expressions, the true purpose of our existence, and the true meaning of our life's passing and its temporary journey, that one day it will be culminated by our end destination and forever destiny.

When we realize and recognize that our created and formed expression of life and its powerful spiritual undeniable origins, that exists within the limits of our own very fundamental and structural foundation of our breathed existence as a forever living soul, that was brought forward and emancipated, and liberated from the influences of the most powerful elements of life in the Creation, by the very own Breath of Life and DNA of God's own unlimited wisdom and infinite knowledge, the One and the true Creator of all things, visible and invisible, and their spiritual, psychological and physical forms and shapes in the entire Creation, the only One and true Almighty God, we will be able to realize, and also we will be able to sense and to recognize who really it is after us and after our living Soul's essence and its spiritual fragrance, and after what has been deposited by the powerful Breath of God within the hidden chambers of our most profound parts of our living Soul, who really is the enemy of our Soul, and why there is and exists a real fight for the very end destination and forever destiny for the living Soul's breath and its uncorrupted DNA origins that the living Soul received from God, to be able to capture it and to hold it in its robust deceptive and influential schemes, all the authentic and powerful living Soul's information and data functions of its forever expressions reflected by God's own image and likeness and its forever living eternity and its permanently activated connectivity and signals within the presence of his Creator.

But how in the truth of the matter, we can be able to recognize and realize the real and the dangerous deceitful influences that are being released continually and non-stop against our own Soul and its eternal survival, by the natural enemy of our Soul, that it is filling the air and its entire atmosphere presence all around us within our own surroundings of living and moving expressions and manifestations, with its very own and powerful deceptive waves of information and data structures, that can bring at times much confusions and deceitful revelations, that will really blurry the Mind by injecting and infecting with its purpose designed schemes, all the chambers of our complete consciousness roots that are located within the powerful thought mechanism system bestowed and ordained by our Creator upon us the humans, that we may be able to function and to be able to operate in our created existence as once was our purpose and intent for the Order in the Creation's magnificent and perfect transcendental realm manifestation and its living expression?

But how in the truth of the matter, we can be able to recognize and realize the real and the dangerous deceitful influences that are being released continually and non-stop against our own Soul and its eternal survival, when the absolute truth of the Almighty God, it is so many times and it is so often perceived by us very subjectively within our own way of understanding it and process it, and it is so often influenced even by our very own made individual belief system that we may be influence to adhere to it and hold it as being accurate, but that it is not based on the Word of Living God, but it is based on our own individual past and its very present living experiences of our lives, and it is so often at times even being perceived by our own known or maybe at various and multiples of times, by the unknown of our own hidden but very strong and natural biases, that we as humans are tending to accumulate them and to possess them all along the living years of our lives due to our life's struggles for survival on this earth's temporary journey of a live spiritual expressions encapsulated by the winds of the always turning and passing wheel of time, and are being limited and bounded by its physical and its material form within its allowed functions, expressions and movements?

But how in the truth of the matter, we can be able to recognize and realize the real and the dangerous deceitful influences that are being released continually and non-stop against our own Soul and its eternal survival, when our own Mind in its very powerful consciousness behavioral and systematic approaches of its living mechanism structure for processing the vast and at times what seems to be significant blocks of unlimited information and data, that it is coming on a daily bases upon the complex humanity's structured and its very active thought processor foundation, in a never ending released assault from all the places and from all the angles of life's own understanding and its own movements of its forward expressions and abilities, that it is causing the absolute truth of God to become blurry inside our own mind structure and its fundamental purpose and functions, due to the many realities and factors that are being very fervent able active, and also that are being very able to mold it and to shape it and to affect it in many different ways and in many other forms, even our very own way to be able to perceive the understanding of the absolute truth of God, and the truth's eternal living purpose for all living forms and shapes and their expressions and movements in the entire Creation and for the whole of the Creation and its complex existence.

But how in the truth of the matter, we can be able to recognize and realize the real and the dangerous deceitful influences that are being released continually and non-stop against our own Soul and its eternal survival, when the confusion and the manipulation of our own Mind and its practical consciousness ability to process and disseminate the information and its data signals received and revealed from the absolute truth of the Word of the Living God for our soul salvation, becomes blurry and really strongly affected and also being infected at the very root of our own structural and fundamental thought process system and its mechanism functions, by our own upbringing and growth that we were being exposed to even from our very infant stages of life, being molded and breaded and seeded by a powerful cultural environmental and its very powerful societal influences around us, that we all were been at various times exposed to, or at times when we were even being born into a such robust and systematic life environment and its belief system and structures that operates in its entire manifest expressions, completely parallel and even at times foreign to the absolute truth of the Creator and his valid message for humanity?

It is there a strong link and a real correlation network system of processing and disseminate raw data and its hot information, between how we can understand it and how we can interpret it, the true revelation that it is received from the absolute truth of God and his true message, and between our own thought application process system and its manifestation that can capture and receive the true revealed information within the depths of its own structural and fundamental mechanism of its powerful living expressions of thought, than activate and release them forward through the filters and through the receptors of our own belief system and portals that are being activated and fueled by the very multitudes of many various and vast applicable moral values, that we learned to live by them all of our entire exposed lives, then also teaching ourselves to be able to accept their activated expressed functions based on our cultural exposure and its powerful at times very undeniable societal influences, that can be bestowed upon us and instilled deep within our own believe system and frames of its active manifestations, even by our own families that we were born into, or even by our own communities we want so bad to be able to assimilate with and be part of them and to be accepted by them at times, or even by our own countries and systems and places where we are all living our daily lives, that can and it will be able to blurry our understanding of God's truth, and it can really dangerously influence our mind and its very own consciousness by manipulating our own structural foundation of our thoughts, on how can we really view it, how can we really process it and how can we really interpret it, to be as an active response and also to be as an understood that it is manifesting its actions towards all of our living surroundings as a visible, and as a tangible act being seen by others as to be our trust and belief and a true obedience towards our creator's true message and his true revelation received for the soul of humanity, and for its forever restoration process of redemption, and for its forever and eternal destination and destiny that not ever a living and breathing soul will be able to escape it and exchange it after its allotted time of restoration and redemption expires.

It is a very critical and it is a very powerfully vital reality, for our own spiritual health and also for our own physical and psychological health, the undeniable importance to be able to realize and to be able to recognize our own selves created and build motives and desires schemes, that are very many times structured and shaped in such a way that it may be able to reflect us through a distorted reality and its own continue search for our own unsatisfied images and their always shifting mirages, of who we really believe and think that we are as created beings, and what it is our fundamental purposes and desires as a living soul that its only true, and its only active and its only forever expression for now, it is being encapsulated and bounded within the limits and the barriers of the time and its own mortality phase of existence, and that are all based on the always movable foundations of our own constructive and living expressions for our own fulfillment and desires of our temporary life's manifestations and its achievement forms, to be able to approach and to be able to build our faith and belief system with a very reverend and clear understanding of God and his absolute truth, with and open but very strictly and very humble mindset, that it is being fueled and propelled forward by a clean and by a sanctified spirit and its consciousness, by the blood of the Lamb of the Living God and by his Holy Spirit, and realizing and knowing and acknowledging that our own self beliefs and its systems, and our own self biases and our own self way of understanding about the revelatory absolute truth of God and its very true message, and if our own mindset and its consciousness it is left uncalibrated and unchecked by the true revelation that comes forth only from the Word of the Living God, can dangerously be able to influence us all, and it will be able to influence even our own thought process mechanism, and it will be able to completely affect and infect our own self way of perception and its focus visions that were already being forth established for our living lives as human travelers on this earth and on the earth's temporary journey of its holding expressions and its powerful influences and controlled functions of the earth's own manifestations upon and over all of the humanity's spiritual and physical senses and expressions, and also if it will be left unchecked and uncalibrated by the Word of the Living God, it will be able to affect even the very living soul's eternal end destination location, and that location will also be the living soul's forever place and its forever and reserved house of the soul's unchangeable destiny.

I believe that it is imperative and also very critical for us to be able to develop the ability to start recognizing and understanding our own will, our motives, and our desires, even our very own instincts and biases that we as humans are exposed to and also we as humans are prone to start to save them and to accumulate them into the fundamental fiber and the blocks of our frames and to build foundation of our build images of their reflected and living build structures of identification, even in those various times when that desired and searched after its reflection and its oneself image for an approve identification does not mirror who we really are and who we want to be, but it does not matter its reflections or what their images and their appearances may seems to be and reflect, because the one true process of an approved identification it is not based on the many shifting reflections of our shadows, but it is based, and it will be based on our own activated and self-expressions and their manifestations that are built on the powerful template of our own self-awareness mechanism system, that it is so essential and it is so important and it is so very vital for our living lives, and this powerful and activated self-awareness mechanism system it will help us to be able to align ourselves, and to align our goals, and align our dreams and desires, align our very own willpower, and align our own reasons and understandings, align our very own emotions and feelings, with the powerful and true revelation received from the Word of the Living God, that it is the only true existence and source of the living life, that was given to humanity to be able to keep its self-awareness capacity calibrated and its discernment's ability working and fully activated, even at the very low end in the depths of humanity's core foundation within the humanity's own complex and powerful fundamental structures of their senses and their networks of expressed operations and functions, by being able of understanding and acknowledging that God's powerful and true revelation of his true Word of Truth has been released for a divine and for a continually sustainment of God's breath and his breathed life into the very depths of humanity's own soul and into the very soul's unsearchable and untapped deep of the true living soul's evermore expression of existence.

In the accordance with the powerful revelation that was brought forward by the holy scriptures, from the Gospel of John starting with its very first chapter we can learn about God's powerful and true revelation of his Word that has been revealed for humanity's continued expression and for the humanity's continued sustainment as being the only trustworthy carriers and the holders of God's own activated and breathed life, that was deposited into the very deep depths of the humanity's soul active existence, by the power of God's own infinite wisdom and its accelerated produced knowledge, from which he released his own unlimited and everlasting steadfast love for his entire Creation that was formed by his own hands, and even now in our very present and living time, God's own everlasting love and his eternal grace it is active surrounding and it is encapsulating his majestic and completed works and all of their living forms, and all of their live expressions and all of their living manifestations in the entire Creation, with his very own infinite and divine wisdom and power of love, that are revealed to all of his Creation and their very own living organisms and their moving expressions, being them activated and allowed to manifest their presence in the heavens above, or being them started and allowed to express their own manifest presence on to earth below, within the very deep depths of the true unlimited living everlasting and eternal power of love, in the precious and mighty fulfilled name of our Lord and Savior Jesus the Christ, the true Word of the Living God that became as a human in the flesh and lived for an appointed time on the earth among us, the humans, the Lord Jesus the Christ, the True One Fullness of the Almighty

God's majesty and glory, the True One Fullness of God's own amazing grace and God's own absolute truth.'

Gospel of John, chapter one, verses one through five, 1'- In the beginning was the Word, and the Word was with God, and the Word was God. 2'- He was at the beginning with God. 3'- All things came into being through him, and without him, not one thing came into being. What has come into being, 4'- in him was life, and life was the light of all people. 5'- the light shines in the darkness, and the darkness does not overcome it.

Let's also go ahead and read what the scriptures are telling us about the revelation of God's own Word to humanity in verse 14'- And the Word became flesh and lived among us (the humans), and we (the humans), have seen his glory, the glory as of a father's only son, full of grace and truth. It is essential to go ahead and read the summary of this robust and accurate revelatory information and its result from the Gospel of John, which is letting know humanity's living Soul in verse sixteen that'-, From his fullness, we have ALL (the humans), received, grace upon grace.' Hallelujah.

I am trying to strongly emphasis and bring forward to our understanding this powerful point of view from the scriptures and its writing words that are revealed to us from the pages of the Gospel of John, because it will help us to start developing the real needed self-awareness mechanism system that we ought to operate and live our life by, and more than anything else it will really help us to be able to approach the absolute truth of God and his true revelation, not through the opinions and their fast focus view lenses that are structured and based on our own many different ways constructive structures of our own way perceived and fundamental core understanding, that may come into our lives, when we were being exposed to, or even now when we are and may be exposed to their very multiple various influences that are very much alive around all of us, and that are the result, and also may be the result and the root cause that was, and that it may be created by our own upbringing, or by our own cultural teachings and their learned customs, or by our own and very real societal manifestations of our own many expressed surroundings and their identifications, or may be even caused by our very own life expressions that are the results of our own very real life and its powerfully undeniable experiences we had lived, but through the living and powerful self-awareness mechanism and its systematic modules, that are being activated into the depths of our whole complete and its entire structural and functional frames of our very own encapsulated and complex living forms that are taking the shape and become the very active expressions of who we really are as humans that are bestowed upon, with a living and with a breathing soul, those powerful and self-awareness modules that are in true being sources and activated and released from the above, but their signals have to, and must be captivated within the fundamental grounds and roots of the humanity's living soul, in order to be anchored and steadfast hold by the Spirit of the Living God in the only True One Fullness of God, in the One and True unshakable foundation and in its revelation in the creation. that has been already established from the very beginning of time by the Almighty God, for the very salvation and for the very true redemption of our humanity and its soul, that it has been already activated and fundamentally structured and grounded into the depths of the spoken Word of the Living God, and the salvation and the redemption of the humanity soul it will be fully fulfilled and it will come to pass, not by the many ways that are presented themselves to all of us, and that are actively manifesting their teachings all around us and within our expressed living surroundings, with their extremely and very powerful revelatory elements as being the help for the humanity's resolves, and with their very own sourced forward and looking very realistic fundamental build structure of expressing their active thoughts, that are fuel and propelled forward on all humans, by using their very powerful and their very deceitful approaches, through which they are trying to capture the humanity and its living soul in the web labyrinth of their multiple manipulative schemes and their dark influenced deceptions that are actively affecting the humanity's entire mindset and its entire active consciousness and its entire controlled behavior pulses, due to their overloaded raw information and data that it is continually being released by design to cause much confusion and doubts to all of them that are exposing themselves to their signals and to all of them that are receiving and accepting their many structural schemes as being founded in their own truth of its living expression and interpretation, but by God's own absolute Truth, and his infinite wisdom, and by the very own wisdom's deep and unsearchable love and unlimited power, and it's very deep knowledge, and by the true holiness, and by the true divine and breathing power of the active and unmovable Word of the Living God, and by the Almighty God's forever and eternal standing of his lasting and living promises for all of humanity's soul, and for all his majestic and eternal creation.

When the Lord Jesus Christ, that was being revealed to humanity as the Word of the Living God that became flesh and lived among us in the fullness of God and in his grace and in his truth, in the accordance of the words of Apostle John's writings from his gospel that I mentioned in the previous paragraphs of this book, was being asked the question about what it is the greatest commandment in the law, trying to test him in that very and real moment when the Pharisees had gather together, after they heard that the Lord Jesus Christ he had silenced the Sadducees previously, when the Sadducees got together to ask and test Jesus with matters and subjects they did not hold true or even believe them as true, but wanted to bring forth to their attention Jesus's own answers with the intent to trap him in their own philosophical and ideological belief system build within their own structural and fundamental frames of their activated thought and manifest mechanism, that was being activated and fueled from within the depths of their own dangerously mindset approach and understanding they had as being as the approved thoughts towards the Word of God and his commandments and his law, without realizing that he, the Lord Jesus the Christ, that was standing right before their physical eyes, he was the true Word of God, he was the true image of his commandments and he was the true image of the law of the Almighty God, the Lord Jesus the Christ, the true and everlasting image of the completed fullness of the Word of God, the Lord Jesus the Christ, the true and the only everlasting and eternal image of The One, that truly encapsulated and activated within himself, all of the very real and power expressions of life's expressed existence and life's forever living and sustainment attributes, for all of the requirements that were established from the eternity and needed to be implemented and activated for the redemption and for the salvation of the human and its living soul, the Lord Jesus the Christ the fullness and the fulfillment of the Word of God, the fullness and the fulfillment of the commandments of God, and the fullness and the fulfillment of the law of God, he answered and said the following words according with the writings that are found in the Gospel of Matthew in Chapter twenty two, starting with verses thirty four to forty and I will write the entire passage for a better and clear understanding. Matthew chapter 22: 34-40," When the Pharisees heard that he had silenced the Sadducees, they gathered, and one of them, a lawyer, asked him a question to test him. Teacher, which commandment in the law is the greatest? He told him, "You Shall Love the Lord Your God, with All Your

Heart, Your Soul, and Your Mind. Jesus revealed to him what is the Greatest and the First commandment. And a second is like it:" You Shall love your neighbor as yourself.

On these two commandments hang All of the Law and the Prophets.

Why I am bringing this robust information revealed from the scriptures for us to be able to learn from it, into the front view focus and into the very critical attention of all of the readers of this book it is because we are all living in a very tough time of a real sad spiritual deception that came and settled its very powerfully seductive eyes, upon the Soul of the entire humanity's capacity and its significantly activated capability sensors and receptors that are receiving and capturing non-stop all the information and their data signals that the humankind it is exposed to daily, through the very powerful and influential channeling of the one deceptive ruler known as the ruler of this world and declared by the scriptures to be known also as the prince of the air, and it is becoming very strongly clear that it is very imperative to our own Soul's health and its survival, that we are to be able of processing and also to be capable of analyzing the dissemination of all the raw information data signals, that we are all receiving into our mindset's processor and its thought system mechanism, through the only true revelatory light and the light's life guiding and its living instructions that are being even now, even in these very dangerous days of our lives when these very perilous times of deceptions and their own systematic and multiple complex manipulative schemes are attacking and assaulting the humanity continually with their blinking signals and power signs of confusion, at the very cross roads of the humanity's existence on the pathway of life that it is being located within the humanity's own complex and complete consciousness and within the mindset of the humanity's life expressions chambers of their active thoughts, that even now are still being released for the humanity's help and survival from the Word of the Living God, and by the power of his Holy Spirit.

The answered words spoken by our Lord and Savior Jesus Christ, when he was asked by that one Pharisee, that also just happened to be a lawyer, but I am not going to talk about this at this moment, the question," what it is the greatest commandment of the law," reveals the true purpose and the true function for the entire humanity's living soul existence as being part of God's magnificent creation, and this powerful revelation brings forward the true reality of our own living and manifested existence, within our purpose living life, at least for now when we the humans are really being categorized under the classification of the eternity's book of life just a passing and faded breath of air, and just being mortals and travelers on our designated road of life destiny, we the humans with a very breathing and living soul, that are also expressing our existence in our own temporary journey on the earth's paramount activated map, we the humans that are the true carriers of God's everlasting light and are the true holders of God's own breath of life, that were being breathed and deposited into the deep and into the very depths chambers of our own living soul, by the Almighty creator himself, that we the humans shall love our God and our Creator, with all our heart and with all our soul and with all our mind, and this "the greatest commandment" it was not revealed to the humanity and released forward by the Lord Jesus Christ himself, the Living Truth of the Word of God, under the attributes of the power of the suggestion, or under the many other powerful attributes based on their own suggestive' s positive thinking and their own critically ideology and dogma, within their very own foundation of understanding and resolves, that are being many, many times masked by their very own powerfully indoctrinations that are fuel by their own mechanisms and structures, but in the true sense of their matter, they are being revealed for their continually searched desires to be able to achieve unlimited power and control over the masses and over the others, but this "the greatest commandment" it was revealed to the entire humanity as a "shall", and there is no other way around it, no matter how much we will try to reason it, or how much we will try to keep spinning our own selves around it, to the point that we may want to make ourselves believe that within our short sight view and in its limited but active compulsive understandings, we may be thinking that we may have, or we may be thinking that we are really possessing the true and vast accumulated understanding and knowledge towards the power of the absolute truth, that the word "shall", it finally reached the threshold of our interpretation point, that it may, and it will may become able to be fitted within our very own structural forms and shapes schemes and their real induced power grab of our own selves physiological thinking, and it will really be fitted and suited for our own many driven narratives, but we the humanity, "we shall love our God with all our heart, we shall love our God with all our soul and we shall love our God with all our mind", and we as humanity we shall hold and implement within our living life expressions, the second, " the greatest commandment", that it is just like the first one being revealed and ordained by the Lord Jesus Christ as to be also, " the greatest commandment", by bringing within the glimpse of possibility and within the limits of our true functions and its perceived understanding of our own activated thought mechanism system and its processor's sensors, the notion of the revealed truth of the matter for all the humanity, that there does not exist any distinction ,and also that there it was never been established from the heavens above, a different standard and a different pathway for their implementation, between the first," the greatest commandment, and the very second following commandment, also that has been revealed to us and known to be "the greatest commandment", that we the humans may hold it and may adhere it, and actively work to implement them, as the commandments had been revealed to us, and as the commandments had been spoken to us by the living Word of God's own fullness and fulfillment, that it is being rooted and grounded into the precious name of our Lord and Savior Jesus Christ, when the Lord was asked one question by that Pharisee lawyer, and he responded with not one, but with two very powerful and true answers, and the second Lord's answer, that it is known as being the commandment that was revealed within this very true and powerful statement," Love your neighbor as you love yourself", because their very active implementation and their very fulfillment of All the Law and the Prophets depend, and, or hang, "the word that has been also used and written in some of the many translations of the scriptures, that are being truth encapsulated, and that are being the life's light only true guidance, and also that are being the truth and the wisdom's frame and instruction, that the entire humanity and its living soul may be able to understand them and that they may be able to follow them", because on these two very powerful revealed commandments and on their true fulfillment cause that are resting within the statements of God's own revealed statutes and their strict ordinances for the humanity, and if we strive to understand them through their true purism observance in reverence, it will be the true root cause action event, that it will really help us and our humanity's living soul, to be able to evolve forward, and fundamentally grow towards achieving and towards reaching their desired and final end results destiny, by being able to accept the reality of God's revealed forth commandments, and by fulfilling their true and their divine implementation.

To be able to at least start understanding a glimpse of these powerful revelation released upon all the humanity by the spoken and living words of our Lord Jesus Christ, blessed be his holy name, in that very divine moment when the Lord answered all them Pharisees that came to test him, in regarding their asked question about what it is the greatest and the higher commandment of the law, we need to accept in truth the actual realization of the fundamental importance that we as the humans with a living soul, we have to start looking inward into the depths of our own selves beings, and allow the spirit of the living God to shape us into the Word of God, that will then activate in us, the must needed building character blocks of our own very strong and fundamental structure foundation for our own self-awareness mechanism expressions and its functions, that it will really help us to start developing within the very deep and depths of our own living being, the capacity to be able to understand how our very own and living Heart, how our own living mind, and how our own living Soul, are expressing their own individual ordain functions within their own allow map of their manifest location for their purpose, yet they inter-exist and they are also very inter-depended within each other's proprietary functions, and that they are also prone and able to, due to their natural and undeniable connectivity sensors and blending signals produced by their own created and overlapping receptors and their received signals within each other's gray areas of expressions, that they are being able to really affect and influence each other's motives and desires, and each other's feelings and emotions, even each other's reason and understanding, within the complexity of the entire human being's expressions and the Soul of the human's whole fundamental and actual structural mechanism and its purpose-produced functions.

For a better understanding for the readers, I will go ahead

and ask few questions in the regards of the matter of life's purposes and their life's functions, and here they are' the question for the humanity true meaning of life's entire existence, and the question for the society true purpose of life's fundamental expressions, and also the question for the humanity true purpose of life's whole manifestation, for us as human beings and for our very own life's temporary journey on this earth that we are call it home, and that it is being bounded within the limits of our own physical and mortal being form, but yet we are living with an undeniable and with an unspoken genuine and living forever burning desire inside of us, that it is making us, the humanity to be on an constant moving strive, by always searching and by always being propelled and by always being driven forward towards reaching our own divine end destination, that it is the original and the everlasting transcendental realm and its paramount location that was already created and prepared for our very own life's immortal living and for our very own unchangeable life's eternal hope.

It is the Soul, our true purpose for our life's existence.

It is the Heart, the true purpose of our life's entire Expressions.

Is the Mind the true purpose of our life's entire Manifestation?

Why it is strictly and very imperative to be able to distinguish between the Soul's own existence and the Heart's own expressions and the Mind's own active manifestation in our divine quest for reaching eternal salvation and also for reaching the humanity's living soul everlasting end destination and destiny, in the midst of all of the storms and in the midst of all of the turbulences of our living life, that are trying daily to shift humanity's purpose and their view focus, from their very real searched desires for the eternal hope, to become just a temporary image glimpse of its sad and its painfully and unforgotten past, from their very own and everlasting living sounds of their fully active joy, to become just a passing sound of a forgotten dropping tear noise and its very own undistinguished sights of its very deep pain, like being as the beautiful grass that may be very living green colored first thing breathing in the morning dawn, but by the very evening time, due to the scorch of the heat of the sun's burning rays, it becomes just a lifeless and a dry shadow reflecting just a painful death, in a place that once was full of a living life, and it is very imperative because it will help us, and it will also help our very own entire humanity created being and its expressions of life, from the top of our own consciousness built in receptors and their very powerful capacity processor and its true abilities, to the very bottom of our own feet's sole and its very powerful built in receptors that are very much alive within their own active module and capacity senses fueling and propelling forward their very own expressions within their very own moving abilities, to understand the very critically and powerfully importance that it will enable us to accept the guidance of the Word of the Living God, and the lead of his Holy Spirit, that will activate in the depths of our whole and entire humanity being, the much important and needed self-awareness mechanism systems and its very own powerful platforms of their unique and true living structures, that will allow us then, to be able to understand the true fundamental mechanism structures and their own true and revealed sources, that are continually fueling their very own and powerful influenced desires, and that also are continually fueling their very own and powerful influenced control functions, that may allow them and may empower them to start planning the capturing, within their own deceptive webs of dark influences that are being very active under their own master's spiritual control, the humanity and its very own living soul's existence, the humanity and its very own heart's expressions and desires, and the humanity and its very own mind's consciousness and its always active manifest behavior.

I am going ahead and will start answering these three questions that were asked in the above paragraph regarding humanity's Soul, humanity's Heart, and humanity's Mind. I also will cover in a few words each of their robust purposes and their functions, which are all very tight encapsulated within the unique and complex design of humanity's shaped and formed structure that was being made and masterfully created and breathed to life but the unlimited power and by the infinite wisdom and love of our very own maker and the Creator himself, for the Soul as being the sole source of the humanity's life and humanity's existence, for the Heart as being the sole source of the humanity's energy and its very living expressions, and for the Mind as being the sole source of humanity's life and its very active movements and their living manifestation.

Humanity's living Soul, it is in truth, the most powerfully activated life's purposes and functions for life's entire existence and for life's whole living and breathing expressions that is being manifested within every single human and its living being, because the living Soul it is carrying within its deep depths of its created chambers of its expressions and own functions, the most potent and essential critical element of existence that it is needed for the entire human life's containment and the whole of the human life's continue sustainment, that it is already being established and located within the very divine foundation of the Almighty God's own built and magnificent Creation, and that compelling and critical element of life's existence and its purpose, for human life's very own containment, and the human life's very own sustainment, it is everlasting and it is the eternal sound of God's breath of life, that had been released into the depths of the

Soul by the Creator himself on that very important sixth day in the Order of the Creation, when he breathed into the human's nostrils. After that, the human became a living soul. This is revealed to us by the living Word of God from Genesis chapter two and verse seven:" Then the Lord God, formed man from the dust of the ground and breathed into his nostrils the breath of life; and the man became a living soul.

Humanity's living Heart is also, in the truth of its matter, the most powerfully activated life's purposes and functions for life's entire expression and for life's whole living and breathing expressions of humanity's strong feelings, powerful emotions, and powerful desires and willpower, that can produce natural life motions and expressions. Ultimately, it will actively start creating compelling and real influential motivators within the human being's living expressions due to the Heart's influence and control over the feelings and the instincts and even over the deep intuitions of the human's built and formed complex and fundamental structure.

To be able to start focusing on the understanding of their compelling attributes and the very active complexity of their very own purposes and functions that are continually operating within humanity's living heart's fundamental foundation of its built structure, we need to be able to realize that our very own human heart and heart's very own powerful capacity and capability functions, that God has bestowed upon the heart living and beeping purposes, we need to start understanding that our very own human heart's nature has the sole power ability to be able to control and to influence and to affect all aspects of humanity's very own life and expressions with its control and authority power that has, and if the heart is being left unchecked and uncalibrated by the Word of the Living God, both human expressions, the physical life expressions of our humanity and the very inner spiritual life expressions of our beings, will be actively and continually fighting against each other's motives and desires.

The humanity's living Mind, it is also in the truth of its own matter, the most powerfully activated life's purposes and functions for the living life's entire moving and for the living life's continue manifestations that from the very first breath of the air when a human being starts its very short life journey on his temporary spectrum realm of his very own life's existence, until that very moment when the human being it is taken into its lungs it's very last breath at the air, when its allotted time will expire at the end of his short and temporary living journey on this earth's presence, the human's very living Mind it will be non-stop purposely controlling all of their active motions and functions that are being sourced and that are all being revealed forward to a manifest action, from within the depths of their very powerfully built and complex design of their created and also appointed executive systematic chambers, and from within the foundation of their very own multi mechanisms of active coordination, for all of the humanity's very powerfully manifest actions and also for all of humanity's driving forward motions and sensors, and they all carry and forms together a very vital and a very important part of all the humanity's constant and complex activity and their very non-stop manifestations, through which their very own existence that it is being fueled by their very own and living soul, and also through which their very own expressions that are all being fueled by their very own and living heart, that it will enable them to be all purposely and actively synchronized and also single bounded together and all core-connected by their very own inter-depended and overlapped functions, and by their very own and unique inter-existence and purpose structure that it is revealed within the depths of the deep and the unmovable structural and fundamental foundation of the humanity's magnificent design and also revealed within their very own complex creation by the Almighty God' s infinite wisdom and his unlimited knowledge, that makes possible for the entire humanity and their masterfully created and formed human beings, to be able to accept and to be able to recognize the most imperative and important aspect of all of our true life's existence and all of our true life's purpose, that it is to be able to worship the Lord our God and the Almighty Creator, and to be able to fulfill the commandments of the law of the Almighty God, that in their truth are all being bounded together into these two divine and life giving commandments that were revealed to all of the humanity by our Lord Jesus Christ himself, the true and Living Word of God, that we the humanity, we shall, and I will quote from the scriptures, Mark twelve verses thirty and thirty one, "You shall love the Lord your God with all your heart, and with all your soul, and with all your mind, and with all your strength; the second is this: "You shall love your neighbor as yourself.' There are no other commandments greater than these", and the Lord added this powerful statement to his life-giving words, saying that on these two powerful commandments hangs and holds all the commandments of the law and all the prophets.

  To be able to start to understand what the Lord Jesus Christ meant by his answered statements that he had at that time revealed to the whole of humanity in regards to God's commandments of the law and the prophets, and how can we all, the very humans, that are being at times so limited in own capability and ability of understanding our very own mind processor and its very active and influential operative systematic actions and their accurate functions and purposes, it is very important and very critically imperative to allow the Word of the Living God and the forth revelation of his

Holy Spirit, to help us and to guide us all, towards a more profound and divine knowledge and its power of understanding, that are already available and have been released into the creation's active form, from the very depths of God's own infinite wisdom, and that are also been revealed forth for the entire vast design and for the creation's very own active expressions, through which we all that are known as the humans, we may be able to start to recognize and also that we may be able to begin to realize the importance of the much needed and of the much searched after, that it is the power of knowledge and the ability of understanding of our own selves, and the power of understanding of who we really are, and where we have been placed by God on the creation, as the very unique and majestically created and formed complex built of a human being with a living soul, that have been empowered by the Lord God and the Almighty Creator that we may be able to function and to be able to manifest our living and expressed existence as being a very important part of God's creation, and also that have been empowered to be able to worship and serve our Creator, with all of our heart and with all of our mind, and with all of our soul, and with all our Spirit, and with all of our whole and complete given power and strength from the Almighty.

As I did mentioned earlier in this chapter, that the humanity existence it is continually being facilitated and sustained by its very own living soul, that in its truthful and in its eternal element of its originality, the eternal and the living soul it is the true sole activated identificatory built mechanism, and also it is the sole marked and tagged complex system fingerprint for the humanity's very own living spirit of life that have been received and that have been ordained to existence by God, and that have been forward activated within the entire form of its existence, deep within the very expression of the entire living human being, by our Creator and God when he himself created and formed us in his own image and in his own likeness, in that very powerful and majestic moment when he the Creator of All, in his true own sourced and infinite everlasting love, breathed in the human's nostrils his very own breath of life, and this is not a theological point of an structural and argumentative opinion that I will want to debate at this very moment in this book but maybe in my future writings I will, but I do want to say that I sincerely believe that our very own living Spirit, it has been identified and marked and tagged for its eternity existence by its own living Soul, and because of that, as every single whole being human and its body, can be identified by their fingerprints markings and also by their own retina of the eyes senses, that are all being developed in their very true nature and in their very unique senses within each and every ones structural frames of their own traits within the living human body, being so careful mastered and also being so strictly unique, that within our own place of living environment does not exist in their true active expressions, not even two, structural and fundamental and created chambers that are producing their very unique receptors and their very own sensors and senses of their capability to be able to receive and send their own signals frames of their own true sourced identification, alike, and it is going to be a soon coming day when every human being that lived in the past generations before us, and when every human being that are living in today's generation, and when every human being that will be born even after we are long gone from this temporary realm of our expressions, and for how long living life will be sourced, and also maintained and sustained in this established and created form structure and expression by the Almighty Creator as we are experiencing it, one day we will all stand together before the Eternal and the Holy and Everlasting living Throne of our Lord God Almighty, and there will be not any sounds of confusions and not any questions about it, there will be not any escape movements or any other spoken arguments subjects of denial, in that very divine and sublime moment of its ordained and its appointed time in the creation, when every single one human being and its very own living human spirit of life, it will be brought up and presented to stand before the Throne of the Almighty God, and every human being that ever breathed God's own breath of life, it will be called and forth identified by its very own living and eternal soul, that also it is known to be the only created and the only living expression in all of the entire creation's paramount of forms and divine structures in their landscape, that have been breathed into existence, by God's own breath of life and by God's own nature and substance, to be able to facilitate and to be able to coordinate the functions of all of the entire living human beings and their systematic and fundamental complexes that are founded by their very own active and expressed movements, within their very own built and manifest actions mechanism, and within the very location of their own complex and powerful networks of their own activated and always sustained manifestations by the Creator's own connectivity for their own life and for their very own powerful built in capability and capacity receptors chambers, that are being very active manifested by having their own true signals and their own true and all senses being attached, hooked and also all connected within the very deep depths of the soul's own foundation of its eternal and divine structure of the soul's express existence, thus making the living soul the only one true and unique masterfully planned and designed and created living life form by the Almighty God's own breath and his breathing expression that exists in the all entire creation, and the very living soul has the appointed capacity to be able to open its expressed location and their activated living chambers, and to be able to receive large and vast blocks of information and data, and also the soul it is very powerfully indeed able to also captivate and to hold the very received information and data within its own structural and living form, from where the living soul will be able to actively coordinate forward from within the very own deep chambers of its powerfully living expression, all of them signals and all of them information of all of the humanity's own send and the humanity's own receive communication and raw signals and also their very active senses, that are all being manifested continually inside the humanity's never stop living life expressions and their power function modules, that are all majestically activated and created for the living soul's eternal purpose, which is to be the true central nucleus function and also to be the living and strong and divine bond mechanism system that it have been created and activated by the creator himself into existence, between the very powerful and eternal humanity's whole living spirit and the spirit's very active and manifested desires, and between the very powerful and complex humanity's temporal and mortal body and the very mortal's active, expressed and manifested desires.

Going a step forward for discussing this very and accurate analogy of the humanity's living spirit and its eternal and powerful desires, and of the very analogy of the humanity's temporary body and its created within its live and its living organism of its identical flesh structures that are being activated and fueled into the existence by their very powerful but yet mortal desires, we do need to be able to realize and to be able to accentuate and really incline ourselves heavy towards the accepted reality that it is being very unlikely to be ever bypassed and to be ever neglected in our own realm of expressed existence, and this reality it is that, not only the humanity's eternal and its living Spirit, and the humanity's temporary and its mortal body and flesh functions are meeting and connected within the deep depths of the humanity's living soul, but also their both living and manifested expressions are being very active against each other's given life destiny and purposes by trying to overpower and in attempting to influence and to control each other's expressed desires for their own end result and survival benefit, and this violent and brutal fight for their own express existences it is being aggressively fought within the soul's own structure and within the soul's life and deep activated connectivity and network chambers that are all together being and forming a very complex and systematic part of the humanity's living soul.

Let's go for a quick moment back to the scriptures and see what the Word says in regards of this very active fight and battle process that it has been taken place without ceasing from that very first day in the entire creation when the disobedience produced pride and corruptions arose and took a living shape structure within the very human's expressed form, infecting the divine complexity fiber of the human's designed and defined shape and form in which the human had experienced and lived in its very own and powerful uncorrupt and majestically beautiful, as an complete and a divine created human being to express life within the presence of God's own perfect and heavenly transcendental realm of purpose, functions and existence, but had fallen short of the glory of God or I may say that had fallen from the glory of God, and because of that process of disobedience today these words of the Scriptures are ringing so true, and in accordance with the man of God writings from the book of Galatians, chapter five and verse seventeen where he says and quote " For what the flesh desires is opposed to the Spirit, and what the Spirit desires is opposed to the flesh", unquote, but in the very beginning stage of its creation the living human being and its living soul it was not like that, and every single one of its functions, and all of their whole purposes of the entire human existence and their very unique expressions, that have been forth created and activated together to be able to work and to exist and to manifest their bestowed and appointed existences in a total complex and complete synchronized operative system, that initially have been designed in their unique life expression forms, that had been created and also that have been revealed and presented to all of the entire living creation, as being the eternal and the forever crown jewel of God's own infinite and divine wisdom, love, knowledge and power.

Understanding the actual reality and the nature of all the elements and the powers in the creation that are really surroundings us all, and what are their real motives and desires for our true living human expression of our life, it is very vital and imperative for our salvation and for our eternal destination, but also it is the same and equally important and very critically and essential to be able to understand the actual reality and nature of all the elements and their structure and their massive powers that are being currently very actively expressing in the creation their own motives and their own desires deep inside all of us, the humans, within the limits of our own powerful self-constructive built, and its complex design of our very own wellbeing that has been created and activated by the Almighty God, in the shape and in the form of our current and existent living human body, that it is also being kept active and alive in its own constant and multi operational manifested functions, by our very own living Spirit, and by our very own living soul, by our very own living heart, and by our very own alive mind, that are being all tight and bonded together to form the needed and the very imperative and fundamental structural foundation, that it is able to build on, and to maintain and also to be able to sustain our very own human identity and our entire life expressions and manifestations that are being reflected within each of us, the humans, that have been created and allowed to be a part of the whole humanity's life, and also a part of the humanity's true and its powerful living existence.

I am emphasizing the importance of being able to start recognizing and understanding at the least, to a glimpse of a sincere reality, the very powerfully acting behaviors of all of our internal produced motives and desire, that are all being propelled to life and also that are all being coordinated for their very own active manifestations and for their own expressed life functions, by our very own living heart, and by our own living mind, by our very own living soul, and by our own living spirit, that are carrying their very own self identities and have their own shapes and forms, for their forth and active expressions and functions, that are being all existent and activated to be able to be manifested themselves, within the very powerfully and the masterfully designed and created human living being, in its entire structural and complex human life form, that are all being framed together into a completed systematic and mechanism of live functions and living expressions, for their very own spiritual, and physical, and their psychological abilities, that are all being together deep encapsulated into the same fabric and into the mere fiber expressions of the entire humanity and the humanity's completed and activated human's divine wellbeing and strong foundation, that holds on it, and also that maintains on it, and also that active sustains on it, the entire life's manifested and their powerfully living expressed structures, for God's created human's very own body and mind, and for God's created human's very own Spirit and soul.

This is the very reason I strongly keep the deep emphasized pressure point on this very real and powerful subject of the matter to be able to start recognizing and to start really understanding our very own internal created motives and their powerful desires, and how they are coming to life and to a real existence and how our very own internal created motives and their strong desires that are so many times so powerfully being expressed around all of our surroundings, and that are being so very effective coordinated, and also being so active manifested, through our very own living heart, and through our very own living mind, and through our very own living soul, and through our own living spirit, because it is very imperative and it is very crucial to our own overall wellbeing and functioning as human beings, created be the very own hands of the Almighty God, to be able to express our own human existence that it is being in true encapsulated within the masterfully design purpose and functions of our own living human beings in God's creation. These powerful elements of life that as I mentioned in the previous paragraphs of this book, they have been created to be able to carry and to express their very own independent identities, but together they are bonded to form a unique and a complex and a total powerfully activated interdependent mechanism system within our own human being form, and our true given abilities from the creator to be able to understand and to be able to recognize, and indeed yes, as it was originally intended to be operative and to be expressed in the creation, and to be able to align their powerful capacity and their very own capabilities that are all producing their own energy pulses and strong living signals, to be able to align them from the depths of our human being frame with the Word of the Living God's power source, it is crucial and imperative and it is vital and in the same time it is undeniable essential for our very own spiritual, and for our own physical, and for our very own psychological overall health during our very short and temporary journey of expressing life on this earthly realm, and also it is very imperative for our own eternal salvation, and for our final end and destination of our own humanity destiny, and ultimately we need not only to recognize this, but we do must accept the true fact that this very powerful understanding of our own self inner core foundation of our working mechanism system, it's very true powerful active functions and its true purpose and existence that in its reality it does contributes to our all humanity's divine wellbeing and its strong core foundation, that holds on it, the entire needed maintenance and sustenance of our entire life's powerfully living and breathing structures, and it is also very imperative and critically vital for all of our very own human beings and its eternal existence, and this process of self-emphasizing the importance of being able of understanding and recognizing the very interconnected divine nature of our own internal motives and their desires, and how they are all manifested through their very powerful and their various elements of our human being expressions, at their multi levels and structures of their own built systematic operations and complexed functions, being them activated at the level of the heart, or being them activated at the level of the mind, or being them activated at the level of the spirit, or being them activated at the level of the soul, we need to highlight the strong idea that our very own motives and desires are being activated and also that they are and will be always and constantly in a fast forward motion, that are being all propelled to a life expressions of manifest purpose or desires by our very own and living heart and mind, our living soul and spirit, that have been created and that have been also allowed to be able to express their very own manifested existence from the very inner depths of their active living and its structural fundamental shape that are forming and overall are completing the human being existence, to an outside living and manifested expressions of their own created motives and desires that are being released and then are being captivated and also that are being absorbed within the eternal transcendental realm of its everlasting origin, by the Almighty God and the Creator, is by its own design a majestic part of the overall applicable functions of humanity that are being located within the revealed and eternal and infinite wisdom of God's own expressions that have been released from its everlasting roots and origins, within the allowed limits and borders of God's very own works that completes and also compliments his magnificent and his divine creation.

Now that we are starting to understand, through a small glimpse of hope, the real massive and immense magnitude of our human being's built-in capacity and its very own powerfully systematic mechanism of our internal human being processor and its accurate active functions, I would love to take you all a little deeper into this journey of our humanity's expressions through their applicable thoughts. I am going to ask this powerful question:

" Can at various times in our very own living experience these compelling elements of life that are carrying their own powerful identities and active functions within our complex built human mechanism structure, the heart, and the mind, the Spirit and the soul, will try to affect and will try to influence each other's motives and their expressed desires, or even at times trying to overpower each other's motions and expressions, and if the answer it is yes, and not if it is yes because we know already that the answer it is indeed yes, how often they are actively being manifesting their motives and theirs own expressed desires alongside each other, and, or even at various times being strongly and very active displayed against each other, at the core health expense of the overall and wellbeing of the humanity's purpose in God's creation, that it is being represented and expressed in the divine, ethereal realm of the majestically created human being complex and completed form?

Yes, it is indeed very possible and very actual for all these powerful life-sustaining and initially created elements within all of us, the humans, that God had designed within the humans to be able to keep and to forward propel the human being to an active purpose and function as a complete living and breathing expression within the vast paramount landscape of God's creation, that is known to all of us as being our heart and mind, the Spirit and the soul, and also we need considering that their very own powerfully independent identities that they all possess, can effectively try at various times to affect and also to try to influence each other's motives and to possible even overrule each other's very own manifested and their natural forward and expressed desires.

The question that keep arising again and again on this topic of the matter it is, why these powerful and original elements that are structurally formed and active synchronized together as a living and fundamental part of the entire expression of life in itself that are containing within each other's received and bestowed capacity from the Creator, the very structural networking capability of their own signals and their own communications functions that are in an forward coordination with one another for the humanity proper function and for the overall wellbeing of the entire created and complex human being expression, are trying to affect and even to influence each other's purposed and created functions that possible can cause a very real dysfunction and a real imbalance and even at times destruction within the overall health expressions of the very living human being's manifestations that all the humanity are expressing on their very living and active platforms of their own spiritual, and their physical, and also their psychological stages of their very existence?

Maybe what was intended in the originality of their appointed and activated functions from the very beginning of their creation, to be able to interphase within each other's systematic capability of their capacitors and receptors, being capable of sending and also of receiving, to and from, their each other's living life signals and their actual life senses, that together they may be able to be operative and cooperative within their very unison bond frame of their own and unique functions for the maintenance and for the very active sustainment of the overall health and proper expression and manifestation of the very human being's existence that was created in the image and in the likeness of the Almighty God, it did got corrupted and also became infected at the very deep core of their own structural foundation of their expressions by other living elements and powers that exists in the overall creation, that were actively surrounding the human, and also here comes another question in the forward view of this very real point, by whom this once perfect created human being got its original and uncorrupted living reality affected and strongly influenced, and what were the objective scopes and their own very manipulative reasons of these other powerful elements in God's creation to seek to corrupt and to seek to capture the human being within their very own powerfully and many deceptive ways, that they may be able to keep the human being capture and bound very far and away from the absolute truth?

Now that we understand that these powerful original elements of life, will try to influence and will try to affect each other's very true expressed motives and their desires, and also knowing that in the beginning it was not like that, and all of their anointed and appointed purposes and functions were in true created to be able to help and to be able to complement each other's very true expressed motives and their desires for the overall functions and also for the overall wellbeing of all of the humanity's complexity of its very own divine existence and for the very overall health of process functions of the human being's life and it's very own and living expressed attributes in all of the creation, we clearly can deduct from this very presented information and come to the forth knowledge of its very own understanding light, that what really had been happened, and what really had been changed from their originally masterfully designed purposes and functions that at one time had been all aligned together within the fundamental and the structural foundation of the entire human's living expression and manifestation within all of the creation's vast landscape, it had been indeed caused due to the very powerfully acting external influences and their actively massive waves of their own released forward manipulation and schemes against the very own human's wellbeing complex and its living structure, and that once they had been able to reach deep into the human being's own inner core and that once they had been able to affect the deep and the very inner human's own living functions and the very human's built in structures and the human's very own and expressed and strong living fundamental foundation, their strong influences had the power to be able to create and to establish between all of those real and very powerfully original elements of life that were created by the creator for the human's own life sustainment, and that even today they are all together being very actively manifesting their own true nature and presence within all of us, and for all of our true living purpose and breathing existence, because without their true living expressions, we the humans, we will not be able to exist, never mind to be able to operate and to communicate within our very own surroundings as it was originally intended to be for the humanity's divine blue print and its masterfully design and executed plan, that was revealed to all of the creation from the very deep and infinite wisdom and knowledge of the Almighty Creator himself, a very powerful and deceptive built and framed network of inter-communication systems to be able to accommodate their very own formed and structural complex for their powerful actions, that are now being fueled and also sourced forward from within themselves, to the very inner core fabric and fiber of the humanity's own fundamental capacity of processing its very own human being's expressed behavior, that have been in the truth of the matter, very affected and very deep infected at its very own structural and internal core, and due to their new created expressions that are being active within the purposes of their new functions, through which they are now revealing their true inner core search for their own influenced power and control to hold over the other elements of life that exists within the very completed human's structural being, and also by actively prioritizing their very own strong but corrupt motives and their own desires over each other's own power functions due to their very blurry and their true misalignments and vision focus that are now being created and exists between them all and from where all of them are being very actively causing heavy damages and also real dysfunctions and also a very strong and turbulent turmoil that are forth creating a total imbalance within the very inner core of the humanity's own living and the humanity's breathing expressed functions and existence.

I did mentioned previously in the above paragraphs that in the beginning it was not like that, and their appointed and anointed capabilities and abilities that have been released and bestowed upon each and every single one of these very powerfully original elements of life in the creation from the almighty Creator, were strictly designed with their own schematic structural frames and accurate active functions, that they will be able all together to interconnect and all together to be able to interfaced with their each other's produced purpose capacitors, for their own living signals of life expressions, and by doing so, allowing our very own heart and our very own mind, our very own Spirit and our very own soul, to be all together grounded and rooted into the one single point of power and trustworthy connectivity source, that it has been created and activated to sustain from within, all the motives and their desires that are in a continue forward motion between all of them powerful elements of life that is a natural and also a very critically and vital necessary part of the overall complex system and functions that makes and completes our human being.

Let's go even a few steps further into this powerful analogy of the subject of this matter and let's start to cover it with a few examples that can be applicable to our very own living expression of our daily life, that are all being very true within their own way of their very powerfully and their undeniable influences that are captivating the overall wellbeing and health of the humanity's feelings, emotions and their nonstop daily palpitations and their intense pulses on the paramount landscapes of their manifest existence, and for this very first applicable example, let's consider that some of our own living mind's very strong and powerful motives and their desires that are keep coming from within the mind's own depths structure to existence in our life, but they are in an active and continue conflict of their expressions, with the powerful motives and their desires that are coming forward from our own living and powerful heart's own depths of its functions, that are also being birthed and are coming to existence in our living life, and in this case scenario how can we as the humans be able to re an accurate natural and feasible solution that will help us to be able to mediate and also to be able to powerfully navigate within the limits and the boundaries of our living expressions in the creation that will help us to be able to hold the manifested and the existent actual center line of implementation actions without any compromise for the overall health and wellbeing of our own life and existence?

For the second applicable example on this subject and topic, let's go ahead and consider for a split second the powerfully motives and their desires of our own living spirit that as I also mentioned before in this book, it is being identified in the entire creation and before the throne of the Almighty God by its very own living and breathing soul, that are also arising and coming forth to their own life and their expressed existence from within their own search for implementation and fulfill actions of their own breathing and their own living connectivity applications that are sourced from their very own and active systematic mechanism functions, that are all together live calibrated and synchronized within the creation's real divine and spiritual purpose and within the creation's manifest expression, and when our very own living spirit and our very own living soul are together releasing their motives and their strong living desires, that are many times in a straight and a very direct conflict of purpose and functions with our very own powerfully motives, and their strong living desires that are being released forward to life from our own physical human body, by our very own living heart and by our very own living mind's understanding, and in this case scenario how can we as the humans be able to come to a real and feasible solution that will help us to be able to mediate and that also it will help us to be able to strongly navigate the waves of their own released and active information within the limits and the boundaries of our living expressions in the creation that will help us to be able to hold the manifested and their true existent center line of their implementation actions without any distortion and compromise for our own internal inner core overall health and for the wellbeing of our own life and existence, and also to be able in the same time to create and to activate and to sustain within our very own structural and deep foundation a strong and a divine true living balance mechanism system and connectivity network that will be able to maintain and to operate all of their activated motives, their activated desires and their true activated signals and senses, that are together all being a part of a nonstop and a continue activity that will always be manifesting as long as life holds as we all know it, between our own humanity's true expressions of their very own and strong powerfully spiritual needs of the human being, and between our own humanity's true expressions of their very own and strong powerfully physical needs of the human being?

Overall, the process that was established by the Creator to be as a mediator and as a true divine and active center of balance between these powerful elements of life that are all being already identified within our very own inner core and its structural and fundamental activated source for their very own and forward proper purpose and functions within the humanity's dynamic manifestations of its very human being's expression of life, it is an ongoing process, and for us all the sooner we will be able to start learning, and also to begin recognizing the reality that surrounds us all, and if we will be open to, and become receptive to its living pulses of their life's meaning, it will surely guide our pathway and also it will vigorously stir us, the humans, towards their genuine and activated center of balance that it has been initially created and established by the Creator from the beginning between all of these powerful elements of life that are still residing within our being, and the closer we get on our life journey towards this activated center of balance of the living's true purpose and functions that are already in existence between all of these very powerful elements of life, the easy will be for humanity to start learning and to start to recognize it, and the result of this process will enable us the human beings, to be able to more effectively manage all of them very powerful and accurate undeniable strong internal interactions and their own interdependent active expressions, that it is also the key to be able to achieve in truth, a divine sense of inner harmony and a healthy spiritual and a healthy physical wellbeing.

But to be able to start managing our very inner being active expression from within the deep of our own fundamental foundation of the true created and its activated and forth powered life sustainment attributes of our life's true center of balance, that it is being already established for the entire humanity's manifest expressions and their vital purposes and functions by the almighty God, we will need to turn ourselves from our own deceptive and manipulative ways that are been driven forward from the chambers of our very own self-corrupt understanding, that will picture before our own living eyes a very strong but distorted reflection of an always shifting reality of life, and we need to return back to the foundation of the absolute truth of the creator that will help us by the power of his Word and by the power of his Truth and his Living Spirit, to get plugged back in, and be reconnected into the fundamental and the structural living core fiber of humanity life's design purpose, that it is still being very actively manifesting within the inner deep and depths of our very created and appointed capacity of our self-awareness mechanism and systematic strong structure, that it is so critically vital and true essential for our own overall well-being as humans, by helping us all to be able to start recognizing our own strengths and weaknesses, our own morals, and values, and beliefs, our very own actions and our behaviors, and by doing so under the living guidance and the instructions that are coming forward from the Word of the Lord, that it is the only true light of the world for the humanity path, it will very positively increase and also strongly improve our overall systematic functions of our entire self-awareness mechanism propulsion, that it is a true and a vital divine component built within the human being's expressed life by the creator himself, to release help for all of our humanity's living beings that once they will be able to tap and access its powerfully live activated module of expressions, those very humans may be in truth able of reaching and achieving a healthier spiritual, physical and also a psychological state of awareness, that will be able to fuel their very own unique life's purposes and their living expressions.

While I was meditating on the spoken words of our Lord Jesus Christ when he answered to all of them Pharisees that came to him with that question about what it is the most higher commandment of the law of God, trying to be able to find and to be able to connect with any feasible and settled explanation that it will really help me to be able to elaborate the powerful meaning of his true spoken words, I realized that Jesus's living words" Love your God with all your heart, and with all your mind, and with all your soul", it did indeed transcended from the very realm of our own physical reality and from our very own active capabilities that are living within us, and that are also bestowed upon us all that are known as to be the human beings with a physical body, and it did reach deep into the realm of our very own powerfully spiritual reality, and also it did reach into our very own and true activated functions and their bestowed capabilities that are within us all that are known as to be the human beings with a Living Spirit, and by doing so the Lord Jesus Christ, has been indeed forth revealing to all of the humanity the very true and the very real power of the Oneness, that it is being actively living within the humanity's very strong expressions and their very unique functions, within the overall and majestically created complex and true completed human beings, that are all being allowed and also that are all being guided by the light to be able to express and to manifest their created and their divine living life, and their very own breathing expressions, in the very immense vast expression of the multi-levels paramount landscape of the Almighty God's eternal creation, as human beings that are surrounded by their temporary and mortal realm of their very own attributes of their inherited physical body and functions, and as human beings that are also surrounded by their everlasting and eternal realm of their very own attributes of their inherited spiritual being and functions, by having both realms of their very powerfully own and true living expressions, encapsulated very deep within the very fabric foundation of their very own fundamental fibers and structures that are being all sustained, and that are being actively maintained, by their very own and powerful breathing and living soul that pulls its very eternal and its everlasting identity directly from God's own breath of life.

I strongly believe that when our Lord Jesus Christ released forward in the creation these life sustaining revelations by the power of his true and spoken living words for the entire humanity to hear them, that their very human being expressions may be able to embark on their very own journey for their own life's fulfillment, by always searching and looking for the true light that it is shining upon their divine life's center of balance, for their very own living and active existence within the purposes and the functions of God's creation, the Lord indeed brought forward to life this very powerful motion of his true and live expressed answered statement, that to love our creator and God, with all of our heart and with all of our mind and with all of our soul, it is the very first and also it is the most high and pure commandment of the law for our very own breathing and living human being existence, for us the humans that are actively seeking to integrate all of our physical and all of our spiritual abilities aspects of our whole and completed being expressions towards the fulfillment of this very true and very powerful commandment, that it is to love our Lord God and our creator with all of our physical heart and with all of our spiritual heart, with all of our physical mind and with all of our spiritual mind, and with all of our spirit and with all of our soul, the very breathing and powerful living soul, that in the truth of the matter for our very revealed existence, it is the very strong foundation and the divine structure that fuels and activates forward to manifestation, both of our living expressions in the creation, our very own physical and strong body identity, and also our very own strong spirit and our very own strong spiritual identity, that completes the oneness definition for the human expression as an encapsulated whole, and as a completed created and fully activated human being, by the power of the Almighty God's own hands, that have been designed, planned and sourced into the very human living and breathing existence from within God's very own infinite wisdom and from within the foundation of his very own pillars of life's creation that holds on their unsearchable depths, the entire structure and the nucleus of the everlasting eternity's purpose and its divine functions.

Considering now that both of these very real powers and their strong influences that surrounds us all at any giving and living moment of our own life expressions in time, the very true and the very undeniable internal power of influence that exists between our very own and powerful original elements of life that are all still residing within our very own internal core mechanism structure, that in their very truly and appointed functions that have been bestowed upon them all from the Almighty creator himself, these very powerful elements of life within us all, that are indeed the essence and the substance that forms our oneness and our true nature that completes our very own and active living human being's created, and formed, and breathed expressions of life, and also there are in the creation the very real existences and their truly undeniable actions of their very own and strong and very powerful external influences, that are actively revealing to us the humans their sources of influence that we may be able to know them at times by default and design, or at times they are keeping their very own sources of their influence hidden and unknown to us, or even at times when these powerful external influences are going forward and actively are trying to manipulate and to confuse the living humanity's very own consciousness by molding and shaping its moral behavior by making the humanity starting to put their trust and belief in them, believing that their own released information are there for the real strengthening of the very complete and the overall health of the wellbeing of humanity, yet many times their very end result of their released informative actions upon humanity proves the real and painful opposite reality for all those that are being entangled and that are being captured by their strong influences and revelations, and now if we truly are considering and recognizing the existence and the actions of these powerful elements of life, the internal living elements of life and their very own power of influence and the external living elements of life and their very own power of influence, that are together in their own truth the very truly building factors, that can help and improve our very own overall process and functions of our living expressions, or that can be in their truth the very truly damaging factors that can hinder and really distort and damage our very own overall process and functions of our living and breathing expression, how can we as the humanity be able to develop and activate our very own much needed internal defense mechanism system capability, that will help us to be able to align them all and to protect all of our very own living elements of life that are truly residing within us all, activated and also connected into the living and activated foundation and structure of our own human being's life center of balance, that also in the same time it will really help us and it will allow us all, to be protected and to be shielded from the very real external powers that surrounds us, and from their very dangerous manipulative influences that are all aiming straight towards all of humanity's deep overall spiritual and physical health by actively and continually trying to capture and to influence, and also to affect even the humanity's very own and eternal end destination and also the humanity's everlasting destiny.

In order for a truly constructive and proper building foundation and structure for our humanity much needed and critically vital, and imperative functions of our very own internal defense mechanism system that has to be fully operative and integrated within the divine modules and their functions, of our very own self-awareness capacity and its multi prong capabilities that are truly being activated in our living life expressions by the Almighty God, by the power of his word and by the power of his owns spirit, we need to really start to understand at least to a very minimum cause effort, the much needed and the very vital and critically importance of knowing our own lives' purposes, by starting to recognize the importance of finding and striving to get as close as possible to our very own center of life's balance, that in return it will truly help us all, the humans, to be able to acknowledge the very crucial importance of a true living and balanced life, for our very own complete and overall well-being health functions of our entire living expressions that are all being in truth manifested within us all, and also that are being active manifested outside of us all to our living surroundings, by the very true attributes and reflections of our own active and consciousness stages of awareness, of our very own physical and emotional stage, our very own spirit and our spiritual stage, and our very own psychological and mental health stage, and I will like to add to this statement that as longer we have the breath of life in our own lungs and as long our living life expressions are alive on this temporary journey of our lives, these very powerful expressions and their manifestations will never stop and it does not matter if we are releasing them forward from a life expression that it is balanced within the center of their proper purpose and functions, or if we are releasing them forward, from a life that it is completely out and away from their center of life's proper balance for their own purpose and functions, but how we will be able to understand and to recognize the importance of life, how will be able to identify the values and the priorities in life, how we will be able to correctly assess our own internal relations and functions between our own inner residing elements of life, and also how we will be able to correctly assess our very own external relations and functions that are happening between us all and our surroundings in life, it is truly the crucial and the imperative key of our living life, that will allow us to be able to unlock the door of our very own powerful inner well-being functions and their very strong internal defense mechanism systems of our own self-awareness divine capabilities and their abilities, to successfully be able to finally understand the true reality of our own lives, and also to be able to make us all aware of our very own and temporary living life's purpose and functions, that are all activated for their living expressions, and also that can be delegated forward into our very life's own expression and existence, from a divine and balanced center of our very own life and its living structure, or from a dysfunctional and from an unbalanced center of our very own life and its living structure.

    One of the many reasons I want to be able to cover in more details this very important and critical subject of being able to search and to be able to find and also to be able to get and to be able to manifest our living expression of our daily lives, as close as possible to the crucial and the vital baseline living point of our very imperative life's center of balance and its complex alignment, that indeed it does really has the power to influence and to affect our entire human character and its built, and this baseline living point of our own life center of balance, must be truly established and continually be keep fully activated in an always forward truth between our internal original elements of life, that are all residing and dwelling within the very overall structure of all of us, the humans, and that are known to be, the living soul and the spirit, the heart and the mind, it is because it will truly help us all in the reality journey of our own living life's existence, to be able to develop the much needed and required forth understanding for developing our internal defense mechanism system within the foundation and structure of our own self-awareness capability, and by doing so we will be protected and shielded at the very inner core health functions of our very own overall well-being, from our very own internal built actions, feelings, emotions and will power that are truly very strong and powerful motivators, that can sometimes lead us to act on their desires and their impulsive sensor and signals of influences that in return will affect us and will drive us to make and to move on decisions, that are not at times in the best interests of our very own human beings overall health and functions, and also by doing so we will be protected and shielded at the very inner core health functions of our very own overall well-being, from the very strong and powerfully external elements of life in the creation, that in order to be able to achieve their own end results against the very humanity's existence and its human being's expressions, will send non-stop their own raw information signals and data, and that if their powerful released information and data it will be left unchecked and left uncalibrated and also left unfiltered by our own self-awareness mechanism system as it is being received and captured within our inner core foundation of our very own built in complex of thoughts mechanism processor and its power functions, and it will in return also affect us, and it will drive us towards making, and forward move on decisions that are not at times at their best for our very own human overall and proper health functions, and if they are implemented these decisions will really affect and will truly influence our very own physical, psychological, and even at various times it will undeniable be able to affect and hinder our very own spiritual well-being and our human living expression.

Knowing that our own human's being overall proper health functions and continued growth it is influenced by both internal and external factors that are being actively interacting and interloping together within the depths of our deep chambers of our life's expression, and its active manifestations as a completed and as a whole living being in the creation, the crucial understanding of what life it is and consist of and what it is in the truth of the matter, our life's purpose and its functions, it is vital and also critically important for the humanity's own internal balance process and its external balance process that it has been already established and activated by the creator for us all, the humans, and if we will follow the guidance and the instructions that are released and reveal forth to us all, the humans from the Word of the Living God, we will be all able on our temporary journey of our lives to start to recognize the importance of living a balanced life for the very spiritual and the physical, and for the emotional and for the mental overall health of our lives, we will be also able to start to identify the true values and their true priorities that it will help us all to search and to determine what truly are the things that matter the most in our lives, we will be able also once we identify the values and the priorities that matter the most in our lives and for our lives, to be able to assess them all and start to implement them all by making and executing the needed changes to our own daily routines and our activities, by setting realistic goals in life that will help us all to be able to achieve them and to maintain them all from within the depths of our own very powerful and strong foundation of our continued fundamental and fully activated structure of life, that has been always holding and sustaining all the humanity's very own living expressions and their unique true center of their life's balance within the entire creation existence and its balance.

Before going a little further with my writings of these very important topics and their true meaning of life's reality, in regards for our very own humanity's purpose and functions and our human being's eternal survival, I want to be able to summarize in a few words the very truly importance and necessity of the understanding of these previous written paragraphs, where we covered in a more details the reality that surrounds us all, that we are all exposed to, and that also can, and it will be able to affect and influence, our overall health and its completed well-being existence, starting with the understanding of the Word of God that was revealed to all of the humanity by our Lord Jesus Christ, regarding what it is truly the highest commandment of God's law that if it is implemented it will be able to fulfill all of the commandments of the law and all of the prophets, then we covered the imperative importance of being able to recognize and to understand our powerful internal and external influences, that can and it will be able to truly affect and to influence us all in our daily living life, what and who are those very real and very powerful internal elements of life that are residing within our structural fiber of our living beings, also we went ahead and did covered in a few words about the very crucial, and the vital understanding to be able to recognize in truth also what and who are these very real and strong external powerful influences that are releasing their raw information and data against it, or for the humanity's overall functions and expressions, and what are their reasons and their true scopes for their influences by doing so, and also we went ahead and covered the real needed importance of being able to recognize and to understand our temporary journey of this life and its living process, by helping us reaching and getting as close as possible towards our life center of balance, that it will be able to help us all to truly realize what life it is all about, what life consist of, and also by doing so how we will be able to start the necessary process to be able to align our very own emotions and feelings, and our very will power and desires, within our own selves built human foundation that it is holding our fundamental structure of its living functions that are being very actively manifested by their interdependent and their interconnected live attributes, that exists at all times between all of our very own and very powerfully internal elements of life, and the real and very vital importance of developing the required understanding that will enable us to build the necessary self-defense mechanism system on the very powerful fundamental foundation that it is actively holding our own self- awareness capacity and capability that it will help us all to be in truth protected against all the many external influences and their powerful new manifestations and revelations.

I wanted to be able to write and to express in this very short summary from the previously discussed paragraphs and their topics, before going ahead and write more in details going forward for discussing some of the points that are covering by this very chapter of this book that it is been called the "Truth Shifters", because it will open up and enlarge our own needed understanding that we may be able to start to differentiate and to distinguish, and also it will help us all to be able to start the vital discerning processes, between the many natural and very powerful life influences that are being very active presenting themselves all around our daily living life and within our own surroundings that we are manifesting our expressions, and also at various times these powerful influences that are very real and very actively presenting themselves to us very deep within our own depth and robust structural fabric of our own human substance and our living essence, and to be able to start to distinguish and to be able to begin genuinely discerning their active and influential sources of their revealed information and their raw activated raw data that it is being continually released within our very own human being's expressed functions, and also upon us all and upon our very own existence 'realm as being the genuinely breathing and living humans that are traveling on our short and temporary express platform of our manifested life on this earthly transcendental realm in the entire creation within the earth's real and genuine environmental and physical existence, and it is definitely very crucial and strictly very imperative for helping our own humanity marching towards reaching and achieving their own searched for living goals and their results, and for their very own final end destination, and for their very own everlasting eternity and location.

Developing the much needed understanding in order to be able to further explore these powerful and complex interconnection and their proper functions and their true meaning of their existence, that are all very actively expressing themselves around us and also that are communicating their impulses within our framed living structure at all times, and that have the power to indeed influence and also to help our human overall health and the very human advanced growth, both internally and externally, it does requires us the humans to move on a very strictly and robust multi-faceted approach platform of an authentic living that draws on it a variety of disciplines and perspectives, that it will really help us to mold and it will help us to build in truth within our own inner being the required mechanism system that it is analyzing and it is processing our very own active and truly strong perceptions and their solid visions for the humanity's life existence and the humanity's true meaning and purpose functions, filtered and calibrated and protected within the foundation of the Word of the Living God, and that the more we will be able to accept and to receive it and to understand it, the less we will be exposed to have our own seeing perceptions and our hearing perceptions corrupted and influenced by our very own internal willpower and their feeling, emotions and desires, and also, by the external elements of life in the creation that are actively living and surrounding us all with their very own strong waves of robust manipulative and deceptive raw data of their own released forward information, through which they are actively trying to capture the humanity's substance and its true essence, and the humanity's breathing and living life' fragrance within their own webbing power.

The reason I mentioned in the above paragraphs about the power of influenced perception in regards to our seeing and how God created us to be able to process what we see, and about our hearing and how God created us to be able to process what we hear because it is very imperative towards our constructive and systematic understanding of acting and executing our significantly expressed and our own released thoughts for life, through which our very own assertive behavior it is being activated by and also represented by being manifested within our very internal behavioral functions of our inner being fundamental structure, and also by being significantly actively manifested externally by the very behavioral parts of our expressions that we humans are releasing them forward towards the surroundings that are around us and consistently are in a continually contact with us, and with our very own life's manifesting expressions as actual human beings.

What is the difference between being able to see versus being able to perceive what we see through the systematic processor of our living perceptions and their functions, and if our way of perceiving is being influenced and corrupt, can this indeed affect and influence ultimately the way we see and what we see? We all know that seeing refers to our very natural and physical act of having the ability to detect light that, in return, has the power to reflect and form an image for our own eyes to see and to process and notice it, but to be able to perceive it and to be able to understand what we see truly, it does in truth involves the powerful activating mechanism system within our innermost being that has the capability of processing the information that the power of the brain is seeing it, that the main activated brain chamber of executive functions will be able to interpret the received data and its signals and its pulses in a meaningful and genuinely and constructively for our overall well-being. This systematic approach towards the true capability and ability of our internal senses to understand in truth what life's presented images are before our eyes need to be genuinely activated by the power of the Word of God and his Holy Spirit.

Let's go together and read as a reference and as an example from the Scripture a passage from Deuteronomy, chapter twenty-nine, verses one through four, where the word of God says," Moses summoned all Israel and said to them: You have seen all that the Lord did before your eyes in the land of Egypt, to Pharaoh and all his servants and to all his land, the great trials that your eyes saw, the signs, and those great wonders. But to this day, the Lord has not given you a mind to understand, sights to see, or ears to hear.

Here is the first example revealed to humanity by Moses in regards to being able to see but not being able to process and to indeed be able to perceive and understand what the eyes are seeing, and because we are reading the Scriptures that are revealing to us the humans this robust process of being able to see but not to be able to perceive and to understand in truth what life's actual circumstances can be presented and projected before our very eyes let's go together in read another passage revealed to humanity by none other than the living and breathing word of the living God our Lord and Savior Jesus Christ, from the pages of the book of Mark chapter eighth and verses seventeen and eighteen, where the Lord said,

" And becoming aware, Jesus asked them," Why are you talking about having no bread? Do you still not perceive it or understand it? Are your hearts hardened? Do you have eyes and fail to see? Do you have ears and fail to hear? And do you not remember? I choose these two very powerful examples on this subject, one from the old testament and one from the new testament, one revealed by Moses of the old order, and one told by Jesus of the new order, to be able to make this true statement that some things will never change and both examples are revealing the undeniable truth that what we are expose to see by our own eyes, even seeing the beautiful works and miracles of the Almighty God in our lives or in the lives of others that are all around us, and also we are exposed to hear with our own ears, even hearing about the wonders of the works and miracles of the Almighty God, and this proves that we can be at times influenced and we can have our very own understanding corrupted by our own internal elements of life residing within our inner being, or by the external aspects of life in the creation that have the power to mold and also to influence us all, and by being controlled and by being made confused by their corrupt information, we are exposed and are made very vulnerable to not be able to process life's events with the right discern, and right distinguish, causing the dangerous and the distorted effect that we may not be capable indeed of being able to understand in truth the process of what our very own eyes are exposed to seeing and also what our same own ears are exposed of hearing in reality?

Maybe some of the readers of this book may start asking this question now,' What may this have to do with the dangerous wave of corrupt influences that are fighting against the very soul of humanity's very eternal destination and its destiny, and why being able to tap into the complex structure of our very own internal processor mechanism system that will allow us and guide us all to being able to understand, what we see, and to understand what we hear, through a strictly divine and appointed revelation from the word of the living God for the humanity and through his very own absolute truth, it is vital, and it is critically imperative for the protection and the salvation of our very own soul?

Answering this very question in these few following words, I want to be able to let the readers know that this same reality of our way of being able to start to interpret and of being able to begin to disseminate and to actively process the accurate information that we as humans are all being exposed to daily, and that are genuinely presenting themselves towards our very own way of life to mold and to influence our very own thought behavior and its solid structural foundation of our human character building blocks and its functions, through an uncorrupt and a non-controlled understanding of our very own thoughts, in the truth of the matter and for the actual perception of our reality, this has to do with all and with everything we are doing in our lives and that we are exposed to and have to analyze and to perceive in our daily activities that are all together bonded and activated to cause and also to be genuinely the significantly driving forward forces for our very own life's meaning, purpose and proper functions.

There are so many things that we are exposed to analyze and to disseminate and to perceive in our daily living activities that are being at times influencing our behavior on an single level of exposure, or at various times these daily living activities, combined and together are forming the accurate driving forward force, that it is building our very own much and needed understanding towards the meaning, the purpose and the functions of our own lives, and the way in which our own way of life it is understood can really in truth mold and influence the way we are force to act and also the way our own firm and structural foundation that holds on it our own human character expression and function that it is being built, activated and manifested, and having our very own character built, activated and truly manifested through a clear, clean, uncorrupt and non-influenced understanding of our very own process thoughts and actions, ultimately it will help us all to be able to reach the necessary platforms in our life's expression for self-control and self-awareness that are crucially needed to be activated in our lives, that we may be able to gain a complete and a non-influenced understanding of our own process thought functions that are indeed what constitute the fundamental behavior structure that it is also a true driving force towards the process of being able to realize in truth what it is really our very own human life's meaning, purpose and functions in the vast creation of the Almighty God's plan for humanity.

As a result of our way of living, understanding that our own behavior can be molded and influenced by our very own internal emotions, and our own internal willpower, feelings and also by its very strong desires, and its perceived understanding that our behavior can be molded and also influenced by the external elements of life in the creation that we the humanity are exposed to interact with, and interloop with on a daily basis, being able to analyze and perceive our very own meaning of life from within the protection and the guidance of the Spirit of the living God, that can truly raise and it will raise a high standard and a strong shield that will help us and will also protect us against any influence of corruption and its waves of deceptions, and also against everything else that we as the human beings are actively exposed of encountering in our lives, that can truly move us and force us into the powerful activated forward life's positions from where we are being able of processing the understanding of the meaning of life through a very powerful and strong influenced and distorted perception towards the reality of life that surrounds us the humanity, and if that process it does succeeds, it will make us very vulnerable, and also it will open us all to start to live and to experience our very living lives without the clear vision and without the much needed understanding of its living expressions, that are very crucial towards interpreting and processing what our very own eyes are seeing and what our very own ears are hearing, not under any corrupt influences but in the reality and its truth, it is very crucially vital and undeniable imperative for our very own human overall health functions and for our very own human overall growth as a physical and as a spiritual well-being and living expression that it is being actively searching to be able to find their own human's life's true meaning, through the various and the multitudes of their very active processes of their very humanity life's true purpose and the humanity's true and uncorrupted life's functions within the paramount and the strong structural platforms of their very own daily breathing living life applications for their growth and for their continued and sustained life's manifestations.

    The reason I am using the wording and the phrase " influenced and perceived understanding" it is simple because we do need indeed to be able to recognize if in our own moving decisions that we are facing to make in life while being exposed to the many waves of information that are being continually loading their powerful raw data within the depths of our own structural mechanism functions of operations and expressions of our human being fundamental character built actions, that it is being very actively manifested in the vast complex and interdependent environment system of our multi living organisms forms and expressions of their own manifested lives, that are operating within our very own inner built structure of our own living elements of life that are all residing within us, or that are operating externally around us, but we are exposed to and also prong to received and also to act on their released signals of information and data within the vast interdependent environmental system in the creation, if there truly have been known or unknown, a variety of attributes and subjects of their matter that had and also have the influence and the power to affect and to corrupt our very own human perception at the very ground level of our own expressed existence and because of that process of influence everything that we are all being exposed to receive and to also captivate it within the very capacity of our own capability and ability of our very own motions and senses systematic and living mechanism that it is being used for our expressed and manifest survival, that we as the humans are also use it for helping us moving forward towards the much critically and needed power of understanding within the very applicable discernment functions for the real data and for the information process of dissemination and activation that it is and it will be a truly undeniable leading powerful force towards guiding us reaching and achieving very strong but also very dangerously inaccurate end results that are truly based not on the truth but really that are being based on our own influenced and own biased interpretations of the very raw data and information that we are all processing, and because of that we all are truly being exposed to start interpreting data and information against a conclusion and an end result that it was already being predicted and also foretold due to the fundamental influenced perception of our very own understanding that took place in the depths of our complex and automatic chamber of our own human mind's processing thoughts mechanism, therefore it is critically imperative and important to be aware of the potential differences between our own natural senses and feeling, and their emotions and desires and between the true process of perceiving facts that are helping us to actively be able to engage us truly within the very powerful receptors of our perception in the presented truth so that way we will be all true protected and also guided on the very enlightened road and pathway of our lives by being able to apply truly accurate measurements of life and their true and unique uninfluenced interpretations of all of our constructive and structural complex combined human senses, that are all together being active synchronized within the fundamental and its divine systematic activated foundation that holds our human's true operational structure of functions that creates and produces the energetic fuel pulses and the signals of our very own living expressions that are all being forth manifested by our very own created human living's abilities that are being truly revealed and also that are activated to existence in our lives by our own very strong and very powerful and complex sense mechanism system that it has been bestowed in activated within the very human being's DNA structure by the Creator himself, and these powerful senses that truly can define our living and moving expression in the creation are the sight, seeing, vision, the hearing, audition, the smell, olfaction, the taste, gestation, and the touch, tactile or feeling, and knowing that all of our powerful senses truly can be exposed to be expressed and manifested through an interpretation and through a perception that at times can be influenced by our own internal mechanism functions, and also many times can be influenced by our very own external mechanism functions that are being all activated to enable our existence and survival as a living created human being with a living soul, within the vast creation of the Almighty God's plan, will and desire, and being able to awaken in the depths of our human being the powerful mind's self-awareness conscious and its powerful divine consciousness by the power of the Word of the Living God and by the power of his Holy Spirit, it will definitely protect us all and guide us all towards the center balance of our life, that it is much needed and critically imperative in order to be able to recognize and accept the reality and the truth of our humanity's existence, meaning and purpose.

The difference, being able to activate and use our own God-given natural human senses for our existence and survival, between our sight, hearing, smell, taste, and touch, and how we perceive their powerful interaction and movements within our very inner framed structure, and also how we are sensing their functions in relationship with our very external framed system of human expressions, can significantly affect and influence the exact outcome of our own experiences of life, as indeed the perception or even the corrupt perception that can happen due to the misalignments that are existing between our very own internal elements of life, that can certainly influence our very own structural and moral behavior, and our decision-making, that can lead to very multiple unhealthy and dangerous emotional responses that are not at times in the best interest for our overall complex existence of our living life through the purpose and the functions that are genuinely the active properties of what can and will define us as humans.

It is, therefore, essential that we are always ready and

constantly aware of the many substantial differences that are arising around us all every day, which are the differences between our sight, hearing, smell, taste, and touch abilities, as well as how our pre-perceptions of the very information and its raw data received are and can be significantly influenced by how we the humans are all being exposed to them in life. As a result, we must be aware of the many and countless substantial differences fighting within and around us regarding the connectivity between our sight, hearing, smell, taste, touch, and their designated properties and functions.

Also, it is critical to know how these properties and expressions can expose us and lead our humanity to the applicable human functional processors that interpret signals and senses when actively responding to the data and to the information that has been received and deeply captivated.

Considering that these multitudes of significant potential differences are constantly emerging around us, we need to be more aware of the actual effects that they can have on our senses, sense of smell, sense of taste, and sense of touch, and how all together these strong human properties are developed and shaped by the way we the humans are responding all to their powerful influences. Also, they can be created and shaped by how the human process of pre-perceiving and perceiving the information and data received is analyzed. We must genuinely recognize and realize that there is a solid and undeniable correlation between our sight, sound, smell, taste, and touch properties and how humans are captivating their signals and interpreting their responses.

This robust correlation and networking bond leads us all to the systemic process of perception of the information and data we will receive to function correctly. Also, it will help us and enable us to be able to clearly understand how we receive it and how we interpret it, how we discern it, how we disseminate it, and how we release it forward into active expressions from within the intense chambers of our minds and from within our mind's complex consciousness.

Having a conscious mind that is very aware of its true surroundings when connecting and interacting internally or externally within the limits of its exposed presence of the internal elements of life and their attributes and their functions that are always in a continually active motion, it does not necessarily reflects our human mind stage of it consciousness and its truly strong ability that can achieve a real powerful result to be able to discern between the very actions of the human mind's own conscious awareness attributes and functions and between the reaction of their strong processing abilities of the humanity's very own and powerful human mind's consciousness divine attributes and its functions, and this analogy truly reflects a very powerful reality indeed, because it does makes us realized that just having a very strong and a very aware human mind's conscious, it does not, and it will not necessarily translate and transfers its active responses under the true power and the true meaning of our humanity's living purposes, and that if we will be open to learn it and sincerely will try to truly understand their meanings, this very process will enable us all and it will also forward guide our actions to be able to reflect truly on our own human mind's platform functions and their realistic stages of expressions through which we are all exposed to manifest our own living and breathing existence of our lives, and also this very true expressed process, indeed can be truly activated and empowered also by our very own strong mind's expressions and their fundamental living structural capabilities and their true functions of being able to activate and release forth our very own powerful thoughts and their living expressions to life from the very depths of our own protected and uninfluenced mind's consciousness, by using its strong ability and also its powerful living expressed functions through their own necessary applicable and its divine moral behavior that we as the humans do need and must possess for being able to properly engage our reality of life within our internal and also with our external characteristics and their manifested expressions as a living organism in the creation by being able of using each and every majestic and powerful human attributes that were given and bestowed upon the humanity mind's consciousness from its creator for a meaningful life that will be encapsulated within its divine purpose.

    I want to go a little further on this very topic and its subject regarding our correlation and the connection that exists between the decisive actions of our very own human mind's consciousness works and the mind's natural awareness of its existence within the stages and within the platforms of the powerful mind's natural expressions that are also exposed to be manifested within the paramount of time that it is being bound by its activated location in the creation, and between the reactions that are all leading to the implementations of our very own human mind's consciousness works and the mind's spiritual solid awareness towards its own existence within the stages and the platforms of the powerful mind's expressions that are also being exposed to be all manifested within the vast paramount of time that it is being bound by its activated location in the creation, and by these real divine connections that are being activated to a forward motion to existence, between the strong mind's conscious and between the strong mind's consciousness, the humanity's own human expressions and their living soul, are genuinely the only created and formed beings by the very own hands of the Almighty God, that can express their own manifested existence in a physical and in a natural environment of their own mind's conscious awareness stages and also that can express their very strong embodied presence in a spiritual and also in a psychological environment of their very own strong mind's consciousness awareness stages, and as longer these very powerful correlations and strong connections that are in the existence between our very own human mind's conscious awareness, and between our own human mind's consciousness awareness, are being linked, secured and protected by the Word of the Living God and by his Holy Spirit, away from all the internal and from all the external corrupt influences that are coming daily against the humanity's living soul, it will be able to help us to produce the positive results and also it will truly help us to be able to move step by step a little closer and closer towards the final end destination of our very own expressed and manifested purposes of our living lives, that can and are in truth being forward reflected within and also on all of our internal and external surroundings that we inter-exist with, from within our very own life's center of balance that it is being activated through the various senses and their multiple signals that are all being received and sent, to and from, continually between the strong actions of the human mind's conscious and the strong reactions of the human mind's consciousness, that are being together connected and synchronized within the depths of the fundamental and structural foundation of our own entire human life's expression and existence.

It is a very powerful blessing to be able to reach the must necessary understanding that will enable us to be able to realize and to able to clearly distinguish the many differences that are arising daily in their active and living expressions of interpretation and perception of our thoughts within the deep executive chambers of our mind's very complex and structural functions that have the power to build and mold our very own human character and its powerfully attributes for our very own life's purposes, that exists between the very strong and powerful human mind's conscious and its awareness properties, and also between the very strong and powerful acting human mind's consciousness and its awareness properties, and when we are considering the actual reality that the very human mind's conscious awareness and the human mind's consciousness awareness, operates and reflects their own actions and their own reaction results under two completely and different meanings, that are the actual results of their final product expressions that are all being genuinely based on their own interpretations of the raw information and data that our very own and powerful complex human mind is actively being exposed to act and implement its executive decisions and its expressed actions upon, through the internal and powerful influences of life's many active mental processes of control and self- awareness, that can be truly constructive and forth defined as being led and controlled by a corrupt and by an influenced mind, or it can be truly defined as being led and controlled by an uncorrupt and an uninfluenced mind, that in the truth of the matter it can produce forth the one true result and the one true reflection of our very own human powerful mind's perceptions that are all exposed of being filtered or being unfiltered by their very own thoughts and feeling, and by their very own strong emotions, their own willpower and desires, that are all together truly the fundamental and the structural part of what creates, builds and forms the humans and their active expressed actions, that are classified as being the ones that have strong and powerfully living and breathing life expressions, that have been created by God to be able to actively exist, and also to be able to actively manifest their own functions in the vast creation of the Almighty God, as a true complex organism form of an divine origin in the creation that it is being reflected by its completed designed form and by its very own and fundamental living structure and combination of the human's very strong physical attributes that are all being connected together with the very human's strong spiritual attributes that are active in existence, within the depths of the humanity's DNA's fiber and fabric of its multi-complexity network of systematic life functions that are all being powerfully manifested within their own and unique form of their existence, their own living and their very own lives expressions and purposes.

Being able to recognize this reality and also to be able to express these critical and complex functions of our human mind's interpretation and perception of our own internal thoughts as a result of the data and the information that we are all being expose to receive and captivate their own signals and their own original sources of product and originality, and how in the reality the mind's power of interpretation and the mind's strong perception can genuinely affect our very own human character and our very own life's purposes, it is very imperative and it is also critically vital to our fundamental overall well-being health and functions, and if this process it is recognized it will definitely help us all, the humans, to be able to start approach with a divine discernment the many variations and differences that are arising daily in the active life of our very own humanity's living expressions from within their many depths of their multiple various sources of information that we are all being in truth exposed to receive and to capture them all, within our minds and also being open to the understanding that in the reality of life, these extreme and powerful differences can all be genuinely deep-rooted within the very own complex structural functions of our own human mind's actual expressed capacity and ability that has the activating releasing power to build, and to mold our attributes and their active functions, that are being all together tight and connected and that are all playing a genuinely significant and a very crucial role that it is vital in the shaping of our lives, and an essential role in creating our identities as the powerful overall expression of our own and complete human existence.

Also being able to express this complex idea about the many various differences that exist in our own human mind's power of interpretation and its active perception of thoughts, that can, and that are all truly affecting our human character and also our own moral behavior's attributes that are all actively required towards implementing the process control of our life's purposes through the clarity and through the needed understanding of the working complexities of our very own human mind's influence and its power of persuasion, that if it is being left unchecked and it is being left uncalibrated, it will empowered the mind to be able to achieve at times the true mind's desires for the executive control, operations and functions of our complete and overall human factors that are all being together contributing and influencing our very own thoughts, feelings and automatic behaviors that are exposed to come to their true living expressions and their strong and forth active manifestations through our own mind's very powerful cognitive biases that can lead us, the humans, to be exposed to make strong errors in our judgment when we are exposed to come face to face with the reality that truly it is surrounding us at all times, but due to the mind's own strong cognitive biases, that can really fuel and can influence our own decision-making processes for the living and survival of our human life's express manifestations on this earthly paramount of God's creation, we are lead to make many times these vital decisions for our lives meanings and purposes, and their functions, by using our mind's confirmation bias ability, that can be also classified as the mind's own power of using tendency to seek out active signals and information data that may be able to confirm the mind's own existing belief systems that have been altogether created, activated and also that have been fundamentally structured on the mind's very strong and bias foundation, thus making us all vulnerable and also prone to start to ignore and also to start to bypass any reasonable raw data and information that may contradict our beliefs and our own experiences at times, and this also can lead and force us to make decisions for our lives that are not based on the available evidences presented to us, but that are in truth being based on our very own mind's strong cognitive biases, and also based on mind's strong confirmation biases, and based on mind's power of interpretation and perception biases, and this truly is the undeniable evidence for our humanity that in truth of its matter the mind can truly be accessed and influenced and also pursued at all levels and stages of the mind's living expressions by our very own internal and powerful elements of life and also many times being influenced by the real strong and powerful external elements of life that are living alongside us, and that surrounds us all, the humans and the humans own build humanity in the creation.

Now that it has become evident in our view and focus, the mighty and robust characteristics of the mind's functions and attributes are forth revealing to us the undeniable complexities and properties of our mind's executive purposes that can be reflected in our lives by the way it is shaping and molding our very unique identities and their fingerprint identifications in the entire creation, it is worth exploring a little further the relationship and the strong connectivity senses and their trafficking signals information and data that are always active in a continuous motion expression between our human mind's conscious and the mind's consciousness, and between the very human mind's consciousness and the human mind's sub-consciousness, and between the human mind's subconsciousness and the mind's unconsciousness power attributes, that can in truth work together as a divine and strong synchronized complex mechanism network that sustains and maintains on its powered frames the entire structural and executive functions of our own human mind's complete consciousness, and being able to start exploring more in depths this true and powerful relationship that have been genuinely established between these individual elements that are manifesting their own executive powers of their expressions within the fundamental chambers of our own human mind's activated power for life functions, with an open view and attitude it is going to help us reaching and striving for clarity and for objectivity in our thinking and decision-making processes that are critically and vital to our life's expression existence, by minimizing and blocking as much as possible the solid influences and the strong biases of our own internal mind's attributes functions, and by reducing the very strong biases of our external interacting factors that can and it will be able to cloud our judgment.

Also we do need to know and learn that, however we may try to use our logical ways of interpretation of the actual reality of our surroundings and our living lives, the importance to be able to recognized and to admit that no human mind can ever be completely free from its very own mind's internal biases and influences, or be completely free from its own mind's external biases and consequences, it is critical and very imperative to our overall health for our physical and spiritual maturity and growth, if and when we are considering that our own thoughts and our own emotions, our feelings and our desires are also being shaped by our own individual experiences of our own lives, that have been projected and reflected within the mind's internal or external purpose and functions, by our own cultural backgrounds, including their many social contexts, and to write this very real thought in a more simplified form of expression, it will be written like this, " when considering that our feelings, our emotions and desires can build and mold our own living character, while in the same time our own strong personality, can create and also can develop our very own thoughts, feelings, emotions and desires," and having this power process really understood, it will be very helpful to us to be able to cultivate the much needed self-awareness and its very critical thinking process skills mechanism, that it will help us to be able to recognize and to be able to evaluate our own daily biases and their very real and robust assumptions towards our lives, when we are prone at times to perceive and to interpret these variations of alternative perspectives and their released data information and their sources that may be coming at times against our very own way of understanding, and this also it is critically vital and important to consider the real and the potential substantial consequences and their ethical implication of our own life's actions, and also it is so critical and essential to strive to find the actual center of balance of life that it is required and needs to exist between our very own personal motives, feelings, and desires, and the very overall well-being of others that had their very own individual experiences as a fundamental establishment foundation sustaining their own living lives, that have been projected and reflected within their own internal and their external purpose functions that were shaped under the guidance of their own strong cultural backgrounds and that were founded and based on their own structural living and social contexts.

    I want to be able to accentuate and emphasize the above paragraph's statement that describes the true reality of life that surrounds us all, and because of this undeniable factor, we cannot just become ignorant and act blind to the fact that billions of people living and enjoying life just like us, and that are also looking for their very own purpose and functions of their living lives within the majestic creation of the Almighty God just like all of us, have to be bypass and disregarded somehow because in our very own eyes their very own and real individual experiences, that have been projected and released within their strong internal and external expressions of their lives, by their strong cultural backgrounds and social contexts that have been used to build and to mold their very own feelings, and emotions, willpower and desires that have been then captured within their strong fundamental and structural own mind's set very powerful confirmations biases, and truth be told, there is no human being ever be able to escape its manifestation, by assuming and thinking that other people's own experiences are less of an importance than ours, and that other people's own feelings and emotions, and their willpower are diminished and less of an importance than our own experiences are, and this real judgment that it is fueled by the mind's own systematic frames of its confirmation bias, will make us very vulnerable to bypass the much needed understanding approach to be able to realize that the reasons for the many diversities of many powerful and strong belief systems across our many various cultures that are expressing their own understood manifestations are indeed truly very complex and multifaceted, and because of that reason, our own humanity's beliefs systems that are so complicated and so hard to be processed at times, it cannot be reduced to a simple desire for absolute power and domination, and total control, by certain groups, by communities and also by many self-described denominations, and at times even by many nations, that will always try to infringe and subjugate their own people's true active search for answers to their own life's questions regarding their living existence and expressions, their very own lives purposes and functions, their own created originality as humans with a living soul in God's creation, thus making their search for answers their fundamental and strong structural foundation that holds at times so many opposite and different belief systems, because in their own way of understanding the truth, different beliefs will try to offer different answers to these many various questions of humanity's never ending search, and those different answers many times can resonate in more depth with the interpretation of the people's many various and different ways of being able to understand and to process those answers by trying to validate their own mind's confirmation biases, that were all based on how they perceived and how they interpreted the information and the data that have been received and then captivated within their own powerful mind's consciousness, that can be, and it will be at times strongly influenced by their own individual living experiences, and then released and activated forward as a processed and fulfilled thought, at the level of their very own overall health as physical beings, and at the level of their own overall health as spiritual beings, that are being both together tight encapsulated within the activated depths chambers of their manifested living purposes and from where the completed humankind's being it is being fueled into existence within God's creation by their very strong attributes functions of their own living lives' s expressions, that were created, and formed and then activated from the beginning of times by the Almighty Creator's own hands and by his very own breath of life, that was breathed into the human's being life expressions in the creation.

In closing of this very chapter 'Truth Shifters' I want to summarize in few more words the journey that we together took in describing the reality that actively it is surrounding us, about the complexity of our living life's expressions, about the very powerful internal influences that are working within our own human being's fundamental structure and that are in a constantly moving motion between the elements of life that are residing within our human fabric and fiber's DNA, for our very existence and sustainment, also about the very powerful external influences that are at times coming against our very own's living life's survival, releasing their own corrupt sources of strong confusion abilities upon the humanity's soul through their deceitful information and raw data that are continually beeping their active signals into the depths of our own mind's consciousness with their very powerful desires that they possess to be able to control and shape our very own human character attributes and their functions, and by being able to do so, they will entangle the humanity in their strong robust webs and labyrinths of their own offered alternative reality away from the presence and away from the truth of the Almighty God, that had been released and revealed to all humanity by the power of his everlasting love and steadfast faithfulness towards all the creation's living forms and lives, by his own divine and absolute truth that was brought forward into the entire creation's fundamental building structures by the eternal, unchanged, always living and breathing Word of God, and if we as human beings will open the gates from the depths of our living souls, and accepting the indwelling of the Spirit of the Living God and his Word, it will help us and it will continually guide us all in our search towards being able to reach and to discover the things that matter the most in our very own living lives, while we are traveling on this temporary and short journey of our expressions on this earthly paramount realm, where we are now actively experience and manifest our existence, by helping us understand and realize that we the humans, are also in a non-stop real fight for the very eternal survival of our living soul, and this proper understanding will enable us all to also be sensitive and to recognize that the very vital and the critical struggles of this decisive fight for survival, it is taken place within ourselves own inner expression of our lives, and also it is actively taken place within the solid and external interactions of our very own and strong expressed manifestations with the world all around us, that we are exposed to inter-exist with, and also to interloop with in our daily living, but to be able to gain this divine understanding truly, we must allow ourselves to be driven and guided forward by the truly unrestricted power and the vital protection that comes only from the Spirit of the Living God and his Word of Truth, which has been established as a lighthouse and guidance for all the humanity, from the very beginning from the eternity.

We also covered the vital importance to be able to start understanding and recognizing the undeniable attributes and functions of our own center of life's living balance that it will help us to pay attention to the powerful alignment that it is needed to be fully activated within the depths of our own structural human being's foundation, between our very internal elements of life that are actively residing within us and that are keeping us in a continued expressed motion of life, our own spirit and its living soul, our strong heart and its powerful mind, that are at times fighting against each other for domination and control over the human's overall well-being expressed functions and existence, by trying to influence our very most inner senses and their perception mechanism system that it is being used for processing the human thoughts, that are coming into active existence and manifestation as a result of their own perceived information that it is being received, captivated and activated by the powerful human's very own ability of active sight, hearing, touch, smell and taste, that are also in the reality of their fundamental and structural' s many bestowed operational functions, exposed to be, and are being at times under the power of very strong and corrupt influences that are all working non-stop against the survival and against the end destination place and location of our human being's eternal and living soul.

Covering this topic we also realized the very vital and critical importance of the much needed understanding that it is so many times require to be part of our life's functions to be able to actively disseminate the vast information that we are exposed to daily, to which we are all also opening ourselves in our life, that we may be able to receive internally their strong signals and raw data, through a divine discernment spirit that it will help us to be able to differentiate between the multitudes of many various sources of strong influences, and if we are operating our own expressing living functions without it, we will be exposed to have our own lives moved and carried away on our very temporary journey on this very earthly realm of our living existence, by the wrong waves and winds of very strong and powerful deceptive and manipulative schemes that are being actively fueled and sustained in presence from the expressed depths and dark chambers of our living soul's enemy, that from the very beginning of our creation as being the humankind in God's image and likeness, never stopped searching for ways to affect and to hinder and to influence the holy and divine humankind's relationship with the everlasting father and the creator of the heavenly hosts.

It is good to take a quick look and read the words from the scriptures of Revelation, from Chapter twenty and verses one and two, where the Word of God says: "And then I saw an angel descending from heaven, holding the key to the abyss (the bottomless pit), and a great chain was in his hand. And he overpowered and laid hold of the dragon, that old serpent (of primeval times), who is the devil and Satan, and bound him"... (AMP Bible*), because this will open our very own understanding to be able truly to recognize and to realize that the enemy of our living soul is an actual entity, and the fight for our end destination and place for our eternal soul it is very real, and the waves of powerful influences that comes against the soul of the humanity are natural, and this ongoing battle and fight that started right there in then in the presence of the Almighty God in the garden of Eden did not ended, and it will continue to be fought until the very end to that very last moment when the Almighty God will restore into himself the entire creation's landscape, that very powerful moment when the very human mortality will be swallowed by the immortality, that moment when the corruptibility will be consumed by the incorruptibility, when the inner being and its living soul will be released back into God's transcendental realm, redeemed and restored back to its original humankind's purpose of its executive attributes and functions that once had in the very beginning of his creation when the human being's living soul used to enjoy, while also expressing and living its active life's existence in the compelling image and likeness of the Almighty God himself.

Chapter Ten:
Deceptive Platforms

Mark 13:5-6" Then Jesus began to say to them,' Beware that no one leads you astray. Many will come in my name and say," I am he!" and they will lead many astray."

In the beginning phases of writing this book, I did mentioned that the 'Truth Shifters", are the solid outsourced waves of the very real Deceptions and Manipulations of a Stronghold Bounded Union, that are all actively searching for many different ways to be able to capture the Human Mind's Conscious in its labyrinth and in its own web of their very powerful desires, by trying to achieve total influence and also control over the very Human Mind's own Complete Consciousness and over the Human Mind's Moral Behavior that are expressing their active existences within the overall human well-being manifestations that are happening daily across the humanity's multi fundamental and structural strong foundations that are holding on their pillars the actual living frames of all humanity's established and sustained actions for their very own religious, spiritual, political, economic and social-justice platforms, that have the power to truly define the very human being's purpose and its own attribute functions and existence in the creation.

Now in this last chapter of this book, I would love to be able to write in a more detail about the true and accurate connectivity and networking power that is active and also fully functional, and exists between all of their fundamental and structural levels of express and activate manifestations, between the powerful religious-spiritual, political, economic and justice platforms, that are together forming the very human being's humanity living expressions and character, in order that we may be able to cultivate the needed understanding required for developing our own self-awareness attributes and functions that will help us all, the humans, to reach and to achieve and to also be able to sustain our living life's true purpose, and in reality it does not matter how much we will try to separate the proper functions of these very powerful platforms that are carrying their own identification within the structure of our very human being life's own meaning, through our limited way of being able to understand them, and calling them as irrelevant in their own relationship with each other's functions, and no matter how much we will try to keep them at their top view apart from each other's powers and influences, we do need to be able to realize and also to recognize that in truth, the religion, and politics, and the economics platforms are all together being interconnected in unique complex ways at the very deep depths that exist within the strong foundation and frame that holds and also that molds our entire human being's expressions and character, and these platforms can have and they do have a substantial and significant impact towards influencing each other's functions, and together they are all affecting the entire humanity as a whole, the very human being's expressions for life and of life in the creation.

Along the years of our past generations and even at the present time of our own living, the religion and the politics have a strong and long history of being able to influence each other's true meanings and their functions that they all possess, by advancing forward their own interpretations in relation for the greater good of the overall health of the very human being's true life's purpose and expression, that are being motivated by their desire to be able to achieve control and domination over the masses, and in the order to be able to do so, we can witness so many times how political leaders, their movements and their platforms on which they based their political decisions have been motivated by religious beliefs and also many times influenced by religious leaders, and it is nothing new to us to see how many political leaders in their pursue for achieving positions of power, before any coming elections they are strongly forth aligning themselves with many and specific religious groups or their denominations, and that way, they may be able to gain their trust and support at the ballot box when is the voting time. This argument proves that in the reality of our living lives, no matter how much we may try and want to separate them at the very top, by proclaiming and by screaming and by shouting words of self-made declarations, and by doing so thinking that we may be able to establish and drive a gap and a separation channel between the politics and the religion adjectives, but in the truth of this matter, these both genuine and powerful structural platforms of our very own humanity living and their lives s expressions are both together being scribed and enshrined deep into the depths and structure of our human being's fundamental fabric and fiber of its DNA's acting and living purposes and their expressed functions.

    We do need to also understand that from an overall point of view, the necessity to be able to start to realize that the very fundamental structure and foundation that holds within its pillars and facilitates the strong connections that are all actively synchronizing their very own truly interdependent information and raw data that it is being transferred to and from between these many expressing powers that are forming our humanity's religious, political and economic living platforms, can be undeniable complex due to its natural variety of its originality and functions, causing the search for a common ground for the overall health of humanity's physical and spiritual well-being's expression to be always hinder and never be fully achieved, because of their own strong perception and their interpretation of the information that it is being received and then it is being released forward through different meaning and ways of their process understanding ability that can truly cause many times our humanity to reach different end results, even than when the original good intent had been fueled from the same powerful and structural foundation of the religious, political and the economic platforms' s common desires and goals searching to achieve for the human being's living and breathing expressions an overall health and stability, and while they are sharing the same common goals, it is worth noting that due to their very powerful and strong differences in their force approach towards achieving all these end result goals, it is in fact the very reason that many real conflicts and strives are arising all around the world, opening and making ways for strong corruption and powerful dark influences to be able to enter our own earthly paramount landscape realm, to cause and to produce waves of instability and much unpredictable behavior levels within the humans living expressions, that are the active birthed results that are following the real chaos, and the pain, and the suffering that it is being non-stop released upon the innocent masses in the name of the greater good for the humanity's breathing and living existence.

We cannot look the other way towards the reality of the power of corruption that can influence our own internal and overall well-being's physical, spiritual, and psychological health functions, which are coming against our very own strive and purpose of life from the external influences that can have a strong, negative and significant lasting result against the humans, regardless from where these corrupt influences are releasing their information upon the humanity's living soul, being them rooted and activated forward into existence from the very depths of their religious, political, or even their economic platforms of expressions.

By writing this, I want to let the readers know, and let this be like a disclaimer of thought, that not all the information and the data released upon the humans' life with the solid motive for capturing and influencing humans and molding their character of expression in the vast creation, and that are sending their own and daily dependable live signals from the depths of these powerful platforms for the humanity's living expressions, and are based on their belief systems that include their very own strong religious, political and their very own economic and living functions, are corrupt in their very true own nature and purpose. Some of this authentic and compelling information and data released upon humans from within their own religious, political, and economic platforms does contribute positively to the solid and successful overall health structure, purpose, and functions of our human being's expressions in the creation.

Now that I have addressed this disclaimer let's go back to the topic and continue the journey of discovering together the required and must-need understanding that will help us to realize the corruption's many different complex issues that, if left unchecked, the sin will be able to run rampant its strong waves of their manipulative seed of destructions that will cause harm and a profound impact within the humanity's living expressions that are being manifested all across the world's fundamental structure of existence that is very active on multiple layers and levels and that are all being able to actively express themselves from a single mere individual or human being level to a group level, community level and also national level, that are being fueled and activated forward as a result of their very own religions, political and their economic perception of thoughts and influenced understanding.

In a few more words, I would love to elaborate on some examples of the many ways that these compelling corruption attributes can cause much damage and painful harm to humans across all their levels of living expressions of life, which can come at any given moment under pressure from external influences that can contribute. Also, that can lead to a dangerous breakdown of humanity's executive motions and functions, thus affecting even the overall health of human well-being. Its complex physical, spiritual, and psychological living and breathing active forms encapsulated within the human's built-in solid foundation of its entire expressed and manifested existence also can be affected.

Knowing that there exist many powerful external strong influences, and more than anything else knowing that these influences that we are exposed to interact with can also be corrupt in their originality and nature, can affect and cause much harm to all of those that are getting entangled within their snares of powers, let's go over these true examples that can bring into view focus the reality that surround us the humans, that we may be able to understand, realize and recognize that these powerful corrupt influences can come to us all in many different forms that are being activated across these strong platforms that holds humanity in a continued motion and moving functions, that are being enabled to exist and operate on the political platforms under the influences of the political corruption, that can lead to a lack of trust in the political institutions all around us, that can create anxiety and stress, and a sense of powerlessness in humans, and if the corruption remains uncontained, in many cases this will also lead to real human rights abuses and many social injustices, that can all really affect us and have a profound and harm impact on people's well-being, and on the religious platforms under the influences of religious corruption, that it is also a strong and very powerful external influence, that can produce and have a strong and a profound impact towards our very own human being's belief systems, its human moral values and behavior, that does indeed has the power to shape our perception of the world that surround us all, and that can affect our entire overall well-being's health and operative functions, but setting our searching goals towards achieving the much needed understanding and its revelatory power to be able to differentiate and to distinguish between the strong religious corrupt and influenced power and the strong religious uncorrupt and influenced power, it will guide us and help us to be aware and sensitive to the very religious practices that can be a source of comfort, peace and support for us, as an individual, or as a group, or as a strong community, and even at times as a nation, helping us cope with life's many difficulties and life's many hard situations that we as humans are at times exposed to encounter and deal with along our traveling and journey on this earthly realm, and this will create a very positive impact towards our internal and overall human being's spiritual expression and health, and also this much needed and required understanding and revelatory power, it will guide us and help us to be able to differentiate and to distinguish and be also aware and sensitive to the very religious practices that can become a source of conflict and division, particularly when different religious beliefs and their practices may come in direct conflict with each other's way of perceiving and interpreting the truth and the truth's applicable life's guidance for the humanity's own existence through their own mind's conscious but filtered self-understanding, activating and fueling the sources and the causes that are behind the creation of many different religious conflicts along the years that led and it will continue to lead to painful discrimination and intolerance and many times to brutal violence, that can produce strong and negative impact and also much undescribed harm, for the very human well-being's physical and spiritual overall health, and last but not the least when these external powerful influences can manifest their expressions, on the humanity's economic platforms under the influences of their economic corruptions, that is the one power force leading to the very economic exploitations that it is happening all around the world, and also the it is worth noting that the economic exploitation it is truly the number one cause of humanity's poverty strong living levels of expressions, that are actively harming and profoundly and negatively impacting the very human being's overall physical, spiritual, psychological and mental health.

    The religious, political and the economic platforms to a certain degree do overlap with each other's power functions in almost a similar way that our very own internal elements of life that are residing within our bodies, that are known to be the spirit and the soul, and the heart and the mind overlap with each and with another's one power functions in unison, due to their own executive abilities and their interactivity link powers that they all possess in their own ways, and together in their created originality one time they all have been working for the overall good and health of the soul's breathing and living expression, but now they are actively trying to influence each other in many different ways and because of that many times our very physical health can do have a great impact over our very own mental health, while on the same time our mental health stage can have a great impact over our physical well-being's health, and also together our internal mental and physical health can have a great impact on our very spiritual well-being's health, and that can be a major cause of a real concern when we are exposed to connect and to interact externally on these very strong and very powerful, religious, political and economic platforms of humanity living and their sustained expressions, that all together have an undeniable deep and strong impact in so many complex ways, affecting so deeply all the various aspects of our lives as a human society, including our moral values, belief systems, social norms, economic policies, and political decision-making, and because of that it is critical vital and also very important to be able to consider all these range of different factors that will really help us to develop the needed understanding towards the reality of our own world that surrounds us when we are approaching and embarking on our life journey's traveling on these very strong and very powerful structural frames of life's active senses and their motions, that are holding together within their deep foundation the entire humanity's living and breathing expressions that are all being manifested deep within our internal inner being functions, and also to all of our outer surroundings for the external human being's functions, that are happening all over and across the vast and the very powerful humanity's religious, political and economic platforms, and the more we will be able to start to align their strong and their very unique processes and functions, pushing them on and forward towards the finishing line of being able of reaching and achieving a true common center of balance and a true common divine denominator factor for their own results and resolves for the humanity's overall well-being, the more humanity's very own living and breathing spiritual, and physical and psychological attributes of our human being's overall health and functions, and expressions, will be able to truly start to benefit from their own individual search for the end goal results and from their resolves, but in the true reality that we are all exposed to be living our manifested existence within, it is so complicated, and also at times it is impossible to be achieved when we are considering that so many cultures and their own societies have already built within their fundamental strong and structural foundation of their fiber and fabric of their living existence, based on their very own processes of understanding the very needs of humanity's many real necessities, so many different options and many different ways of approaching and navigating these real powerful platforms that are all deeply enshrined and scribed into the deep humanity's breathing and living foundation that holds on its majestically pillars of the reality our very own and entire human being's overall breathing and living and expression.

We have to start considering that in the reality these many diverse cultural societies have birthed along the many years different ways of processing their own views and their own understandings for the humanity's needs, and that process have resulted in the developing of very strong and very complex systematic diversities when it comes to the topic of relations that covers people's major belief systems and their moral values and behaviors that are based on their very own strong historical traditions and experiences of life, that are also the fundamental building blocks of their strong active and powerful contributing factors that have been in truth the vital sources that fueled their own process development of their own life's living standards, and that very powerful process produced in truth so many different approaches and also reached so many different views and so many different opinions on how to navigate and on how to be able to really understand the vital and critical processes required to keep alive and in an always forward motion their own realities in regards of the religions, politics and economics platforms that took fundamental shapes and forms very deep within their own created cultural expressions, and because of that finding a true common center of life balance between many different cultures in our today's existence, and reaching a true denominator factor for their own individual created common understandings, it is indeed a very complex and a very unique issue that at its very deep core, it is being structured on the very powerful end results that are truly the leading issues that are caused by their very own strong complexity of this very subject at hand, but it is also worth noting to come to our attention that at times it is not impossible to be achieved, and not all hope it is lost, as longer we the humanity that it is bounded as a complex and as a complete establishment form structure, we will be willing to start recognizing the many and the multitudes of our very own drives of a common share values that can unite us, these common share values that are truly in an active existence and that are manifested within the very living frame of every human being's own life expressions, despite the many arising uncommon differences and despite of their own diversified factors that truly exists between the world's established cultures and societies around the world, and this is a very strong but also a truly sincere and very powerful undeniable truth that we do need to start to understand and to consider in our own lives, that the religion platform, for an instance, it is a strong and very powerful driving force that can shape the many beliefs and values of individuals, and of groups and of communities, and yes even of nations, by being able to offer and to provide for them all a moral compass and a divine and a designed guidance for their very own people's actions and decisions, but however, due to the many different and powerful interpretations that are being considered supreme towards their own variations and views through which they tend to perceive their own structural processes and understandings, the many diversities of the religious beliefs across the world has led to so many different ways of interpreting the values and the ethics and the morality for the human being's living expressions in the name of the humanity, but in the truth for this subject matter, these very powerful differences have been the true leading causes that created and fueled so often tensions, and at times so many painful and brutal conflicts among the world's different cultures and societies, and also in a very similar way of their own true living expressions, the politics and the economics are also deeply enshrined in our cultures and in our societies, and they can too as well use their own strong and real undeniable driving forces and existing powers that can lead and shape our very own social and our own economic development as individuals, and as groups, and as communities, and also as nations, that are also very diversified in their own strong nature due to the many powerful cultural influences from all around the world, and because of that many political systems vary greatly across many different cultures, that can be expressed on different levels of manifestation, that can range from being very liberal and democratic regimes all the way up to being very extreme and authoritarian regimes, and these expressions are reflecting the many different values and their deeply core beliefs about the role of the government in their own cultures and in their own societies, and also because their strong differences that are being manifested within their own multiple ways of the interpretation towards the topic and subject of the greater good and common sense cause for the humanity's overall well-being health expressions, these many different cultural and expressed opinions are also a true leading cause that it is the source fueling in truth the many different and major economic platforms that are known to us and across the world as being guided and ruled by their own capitalism, socialism and their communism systems applications, these very strong and very popular influences that have been emerged and birthed from the very deep humanitarian structures and also from the very strong fundamental and core foundation that can hold the humanity's truly powerful diversity that it is being actively expressed all across the human being's own expressed manifestations, that are being all tight encapsulated deep within the very own structural frame of humanity's many powerful cultural variations of their strong and complex social contexts and attributes factors.

Our humanity needs to consider the starting point implementation of the realistic processes that are necessary for the continuing improvements that are all genuinely required for developing and also for reaching the human solid mind's understandings through our very own mind's powerful thoughts processors, which must have their signals activated towards getting our very own understandings and their expressed functions, and if indeed this process it is genuinely being implemented and achieved, it will help us all, the humans that are very engaged and actively navigating these powerful and natural waves of our lives and their always mixed influences that come against all of us, knowing that their information is being released to existence to be able to affect and to mold our living character from the very deep and structural foundations of these very real and robust, and powerful three significant platforms that hold and sustains within their grip of powers our very own human being's existences that are revealed forth by their expressed humanity.

I am going forward and will start writing a few more paragraphs regarding our own human being's strong power of implementation for humanity's much-needed search after the understanding and approach towards the very life's realistic processes and development.

I am calling the following paragraph's title below:

"The Power of Enhancing Human Understanding and Development Through Life's Realistic Processes."

My sincere prayer and focus it is that these few presented points below will really help us to be able to reach into the very real idea that our own humanity does need indeed to be able to produce the willingness to start to embrace in truth these powerfully strong points for divine implementation of our own human life's realistic processes in order to be able to achieve and to facilitate going forward the real necessary improvements that will be able then to foster a much deeper common sense understanding of the very real strong powers of our human being's mind capacity, and this improvement will help us as a starting point to be able to realize that by harnessing these very strong signals of our own powerfully thought processor functions that operates within the vast and powerful landscape of our very own human being's mind's complete consciousness attributes, we can be able to truly activate the required senses that will enable us to start to comprehend many different social and complex concepts of the world around us and that in return will help our very own cognitive capabilities and their real abilities to be able to process and to disseminate different information and different raw data, and if we will be able to reach it, and if indeed such first step implementation of our life's realistic processes it will be realized, we as humans can greatly start to really benefit from their positive results, as individuals, and as groups, communities, denominations, and nations, that are being all very actively navigating their own multiple waves of life, and that are always in a truly realistic contend of battling their very strong myriad influences, and that no matter how we are tend to see or perceive their powers, or how we are being inclined to accept or to reject their raw data, and their own produced and sourced forward and released information that we are all being exposed to on a daily bases, we do need to know in the truth of the matter that these strong waves of our own living lives, and their powerfully strong myriad influences, it does and it will have the true real power and their strong convictions functions activated within their own masterfully designed and strong executed planning of always searching for ways to be able to shape and to be able to mold our very own human being's life image, expression and its living characteristics.

Another strong point in need of implementation that it will result in helping us enhancing our very own human being's understandings and that also it will help us to be propelled forward towards being able to reach a higher living standard for our own human being's expressions through our life's many realistic processes, that will lead to our improvement across all of our overall humanitarian development and structural frames, it is for the power of our own and strong willingness mechanism system to be unlocked in order to enable us the humans to reach a more divine and a more profound comprehension of the world's realm that surrounds us all, by leading and by guiding us towards the vital and the critical process to start embracing with a more holistic approach, the very breathing and strong living life's active expressions that are all being produced by our very own human being's multiple and realistic perceptions and views, and also by leading and by guiding us all the humans to start embracing the humanity's many real and substantial cultural backgrounds that are also being forth here defined by their very own multiple and tangible diversified empirical evidences, that are a mere and a realistic product of every human being's very own rational thinking, and by focusing on these true realistic processes of our lives through this expanded understanding approach, we will be able to gain the ability and the agility to be able to truly navigate and to contribute positively and meaningfully internally within our own inner being's purpose and expressed functions, and also externally towards our own surrounding world that we are exposed to interconnect with daily, in regards the world's own purpose and expressed functions, that also have been together deeply fueled into the existence by the very strong humanity's own diversified power of perceptions that it is being used when producing and activating thoughts into the existence, that are also being strongly based on the realistic relationship of their own multitudes of true and undeniable life's historic experiences that have been engraved and also that have been all together tight encapsulated within the very fundamental deep fabric and foundation of the world's own structural powers and frames that are actively holding on their existent and living pillars of life, our whole and our own entire humanity's powerful living cultural expressions that are being released, expressed and manifested in life from their own strong and very diverse attributes of their unique and complex social contexts.

The third point in need of implementation that it will also have its result really helping us enhancing our very own human being's understandings through the very powerfully life's realistic processes, and if truly can be reached and also realized, it will also help us and guide us towards the center line of our own life's balance that it is so vital and so critical to be activated and to have its senses and all their functions working properly in order that we may be able to reach the must needed overall and healthy growth of our humanity's own human being's expressions and active functions, and this applicable and very powerful point will indeed lead us all towards engaging with our realistic life's processes that it will also enable us with the opportunity of reaching a truly divine and also a strong understanding towards our very own ourselves purposes of life, our own motives and desires that are also the very primary factors that can truly define us all the humans that are being based on our very active life's expressions, by tapping into the powers of our own active thought's systematic mechanism and functions to be able to start the needed process of exploring the real deep depths of our own mind's complete consciousness attributes, and that as a return, it will be able to help us to start uncovering a various and new powerfully and strong insights that it will enable us with the very vital and critical powers of realizing and recognizing the true and the must require necessity of being able to truthfully start analyzing the functions of life on an non-corrupt and unbiased measuring living scale, calibrated by the energetic power of our very own life's realistic processes that are helping us of being able to start sincerely understanding ourselves and also to be able to start understanding our very own interdependent connection and relationships with the strong and very powerful internal and external elements of our lives that in their originality forms are the real fundamental framework providers and also are the holders and the organizers that are keeping and also that are fueling from the deep depths of our own living souls, our very powerfully human being's strong feelings and emotions that are all being actively released forward into their manifested existence internally and also that are being manifested externally from the deep structural foundation of our very own humanity's strong and undeniable powerfully manifestations of our expressed motives and active desires.

By harnessing and processing these very intricate workings of our own mind's complete consciousness and cognitive processes, we can sincerely embarking on the profound and realistic journey for our own life's destiny when sincerely we are looking to be able to develop and to reach the must and required understanding levels of expressions, that are needed when we are searching and exploring our pathways of life that can genuinely yield a various and a multitude of new and powerfully potent insights for our own humanity's living purposes, which in turn will enable us humans to recognize and to really appreciate the critical and the vital importance of being able to start analyzing our life's motions and life's manifest expressions that are in a constantly active existence internally and externally from a point view of impartially, through the filters that are powered by the unbiased lenses of life that will bestow upon us humans the natural blessings of gaining a proper understanding of our own selves motives, our desires and our place in the creation, and also a critical and vital knowledge of our own relationship with do need to have and do need to carry on, with both, the internal and the external powerfully elements and influences of our life, that truly can shape our own actual existence and can shape our behavior and living character that it is being actively exposed and also analyzed by the very systematic and structural frame scale that can and holds on its powerful balance all of our own life's actions and reactions, the factors that are indeed the main powerful forces that are driving into a forward motion the very fragrance and essence of our very own humanity's fervent motivations and their living aspirations.

The fourth point I would like to be able to address it on this very topic it is the subject that it will also help us to be able to incline our focus and attention towards improving our human being's understanding of the surrounding world when navigating the waves and the influences of our lives, it is the fostering power and the activation of our very own self-awareness mechanism system towards the actions and towards the reactions of our lives's realistic processes and their unique but powerful manifested expressions, that it will equip us with the necessary tools to be able to discern and to also be able to disseminate the sourced powerful information and the raw data that are being continually released by these very real and strong influences that can have a real dimensional wide range from the very societal norms to multiple and various cultural beliefs systems that are all being truly based on humans very strong and intricate and diversified perceived interpretations at various levels that can start from a single individual, then expanded to a group, community, denomination and the way I like to word it on my writings, even to nations, and by fostering self-awareness and a deep and sincere understanding of our own confirmation biases, we can approach the new sourced information and their raw data with an open mind, that also will enable us to critically evaluate our own internal and external influences of our own lives and that will guide us and enable us to make informed based decisions that it will align with our own values and our aspirations without dis-considering and neglecting the values and the sincere aspirations of other humans that are also actively navigating their own waves and influences of life on this earthly realm of existence, and embracing these life's realistic processes, we will be able to truly strengthen our very own collective humanity's purpose, and by starting the life's own realistic processes by fostering a more compassionate and a sincere view towards others, we will become more understanding of the human's passions and desires all around us, and this will have a strong and a very positive impact on all of us humans, and this impact it will be in truth beneficial to our very own human's beings entire overall health and life's progress.

    In today's rapidly evolving world that truly encapsulates within its fundamental and structural foundation all of our human being's strong humanitarian manifested expressions, actions and reactions, feelings, desires and emotions, our own and always thinking human mind faces numerous and many different and various challenges in understanding and adapting to the many differential and complex driving forces that are design to shape and to mold our own existence and character functions, and for us if we are being able to start to explore the vital and the critical importance of implementing our life's realistic processes to help us to facilitate the must needed ongoing improvements that are in truth required for helping us strengthen our very own mental capacity, and that implementation in return will enable us reaching a much deeper and a much more profound comprehension and understanding of our own selves and also of the world that surrounds us, and if achieved I firmly believe that this process it will lead us all humans, to be able to establish a genuinely divine and enhanced connections and communications with one another, helping us to start focusing our energy to be able to understand another one's purposes, functions and expressions, and all together activating this realistic and vital fundamental thought process mechanism, we will be able to start to contribute and to build more positively and more meaningfully on the pathway of our own life's journey and paramount landscape striving towards the unique and divine goals of reaching our own human being's collective growth and its enhanced humanity living pulses.

In a summary of the above paragraph called:

"The Power of Enhancing Human Understanding and Development Through Life's Realistic Processes,"

I do want you, the readers, to consider these four very fundamental and foundational pillars that can hold on to their base the entire functional and operative structure for the development and implementation of our life's realistic processes through a deeper and improved understanding that our very own humanity needs to start embracing:

1. Recognize.

Recognizing the critical need and the vital significance of our Life's Realistic Processes enables us all to start embracing the driving forces that can encompass various and many different methodologies and approaches that can align and facilitate ongoing improvements needed for strengthening our human mind's capacity for a profound comprehension and a much deeper understanding of ourselves and the world that surrounds us.

2. Develop.

The starting point for advancing and driving forward as a positive human society lies strictly in the Development power of our human understanding. By being willing and able to start the implementation of our own Life's Realistic Processes, we can open ourselves up to a much more profound comprehension of the other humans that we are all interconnected with, and this will allow us all to move much more profound and way beyond the raw superficial surface level of understanding when exposed to really engage with our life's complex issues that are continually arising on the diverse map paramount of humanity's multiple perspectives that are all driven forward from within our very perceptions, empirical evidence and our own and strong bestowed rational thinking.

3. Reach.

Reaching inside our human solid mind's understanding for implementing our Life's Realistic Processes by energizing and harnessing the robust thought process or mechanism activated within our human mind through the signals and the senses that enable us to be able to comprehend complex concepts and enhance our cognitive capabilities, will help us to start exploring and engaging our very own human mind's active consciousness, that it is the provider and the actual organizer of our very own thoughts, that are being all motivated and guided by human's will power, emotions, feelings, and powerful desires.

4. Navigate.

Implementing our Life's Realistic Processes will help us humans who are Navigating the waves and the influences of the world that are continually arising along our journey. Life presents a constant, powerful influx of diverse and robust forces that can shape and mold our life experiences and how we record and perceive them. These powerful influences can range from broad and diversified social norms and different cultural values that can affect and influence our personal belief systems that are also fundamentally based on our historical experiences.

Giving a chance to understand our Life's Realistic Processes will equip us with the necessary tools to navigate the multitudes and powerful intricate web of influences, by helping us to start fostering our self- awareness mechanism capacity, thus enabling us the humans that are inter-existent and interdependent with one another active manifestations, to be able to begin to confront and to also adapt at times to these very strong and powerful influences of life, these realistic tools that are empowering and leading us to be able to navigate more easy the life's informal complexities, resisting the solid inner pulls of one's conformity, but critically be able to receive, discern, and evaluate the true roots and the authentic sources of all of our own internal and external strong powers of influences we are exposed to interact daily with, before making any informed decisions that many times can affect us and it will affect the very overall health of our own human being's life and its breathing and living expressions.

Recognizing and activating the development of our Life's Realistic Processes while we are exposed to navigate the foundational platforms of our humanity sustained existences where we are all very actively manifesting our own voices and expressions in regards our own Religious, Political and Economics' very strong views and their opinions that are all being based strictly on our own power of perceptions and interpretations of thoughts, are not limited to any one's individual's very own growth and very own development process of understanding, and indeed these robust and realistic processes can all be recognized and activated to be able of being driven forward towards implementation also in significant and collective levels, by embracing and also reinforcing the very diversified shared added value of our own human existence, by increasing empathy, compassion and cooperation that will help the humans to build bridges between diverse communities, by fostering a much deeper understanding and by creating a more inclusive living environments, by closing the world's wide gaps and views that are in existence between the fields of the many diverse understandings of our own purposes and functions as a living human being in the creation, and all together these very powerful processes if implemented and achieved, it will genuinely be able to strengthen the overall fiber and fabric of our all humanity entire core and foundation.

Another benefit of implementing Life's Realistic Processes while navigating the real humanity's three major fundamental and structural platforms of their expressions that all together contains and sustains our very human being's characteristics and vital behaviors is the true benefit of being able to start accessing and also to start exploring the myriad of the information and the many influences that are all very actively being released as points of navigation and of guidance for us the humans, through the awareness and the conscious of our mind's functions approach towards the goal of reaching our very internal and active understanding power process of being able to start analyzing the many ways and the many different sources that are all being going on, in on a continued mode, very active releasing their information with solid and natural desires to be able to capture the very humanity mind's capacity and the same mind's very own express functions, and being able to start analyzing and also to start discerning the roots and the sources of their vast influences of solid information and data, will help us all, humans, to be able to actively start to distinguish between the reality of a sincere, honest, and very strong positive information and its power of influence, that can be built and also mold our very own humanity character, and between the reality of their very corrupt and robust negative information and its power of influence, that also can build and mold our very own humanity characteristic behaviors.

We all know and heard this old saying one time or another that " information is the deep source of power, and that if the power if it is being left unchecked it will produce corruption", and if we go one step forward and eliminate from the phrase the middle part about power, we can just address it with a straight face like this," the information that it is not controlled and also not checked it will then produce corruption", and this real analogy to a certain degree gives birth to the very idea that people with the most data and information that they can accumulate and hold within the powerful grasp of their own mind's capacity portfolio, leads them to be able of gaining certain power, and it is a known fact that power does corrupts individuals, groups, and communities, and this happens when they become driven and focus towards maintaining their achieved power and status and because of that strive, certain people are willing to engage in unethical, corrupt and immoral behavior to maintain it at all costs, and I do want also to write and to mention this very important note, that not all of the many individuals, communities and groups with vast accumulated information resources and data, that helped them to gained and to achieved certain power and status are being influenced by corrupt motives and desires, and it is worth to mention and to be able to address the fact that never the less, also there in midst of our living lives are many people with less accumulated information and resources and with less achieved power and status, and they can too, be truly expose to many corrupt influences that can definitely capitalized on their own opening to operate and to function from a fundamental point of view structure that holds within its powerful frame many strong but also a diversified class of wrong motives and desires, and this proves that there are many different levels of understand powers and that there are many different classes of corruption that can manifest and also occur at many different levels of powerful influences that are also being expressed in various forms and shapes depending on the places and the context of their own living circumstances of life, for an example, the real corruption that can happen in high-level politicians and executives may involve embezzlement or bribery, while also corruption at the low-level officials may involve the process of abuse of power, or even taking bribes for holding on to their own personal gain, and this is also a true leading cause related to the power of corruption to control others, by abusing one's position of authority to engage in an unethical behavior, using very strong intimidation and coercion processing factors that can, and it will lead at times to serious and very painful harm to the very health and manifest functions of our very own human being's expressions in the creation, that happens at all levels, being them as individual, groups and communities.

And like everything else that surrounds the operative

functions of humanity's expressed behavior in the very relationship with their existences as a live living organism in the creation, in a truly and continued inter-existent and interdependent relationship that it is being manifested internally and also externally within the vast paramount of the earthly realm that we the human beings are expressing our presence with very powerful living and also strong realistic factors that are interconnecting with us all humans, also there it is a strong and powerful undeniable relationship and realistic connectivity between the corruption and the abuse of power factors that are active releasing their own input and their very own sourced influences for reaching control and total domination within the powerfully religious, political and economic platforms of our lives that sustains and maintains all of our human being's humanity and expressions and also our forms of how we are manifesting our internal relationships within own ourselves and how we are manifesting our strong realistic external relationship with other humans that are surrounding us and that are interconnecting with us on a daily bases, and while it is being so difficult at times to be able to establish and to really pinpoint the real definitive casual and factual relationship that produces and causes abuse of power and corruption to be so often and real together tight interconnected, helping each other and also reinforcing each other's expressions of their own influenced strength, leading us to start asking these very questions at times: does corruption creates and enables abuse of power, or does abuse of power creates and enables the flow of corruption?, and my own sincere opinion on this very topic is that even if we do not know what may come first the corruption or the abuse of power, and what may fuel each other's very powerful desires, it is understood that corruption and abuse of power can truly coexist, and can interconnect and also can mutually perpetuate each other's strong motives and desires, by being able and by forming a strong and a powerful symbiotic relationship, even thou their own search for domination and their own dynamics may vary due to their own many different contexts of their own complex structural applications, and even thou that I do think personally that the corruption it is the very strong sourced mechanism that enables those in the position of power and authority to act outside the very boundaries of their own roles and to exploit their active positions for personal benefit, the abuse of power or the desire to maintain their once achieved status and gained position of power, definitely it does, and also as well can indeed create, lead and also can be all able to facilitate the processes of corruption, thus making them both the corruption and the very abuse of their power a very well and synchronized designed, of a very tight close bound web networking labyrinth mechanism that creates a toxic environment that it is also prone to conducive and strong corruption practices, a fundamental root from where the very abuse of power and desires for manipulation, domination and control are together thriving forward into their existence within the deep structural foundation of the humanity's very own religious, political and economic platforms, that it is also made possible due to the very corrupt human being's nature, that it is grounded and rooted deep within the humans behavior and within all the flaws that come with it, and that it is being also revealed forward many times by the humans selfishness and greed, or revealed forward by their own strong desires for personal gain or for positions of power at all costs, and whether there are religious leaders that are exerting a total and unquestionable control over their own followers, or whether there are many various politicians that are exploiting their positions for a continued personal gain, or whether there are many economic leaders that are being deliberately manipulating the systems for their own benefits, and these are just a few of the many examples of the very diverse myriads of numerous human influences that are the true leading causes that are producing a variety of very dangerously establishments to sustain the powerfully imbalances that exists in our human society today, and these very powerful imbalances are all together very actively expressing their own corrupt manifestations on all of our humanity's life's living and moving platforms, producing and resulting in the lack of transparency and also in a weak or even at times in a nonexistent accountability and that status creates various and many inadequate checks and balances, where multitudes of mere individuals, groups and many various communities can start act with impunity, knowing that their own actions are less likely to be scrutinized or punished due to their very own powerful complexity and lack of transparency, that can be truly at times also very actively effective while navigating the very diverse and also the very strong platforms of our own humanity's many diversified but powerful religious doctrines, or while navigating the humanity's various political systems, or while navigating the very own humanity's created and built economic structures, that all together can, and will indeed be able to provide in various times multitudes of disguised opportunities for manipulation schemes and control by masking their very own concealment of strong corrupt practices, and due to the intricacies that are involved in all these very strong and very powerful platforms of our living lives, it is so difficult at times to be able to detect them all and to address them all effectively, both the corruption and the very abuse of power dynamics that are together being so deeply ingrained within the deep fiber and the fabric of our humanity's own natural but corrupt DNA.

There may be a few questions for some of the readers regarding the above paragraph where I wrote that both the corruption and the abuse of power are being together profoundly ingrained within the deeps and the depths of the fundamental foundation of our very human being's corrupt DNA and to be able to start answering some of these very questions let's go together and read in the Word of the Living God, what the scriptures are telling us about this very subject, and for a start I will bring in forth view the scriptures from the Genesis, Chapter six, and verses eleven and twelve, where the Word says " Now the earth was corrupt and God's sight and was full of violence. God saw how corrupt the earth had become, for all the people on earth had corrupted their ways". (NIV*).

All the people of the earth became corrupt due to their own way of searching and understanding their own purposes and their functions, regardless the many living platforms of life, where they were all able to manifest their active and their corrupt expressions for control and dominance over the very religious, political, or even over their economic belief systems of their established humankind's own natural and expressed habitat environmental locations for their survival, by bypassing the very instructions and the commandments of their Creator, that from the beginning of life's very own existence, revealed his will and his commandments to the very first humankind created in God's very own image and likeness within the perfect landscape of the Creator's divine in-transcendental realm, but pride and disobedience showed up, these two powerfully elements and characteristic of our very own human being's life and expressions, thus enabling the solid and realistic processes of corruption and the abuse of powers to sow their first ever destructive seeds, deeply to be ingrained and sustained for growth into the foundation of the humankind's manipulated and altered DNA's structure, away from what was once a perfect and majestically the humanity expressed beings in God's creation, blessed with divine and bestowed authority when appointed and given dominion over everything that crawls on the earth, over everything that swarms the waters, and over everything that are flying in the fantastic sky's atmosphere.

We may be exposed to ask these very questions right now: why were the first humankind beings created in the exact image and likeness of the Almighty God with bestowed authority, power, and dominion over many aspects of creation's own expressed operations and their functions, living and encountering the Creator's presence on a daily bases, why and what was there the very root causes that influenced them to bypass and to disregard in their very own disobedience the exact instructions and the same commandments of their everlasting Creator and father? They were living in a perfect environment, with an ideal DNA structure, in an excellent relationship with all the other various and diverse created powers and elements of life in the creation, and what causes their fall and their actual demise from the dominion and from the authority powers that God bestowed upon them that they may rule over everything else that came to existence because of the inherited breathed life that he the Almighty God himself had breathed into Adam's nostrils from his very own wellspring of life flowing from eternity? It was indeed motivated by their mighty own internal pride and expressed desires for much more and, without a doubt, led and influenced by the robust external waves of information and data the eternal enemy of the soul exposed humankind to, with the desire to make the human fall from glory.

I know that there exist today many interpretations and many opinions that, over the years, people from all walks of life brought them forward to existences based on their very own understanding and capacity of being able to truly perceive and comprehend their very own thought processes and mechanism powers, but I will go over the interpretations and the opinions of many. I will take the readers back to the Word of God and let us read together what the scriptures say on this subject and topic. In the book of Genesis, chapter three, and verse six," So when the women saw that the tree was good for food, and that was a delight to the eyes, and that the tree is desired for to make one wise, she took of its fruit and ate; and she also gave some to her husband, who was with her, and he ate.

Based on this very scriptural text from the book of Genesis, I am leaning towards the opinion that the external influences of powers that they were exposed to, few moments before the fall into their new discovered and corrupted nature that has been right there and then framed by a new and altered DNA structural form and shape away from its complex originality, had the power to manipulate them into the false assurance that there will be no consequences for their own disobedience towards the very instructions and the revealed commandments of their own Creator, but their fall process in itself was caused by their very own substantial and powerfully internal motives that were all being birthed, produced and then activated into their expressed and manifested actions by what was saw then to be a tree that was good for food, a tree that was a delight to their eyes, and was a tree that was to be desired to make one wise, so if we take a few moments to really meditate about this falling event into the corruption of the first humankind being, at the very first glimpse we may tend to be in agreement that there it is nothing wrong to be able to find something suitable for food, also to search for the beauty that delights the eyes, and to search and strive for reaching wisdom in life that we may become wise, but also if we will sincerely start to meditate a little more profound on this subject we can indeed be able to discover and find out that the way we are conducting ourselves and how we strive to achieve the end results of our own search, it does makes a difference and it does indeed matter, and definitely bypassing and ignoring the very instructions and the commandments of the Creator and start living in a total disobedience of his will power it is not the way to our human being's humanitarian fulfillment.

Another question that we as humans may really need to keep on asking it is this one: ", If the one that was once pure and majestically created, the very divine first human being's incorruptible living expressions and manifestations of a living life within the perfect in-transcendental realm of the Almighty God's divine presence, became manipulated and also exposed and influenced by its very own internal motives and deep desires that raised and came forward at the surface for implementation from their very own deep foundation that is the holder of their structure for executive powers and functions, and at the very same time became manipulated and also influenced into the disobedience by its own external powerful elements of life that from the very beginning of the existence of the time, have been all there present in the creation, and were actively surrounding with their own information and data, the very own humankind's divine, perfect and living expressions, that was also the root causing the fall and the separation between the creator's own released power-will, his own revealed instructions and his own commandments, and the very creation's own way of perceiving, analyzing and understanding the real power of God's instructions and commandments, through their own systematic thought consciousness mechanism, that had been already exposed to manipulation before, and that can be manipulated and also fueled by the very own human being's strong motives and desires, what about us all, the mortals and the mere living humans that are being already born into this hard and corrupt and imperfect realm of our existential and active environmental world, that has been than from the very beginning, and it is being even now at our own living and present time, actively and undeniable manipulated and also influenced by the myriads of various diverse and real strong rebellious powers of our own lives, that are all continually and nonstop fighting all together against the very creator's own revelation and information, that are still the standing living instructions and still the standing divine living commandments, that the creator of the heavens and of the earth, he himself has been established for them to be the required guidance that the entire humanity shall follow and go by when expressing and manifesting their living purposes and functions within the creation, how can we, in the midst of our living reality that are just a mere mortal humans that are already living in a strong and corrupt state of our own expressions, how can we, truly indeed escape the web schemes of these many myriads of multitudes of destructive influences and their own various and dangerously diverse powers that are propelling forward their waves of manipulations and corruption, that are all together being very actively fueled into the three major moving platforms of our humanity's very own existence by their own desires of actively searching for different ways of reaching and achieving control and total dominance over the human being's mind, purposes and its functions, in order to be able to affect and to influence not only the humans' behavior and their strong internal and external relationships with others in the creation, but also to affect and also to alter the deep fundamental and natural structure of the humanity's own DNA's very magnificent and complexed divine originality, the leading causes that conveys a truly sense of a very real deterioration of our own living humans' societies and their living standards, that will result in the abandonment of the humans' divine and moral principles and active behaviors, in the exchange for the human's own influenced pursuit of their powerful selfish interests, their selfish motives and their selfish desires, that are being fundamentally the very active attributes that are all carrying a strong detrimental and destructive Lego Effect on all of the levels of our own humanity' expressed existences, as individuals and groups, and also as communities and denominations, and we can say also as a whole and entire human society, that are offering the very perspectives that also will attribute their webs of corruptions and the abuses of their own powers to the very human being's own humanity's deviation from God's own divine and assigned pathway in the creation, even to that point of totally disrespecting and also disregarding the very consequences that will definitely follow us all one day.

The humanity's living expressions that are at times being manifested within their ambitions for reaching and for achieving a strong self-pursuit and driven implementations of their own many diversified and many various processes that are grounded and rooted within the frames of their many selfish interests that are being deeply fueled into their active existence by their own multitudes of strong and very powerful selfish motivations that are all keeping on beeping their own living senses and their own signals within the structural executive functions of our human being's very powerful expressions of being able of manifesting our strong selfish desires, that are also causing our very own human beings to start embracing the symptoms of the humanity deviation syndrome's characteristics, away from the true and powerful revealed instructions and from the holistically divine pathway that has been already established from the very beginning by our creator for us all, the humans, to heed them and also to follow them, are indeed the very combined leading causes in our lives for many strong and for many real destructive consequences that can truly infect, and it will, with no doubt be able to definitely affect the entire human's overall physical and also the very spiritual health of many individuals and many groups, and many communities and also entire societies as whole standing entities, by paving the way, by allowing, and by enabling the breathing and the living corruptions and their abuses of power to live together and to co-exist, and to strive forward once they are all being activated to life by the very humans' very own desires and strong powerfully lusts for searching and for achieving various structural heights for their own standards of living, also by their own influences that are leading to many various ways of gaining vast corrupted wealth at all costs, and also by their own proclamations of selfish and at times uncontrolled desires for ways of reaching various recognitions of statues and positions for their life, and all of these powerful lusts and desires can really start to oppress and also can deeply cloud the judgment of our very own human's powerful mind's consciousness and its mind's functions, and also if these truly realistic and negative detrimental processes of life are being implemented, will dramatically cause heavy erosions within the deep fundamental values and behavioral attributes of our entire human being's foundation of life that holds and glues together the humans very own humanity and the humanity's many various faces of expressions that are all being manifested within the vast landscape of our living societies, and the very humans that are being ignoring and that are forsaking their original and inherent moral attributes and acting behaviors of their divine conscious, and are being exposed and prong to succumbing to their very own deceptive and many waves of the powerful dark influences of life, these very strong and very realistic influences that have the real intended power to be able to blur and also to distort our very own humanitarian and purist characteristics and values, even the principles of our very human being's own ways of understanding and processing within our life the needed fairness, and the required accountability, and the search for transparency, theses real holistic elements of our living and breathing lives, that in the truth of the matter are all needed to be the number one priority when we the very humans are searching after the divine morals and their positive attributes of character that we all truly need be able to possess, in the order that they will be able to start positively to guide all of our humanitarian actions and all our humanitarian reactions, and also in order to start to positively lead and guide all of our own breathing and living interactions, internally within ourselves, and externally with the other human beings that are actively sharing with us all, God's own magnificent creation, by being able in reality to start understanding and start recognizing that the fight against the corruptions and their abuses of powers is not only a living imperative moral of higher standards, but also it is a critical and vital practical necessity that truly does needs to be indeed hold tight and embraced dearly within the very deep fabric of our very own humanity's character and mold behavior's fibers, if we as the humans that are searching and that are reaching for ways where we can find and discover the places and the locations of our living lives from where we can be able to start in truth the realistic process of recognizing the vital importance of our very human being's returning to our divine and moral compass, by implementing the processes of recommitting ourselves back to the very human values, instructions and the commandments that have been from the very beginning bestowed upon and also ingrained within the very strong essence of our very humanity life and its pure fragrance, and thus helping and enabling us to be able to start holding ourselves and also others accountable for our very own actions and for our own ethical conduct, fostering and implementing a true culture that strives for integrity of expressions, even than when knowing that within the vast life's spanning of our very own humanity's breathing and living manifestations of this earthly and mortal realm, both the very strong corruptions and their very strong abuses of powers will never be fully eliminated from their very own existent living forms and shapes, due to our very own fallen and corrupted human nature, but by returning, holding and also by embracing our own humanity 's original bestowed inherent morals and their holistic revealed attributes, and by going back and start the must needed processes of walking in and upholding God's established instructions and divine pathway, we as the humans, will be all able to start working towards reaching and towards achieving our own intended humanitarian life forms and expressions that will be then allowed to be manifested forward from a real divine human structural and very active fundamental foundation, and from a true position of our own human being's mind's consciousness, from where these very real strong waves of human corruptions and their very strong abuses of powers, together with their released powerful web influences of deception that are causing so much destructive pain and suffering among the human's living soul, will no longer be tolerated and accepted in none of our societies.

The influences of corruption and abuses of power goes deep behind any one's own individual actions and they can extend and expand, and penetrate the versatile walls of our very humanitarian and societal levels of their process functions, and if these strong and very opposing dark forces are being allowed to be able to prevail by taking a stronghold and a foothold as an acceptable position within the frames of our human being's structural foundation, it will profoundly affect the human mind's systematic processing of thoughts, negatively impacting our very own humanity's collective consciousness and the humanity's behavioral attributes, as a breathing and active living society, producing waves of erode trust among the humans, creating very strong factors and many senses of cynicism and disillusionment properties that can hinder our communication progresses that are all vital to be sustained and maintained on active modes between people, creating corrupt systems of living standards platforms, where meritocracy it is being actively replaced by nepotism, competence it is being strongly overshadowed by favoritism, and fairness does not even exists as a word, due to the many ways people are processing their acts of inequality, through the many influences of a very powerful but also a corrupted human mind's own understanding and comprehensions, the result of the humans deviations from the very instructions and the commandments of the Creator, being exchanged for the many embraced and distorted human values and ideals.

Before I go ahead and write more on this chapter called "Deceptive Platforms," I want to present the readers with a few more points that will summarize the conclusion of the above paragraphs.

In conclusion, we need to be able to be aware and also to be able to recognize that we the humans, by allowing the waves of corruption and the abuses of powers, and by allowing and accepting them as being an everyday expressions of our living human existences that it will create, and lead humanity towards various uncontrolled and unchecked active platforms of our humanitarian forms and manifestations, from where the corruption and abuses of powers are being allow to flourish and also are being enabled to coexist and thrive forward together without any consequences for their pursuit of destructive actions, our very own humans' established societies will be indeed strongly influenced to operate their significantly manifested functions from the crossroad locations of the "risking and undermining" pathways, that it is affecting and negatively impacting the very divine natural core of the very human being's fundamental solid structural foundation that constructs and holds and defines our own living humanity. Suppose these unchecked and substantial negative consequences are left unquestionable and not appropriately addressed, it will produce to our life's living existence robust and powerful detrimental processes of active and alive expressions that will extend way behind the limits of our capability, control, and ability functions. In that case, they will start manipulating our search and pursuit of our lives toward reaching vast material wealth and other positions of power at all costs, no matter what may come. The corruption and abuse of power will infect and erode even the most profound human's moral values, feelings, and behavioral attributes that are all very active and are genuinely realistic as being the actual contributing factors that make us all, the humans who we are, the very humans with a breathing and a living soul searching for the eternity.

It is very critically vital and essential for individuals, and groups, and communities, and denominations, and really it does not matter on which platforms of their living life are they all being navigating their manifested and their strong expressions, to start to truly recognize the powerful and the destructive nature of these solid destructive myriads and their very powerful hostile and influential dark forces that are all working together towards affecting the very human beings overall health and also their own survival, by turning around and by sincerely starting the working strive towards the implementation of the must needed, critically and very vital processes that are enabling the creation of their substantial humanitarian buildings and structures of their very actively living beings, having as their first building blocks of their humanitarian and structural foundation, a strong and also a divine comprehension and understanding towards a truly prosperous culture of active transparency, of fairness and of accountability, a culture that it is being driven on and also forward by fundamental strong morals and ethical values, the very elemental expressed living attributes of our life, that if they are being sincerely implemented, will be able to preserve and also to strengthen the much needed and search after, the very integrity power of our own human being's divine and its own revealed humanity that can be very actively and positively working within the limitless scopes parameters of God's given and bestowed properties and their functions for our expressed human lives, that may guide us and lead us in the truth of our inherent humans characteristic purposes.

For a more simplified way of wording all these points that will follow in the paragraphs below, I would try to expand on this very subject and its topic with a visible breakdown of the corruption and the abuses of power's many different aspects of expressions so we can together start to recognize and elaborate their strong webs of influences and implications.

1. The Corruption Impact on Human Expression:

The solid and negative consequences of corruption and abuses of power can extend far, above and behind anyone's level of living human expression. They can profoundly impact the health and the overall active functions of entire groups and communities, denominations, and even nations that actively create and form broader societies.

2. Corruption the Cause of Erosion of Human Values:

The influence of corruption and the abuses of power can infect and corrode the fundamental living structure and the foundation that holds on its pillars the core values of our humanity: integrity, honesty, transparency, accountability, and fairness. When corruption becomes actively pervasive, it affects the entire overall ethical and moral standards of many humans and many societies, the actual leading causes that are driving real destructive breakdowns in trust, mutual respect, and cooperation among individuals and groups, and this weakens and deeply erodes the values and behavioral attributes of humanity's fiber and fabric divine structure.

3. Corruption the Cause of Clouded Judgment:

The influence of corruption and the abuses of power are indeed the force factors that are leading human being's living expressions to operate and to manifest their causes and their affected functions, far away from the needed and the required sound judgment of a human approach to its humanitarian purposes, giving way to the power of the corruption and abuses of energy to take priority, resulting and leading to a humanistic society that can be characterized, as being a society driven by powerful corrupt forces that are practicing inequality and social injustice, sourced and field into a living existence from robust manipulative schemes of skewed unrealistic policies and outcomes that strongly favor the systematic corruption of a human being's attitude rather than a common good.

4. Corruption the Cause of Selfish Desires:

The influences of an oppressed and a clouded mind's judgment attribute characteristics give birth to and create various selfish and powerful uncontrolled desires in search for self-recognition and power statuses that indeed can be detrimental to the overall health of a society. It can start blinding the vision of many individuals, groups, and communities. In their self-pursuit that it is fueling their corrupt realizations of their dreams, no matter what their produced damages and inherited costs, they actively reject and bypass the morals and ethical implications of their actions that can hurt themselves and many others. When personal selfish ambitions and their very own solid self-desires, the leading opening causes of corruption and abuses of power, can freely bypass undetected and unchecked the filters of our human mind's divine inherited consciousness, they will take substantial precedence over any human being's moral values and its humanistic and ethical considerations factors. These dangerous human beings under the mesmerizing power for control will engage in a heartbeat in various corrupt processes and abuses of power to be able to achieve their selfish dreams and goals in life, which are hurting not only their own self moral compass but their own inherited and bestowed values. They can cause unimaginable pain and suffering for others they interact with and become victims of their schemes. They can deeply create an intense, destructive, solid, harmful, detrimental optimal vision that will affect and will undermine the clear communication, trust, and the very integrity of their mere humans' living humanitarian platforms of life and can affect and undermine the institutions that they are all part of, regardless of their very own religions, political or economic originality, and expressions.

When a human society fails to address and combat the fundamental processes of corruption and the abuses of powers tactics, that human society essentially does not only creates an entirely new pathway for the crime and abuses of power to be able to start flourishing, but also it is enormously encouraging it by paving the webs of the corruption's own ways for easy accessibility into the very structural depths fibers of our own humanity's foundations, that can create and hold on their strong corrupted pillars very week and anemic governance structures, from where the true and the realistic manifestations and their operative and executive functions for law enforcement, for transparency, and for humans life's accountability systematic and standard processes of living, are all being bypassed and replaced by many various means of their humanistic own expressions that are revealed and gratified into their very living existences, that are intended for the abusing and for the targeting of others, that are all being fueled and also actively sustained by a powerfully mixed variety of blends that are the results of the many various inadequate law enforcements and their lack of trust and transparency together with uncontrolled factors and their unchecked accountability, that are all in the truth of their corrupt matter the destructive damaging products of a human society's compromised moral values and their ethical behaviors, that can create and actively produce and facilitate the sustainment and the growth of the corruptions and their abuses of powers to be deeply rooted and also to be deeply ingrained within the deepest parts of our humanity's own established systems of their living lives.

Based on the above paragraph's statement, it is okay to imply that the corruptions and their abuses of powers are both truly inter-connected with each other's results, goals, and desires, and together are forming a giant living tree with crowns that have their dangerous and potent growing feeding roots deep planted, sustained and activated into their existence by being watered, and cared for, and also pruned, by the very humanity's abandonment of their own inherited pure characteristics and their own divine moral behavior attributes standards, in the favor for searching and for reaching and for pursuing at all costs their own vital influenced selfish interests that are all so many times being motivated by myriads of very powerful influences of human life that are being able of capturing within their own web schematic structural frames the very human beings' selfish solid desires and their very own lusting attributes, all these undeniable powerful human expressions and properties that if are being left to stand and to function and to flourish, and if their actions are being left uncontrolled and also are being left to breathe life and to exist, without them being adequately addressed as they are taking their own shapes and forms at any levels of their various manifested expressions, being them accepted, activated and encapsulated at the levels of individuals, or by groups and communities, or by multiple denominations, even by the functions of nations as a whole complex structure, it can sadly lead our very own humanity destine into the dangerous embrace of very strong waves of disillusionment attributes that are guided to an activated life by the very powerfully systematic dysfunctional humanistic behaviors and their own characteristics, that can and it will be able to ultimately cause the endangerment of our very own human being's overall function, health and survival.

While surfing the pages of this book, the readers are meeting and encountering many times in my writings the words that are addressed towards the many various processes of our very own human being's overall functions, and health, and survival, while we are being actively navigating the waves of our life's pathway journey that are all encapsulated within the structural and the deep fundamental frames of the factual foundation that are all together being in truth the systematic mechanism that it is holding our very own humanity's living and manifested expressions, and their purpose and their functions, that are all genuinely being affected and are also being influenced, and molded and also shaped into their active existences by the very strong and the very real undeniable powers that are all together sourcing and creating, fueling and sustaining the very religious, and the political, and the economical' s established platforms for our humanitarian living lives on this earthly realm, and these three significant life's platforms that can define our very own humanity, indeed does have the powers, and it can definitely hold very tight within their own strength and powerful grips of influences all of our entire human being's living and breathing life's manifest expressions and their faithful revealed humanistic and characteristics functions, that can be continuously improved and developed by searching and by implementing the true and the realistic processes of our own lives, through the pure and through the divine understanding that it is being actively released from heavens above and it is also being bestowed upon the soul of the humanity by our Creator's own established commandments and his own instructions for all of us, the humans, that are being in the creation indeed the magnificent manifold works of his own hands.

One of the many reasons I am emphasizing and I am also accentuating in my writings about the importance of our very human being's overall functions and our overall health it is because these very human attributes factors are the real ones that can directly and also can indirectly, in truth affect our very humanity survival that can be also classified in the reality of our temporary living lives as the one actual major living processes that can be, and it will be actively together expressed and manifested on two different power planes and on two different power dimensions, one reality that it is able of exposing the fight of our very own humanity's temporary survival of its physical expressions of its human's own body and own mind entity, and one that it is exposing the real fight of our very own humanity's eternal survival of its very own divine and spiritual expressions of its very own human spirit and its living soul entity, that are being both together inter-existent of each other, and within each other, and also that are being both together actively synchronized and interconnected with each other together within the deep and structural fiber of our own humankind's unique DNA's fabric and its pure divinest operative impulses and signals.

Are we able to recognize that our very humanity's temporary survival of our very own human beings' physical manifest expressions is actively and continually fought on the various battlefield landscapes of the world's many political and economic platforms that are profoundly captivating people's physical and humanitarian lives and that our very humanity's eternal survival of its human's being spiritual manifest expressions it is actively and continually fought on the various battlefield landscape of the world's very diverse religious platforms that are genuinely captivating the peoples' s spirit and its living soul expressions?

A few questions I would like to be able to ask the readers, and I would like to have them sincerely process their very own answers:

Does our human being's temporary fight for survival while navigating the solid political and the economical platforms of our life's functions and expressions of our physical living forms, can affect and also can hinder our own human being's eternal fight for survival while navigating the solid and diverse religious platforms of our life's functions and their various expressions of our spiritual living forms, and if the answer it is yes, can there be established an authentic systematic networking communication between our both the human being's physical expressions and the very human being's own spiritual expressions, that will be able to help both of our human being's living forms that are together existing and expressing themselves within the unique

God's created humankind's design, the physical form in its own temporary survival fight, and the spiritual form in its own eternal survival fight, to prevent the very strong and dark influences of the corruptions and their real abuses of powers to be able to establish themselves and their own natural fundamental strongholds of manipulative web of various schemes that once they are being created and also activated are all being together released to affect and to alter the human being's very survival and its entire overall health and functions, that are all been actively nonstop working within the very strong fundamental and structural living blocks of the mere humans' physical and their spiritual characteristics that are activated within their realistic forms, shapes and attributes of the human being's own breathing and living soul's spirit that it is surrounded, contained and very tight encapsulated, by the properties of its temporary and limited physical body attributes while it is actively navigating the waves of its living existence and of its life journey on these very powerfully strong waves of our own earthly realm's pulses, signals, and influences.

How can, in the truth of the matter, our both living human realities, one of our very own physical expressions and one of our very own spiritual expressions can, survive and also can adapt when the human being's humanity behavior can be so many times actively exposed and so many times dangerously influenced, and manipulated by the extreme and powerful deceptive waves of corruption and their abuses of powers that are always searching and also are always looking for ways of capturing in their web of robust deceitful schemes even the very living and breathing essence and fragrance of our senses, feelings, and emotions, the power functions and also the attributes that can be able to characterize and to define the living lives of all of us the very humans that are actively navigating and traveling the journeys of our expressions within the truly established limits and parameters of our humanity's religious, political and economic powerful platforms for our human's life?

Up to this point I wrote and I kept addressing in one single content the plague of the influence waves of the corruption and their abuses of powers that are sourced and also are bounded together as one entity that it is manifesting its authentic living expressions, while it is being very actively producing intense and devastating negative results that are affecting and infecting the inherent and the original moral values of our very own human being's bestowed upon characteristic functions and ability purposes from our own Creator and God, if we open ourselves up and allow our life to be exposed and to be manipulated into the accepting and also receiving the corruptions and the abuses of powers various advances and their strong charming cunningness abilities to take a real deep root and build a stronghold foundation within the depths of our fundamental and structural human being's core foundation that in the reality holds our own humanity's living and breathing existence of life while we are together as the humans that are navigating and traveling on our busy life's realistic pathways, that are all being already very deep marked and also are being already deeply carved inside our own mind's true power of being able of comprehending and also of understanding the reality that genuinely creates, fuels and surrounds our own human being's established expressions for its humanity's very strong religious, and political, and economical systems, manifestations and active behaviors.

Considering the powerful impact and negative implications of human corruption and their abuses of powers that can take hold and capture humanity's active behaviors while they are all surfing the real waves of their own political and economic platforms of their living expressions are truly affecting the very temporary survival of our human's true nature of our beings own physical and expressed existences in the realm of God's creation, and also considering that the powerful impact and negative implications of corruptions and their abuses of powers can really take a tight hold and also can power capture the humanity's active behaviors while they are surfing the waves of their own established religious platforms of their own individualistic living expressions that all indeed can and are affecting the very eternal survival of the humanity's truly living soul of its own very human being's manifest spiritual existences and expressions in the vast realm of God's creation, I am going forward in the next few wording paragraphs and will write and address them both separately to be able to make a sincere distinguish between the very strong implications and the undeniable real power of the corruptions that can truly affect us all while we the humans are actively fighting for our very temporary physical survival, and also when we the humans are fighting for our very own eternal spiritual survival, and we do really need to know that the very final and end results and the devastating consequences of our active human corruptions can deeply influence all of our own express religious, political, and economic humanitarian behaviors, that are causing a real harm and also strong detrimental actions that negatively power impacts and affects our very human beings overall health, purpose, and also its divine humanitarian process functions, and while I am writing this very passage I also want to be able to address and mention to the readers of this book that in my own sincere opinion I do strongly believe that the most dangerously and the most destructive humanitarian harms are being caused and produced by the fangs of strong and deceitful corruptions and abuses of their influenced powers that are being released against the very human beings own living existence, are truly the ones that are being able of manipulating and capturing within their influences of deceitful powers and control, and within their very fundamentally strong processes of active manipulative schemes, the very emotions, the very feelings, and the very thoughts and imaginations of all of the humans that are actively navigating and expressing their living experiences of life, and their living manifestations of life, on all of the various and established religious platforms for all the humanity, regardless their own fundamental and their own structural cultural backgrounds and their very own social experiences of life, because in the truth of the matter the humans religious platforms can encapsulate very profound and very deeply our very unique human beings characteristics and expressions, producing the real function attributes and their living factors that can indeed without a doubt can affect and also can influence our very own human beings eternal soul's survival and its final end destiny and destination.

Approaching humanity's living realities and their own variously manifested forms, honestly, it is at times so difficult to be able to make factual and definitive solid statements about our very own human beings living souls' fundamental ability to survive the compelling religious influences and their extreme and realistic waves of continually ongoing spiritual manipulations that are using the information of their very own multifaceted deceptive schemes to be able to capture within their webs of strong corrupted powers and confusion the very living characteristics and their behavioral living functions of our very own human beings undeniable and powerful humanitarian expressions and their beliefs.

Even if we will not be able to make definitive solid statements considering the implications that we are all facing due to the many religious multifaceted complexities and formalities that are surrounding all the living aspects of our very human beings' lives, and our expressions, and our live manifestations while we are altogether traveling and sailing the waves of our sea of life, when we are journey on this earthly physical and natural habitat of our human existence, it is imperative and also very critically essential to our living soul's eternal salvation to be able to develop the much needed awareness capability and functions, to start recognizing that the very real powers of a solid corrupted religion system and its religious spiritual manipulation schemes of their multi deceptive webs can indeed have truly devastating negative impacts that will affect individuals, groups, communities and denominations, and also at times even entire nations, not only at the levels of their temporary and physically living expressions, but also at the levels of their eternal and spiritually living expressions.

While economic and political corruption, abuses of powers, and manipulations are often described as being temporary in their purpose, functions, and nature, the various religious and spiritual corruption, abuses of management, and manipulations are producing waves of deceptive living processes for our human beings overall life and functions that are causing not only detrimental damages that are being temporary but also are causing and also are producing very long-lasting and even permanent effects that are transplanting and transferring their end and final results into eternal expressions and sorrows of the living soul's forever destiny. Therefore, it is critically imperative and essential to be aware of the many opportunities that are bringing within their snares of corrupt powers and manipulative schemes many realistic and potential openings that are actively promoting deceptive tactics to control and subjugate others in the name of their structural religious platforms that are being established for humanity's own systematic beliefs and guidance that so many times are all together falling under the very powerful classifications about leading society to new insights towards a new spiritual revolution and enlightenment.

Also, considering the functions and the applications of our realistic processes of life, it is worthy, and it is a true blessing to possess and sustain the natural senses and the abilities that are all required to function correctly in the order that we may be able to factually notice in the truth of the matter, that all those people that are very actively seeking to manipulate and to exploit others and use their authority to enable them to use and to abuse their powers through their own economic, political or religious and spiritual means and expressions may be altogether sourced and fueled by the exact similar motives and similar desires that will enable them to have control and decisive powers over other human beings, even if their operative platforms of expressions and own manifestations are genuinely operating under a total and completely different principles, different structures, and different control mechanism and structural systems.

Religious and spiritual manipulation often involves the use and the influences of a systematic and corrupted religion and its spiritual beliefs that are reflected within the human expressions, which are being used to actively practice total control, to exploit and to subjugate other humans by a wide variety of different deceptive processes and manifested means, that can take many different shapes and living forms, resulting in an array of multitudes of cults and their very corrupt religious extremism, that are being led and guided by many self-proclaimed religious and spiritual leaders, who are been at times willingly or unwillingly, knowing or unknowing, releasing and propagating false or misleading spiritual beliefs and practices in order to maintain and to sustain control over their followers at all costs no matter what may come, leading to solid corruptions and destructive abuses of powers that can have, and it will have very severe and devastating consequence for individuals and groups, for communities and denominations, causing at times an undeniable physical, spiritual and psychological harm, confusions and loss of personal expression and self-autonomy, that are being altogether known as the actual leading contributes and attributes factors that are being able to create new and also false humans identities controlled by their very strong perceptive reflections and shadows, that are also being altogether manipulated and also used to deeply erode the human beings social and vast multi- cultural humanitarian norms, and ultimately producing very strong and powerfully corrupted influential systematic and destructive waves that can genuinely cause abuses of powers, that can, and it will definitely be able to undermine the very fundamental foundation that sustains the entire manifold fabric and the fiber of our humanistic and living societies and their expressed social platforms.

In despite of all these powerful challenges that are nonstop coming and flowing into the living sea of our very humans living lives, from the vast multitudes and also from their own and various myriads of strong and corrupted, turbulent and deeply clouded and mudded flowing rivers that are all being stretching along the face of the uneven earthly ground that it is completely surrounding our very own living and breathing soul's expressions and life's manifestations, I am sincerely and strongly encouraging all of the readers of this book to keep on pressing forward and to never stop searching and never stop planning and advancing their own selves pursue towards reaching their own human being life's living center of balance in God's creation, that will enable us all to be able to start developing a most profound sense of control and awareness and understanding of the actual real meanings of our very own divine, humanitarian and also humanistic purposes and their accurate functions for our life, that can be indeed revealed to us all the living humans, only by the established and fundamental truth of the Almighty God, to lead and to guide his creation.

As I mentioned before in a previous paragraph that I wrote, it is well worth noting it again that not all of the individuals, the groups, the communities and the denominations that are all actively operating their very expressions on these three major platforms of our manifested humanity existences, that are being rooted and grounded into the religious, and the political, and the economic foundations of our systematically implanted thoughts and also their mechanically processed revelations for activating and green lighting our very own humans many various beliefs systems that are encapsulating and surrounding our very active lives, are all seeking to manipulate, and to control, and to exploit other humans, and while we may truly start encountering in our own very lives many individuals, and groups, communities and also many denominations, that are altogether being sincerely working and operating their very strong convictions and expressed functions within all of these powerful platforms of our very humankind vivid expressions for real strong humanitarian purposes and their active sustainment and maintenance influences towards changing other people's lives for better, but truly it is very important and critically imperative for us to be able to evaluate properly their very actions and their realistic operative functions and active motivations that are all sourcing and also that are fueling their very humanistic desires, through the lenses and the apparatus of our very own human divine developed self-awareness mechanism system, that it is needed to be located as close as possible within the frame of our own life's center of balance active character and living behaviors that can be power activated only by the word and the truth of the Almighty God, that it is already established and also being revealed for our very own human beings purposes in the creation, and that process of mind development it will really help us to be able to see the true reality of their very humanitarian active and working matters, and to realize if their motivations are being primary established to genuinely help other human beings and are being based on their sincere humanitarian divine values, or if their true motivations are being primary established and also sustained by their very own waves of active corrupted influences and their strong abuses of power that are being all released upon other human beings with the desire to be able to ensnare and to hold them captive for their own very personal gain and self-benefit at the expense of others.

I want to be able to emphasis and advance together with the readers to a more profound level of comprehension that will allow us to be able to start to understand clearly the divine process link and the correlation that truly exists between the need for implementation the programs of our realistic processes of life, and the need for a systematic development mechanism functions of our very own internal mind's thoughts and their very powerful life applications that can indeed maintain and sustain our very own expressed and manifested authentic living in God's active creation, and the more this very strong and active divine link and correlation between development and implementation it is being actively synchronized together to be able to execute their very individual operations and their proper functions in a strict unison relationship bond for the genuine betterment of our whole entire living expressions, the more we will be able to understand and to comprehend the very motives, and the same desires of everything else that are being active surrounding our very existences within the very beautiful paramount landscape of this vast earthly realm of reality that it is known to us all the mere humans to be our living place and a temporary home in the everlasting time.

In our realistic living environment that encapsulates within its strong fundamental foundation our authentic living humanistic expressions of our humanity developed characteristics and behaviors that are all being sourced and also activated to be manifested and to express their very own motives and their process functions, that can genuinely release forward very strong and very powerful results in a life that can affect and influence positively or that can affect and also influence negatively our very own and entire humanitarian actions, it does becomes imperative, essential and very critically vital for all of us, the humans, to start to develop a strong and a realistic understanding that will help us all in our journey of life to be able to comprehend and also to begin to properly analyze the internal levels of our genuine intentions that are all being driven by own motives and desires, and also to be able to comprehend and to start to properly analyze the very external levels of other individuals' true genuine intentions that are also being driven forward by their alternative motives and desires, and sincerely developing and implementing a structural complex internal mechanism of discernment functions, it will benefit us all internally and externally while we are altogether interacting, acting, and reacting with each other's driven motives and desires of our humanistic express and manifest actions of our daily living.

The process of maturing into a strong human being living with an authentic realistic understanding approach towards the reality of other humans that surrounds us, and that are being actively presenting their very own sourced humanitarian planning and actions that are being revealed by their very own motives and their own desires, towards reaching and achieving a forward pathway they want to establish for a influenced, forced and guided implementations of their own programs that are being all released into the existence under a disguised pretext for the humanity's greater good and its causes, so they say, we do need to be able to recognize these very influential actions through an advanced living process templates and frames that will helps us to be able to start to evaluate at face value their true motives and their desires, and figure it out what are their searched for end results and achievements, by using the proper discernment tools and their operative functions, that it will be able to activate our internal mind information mechanism processor, that needs to be genuinely connected, activated and calibrated by the Word of the living God, and by his own absolute truth that is being already revealed to guide all our humanitarian purposes.

In the future, in writing the following few paragraphs, I am praying that the good Lord will help me to bring forward to the reader's attention in more detail the importance of this very subject that I will call:

"Developing an Advanced Internal Mind Mechanism System for Evaluating Our Humanitarian Actions."

In a world where our very humanitarian actions are playing a very crucial role in addressing the realistic challenges of our human lives, it becomes essential and critically vital to ensure that our very own and other individuals' true motivations and desires that humans use as an active starting point when planning to support and help other humans are being all aligned with sincere and genuine intentions, and by being able to start searching, exploring and developing our advanced internal mind thought mechanism functions that it will allow us to be able to start using and also start embracing the much need it the process of applications for actively evaluating our very own motive and desires it is imperative and vital. Also, having the spirit of discernment bestowed upon our natural senses by the Creator, enabling us to start assessing the motives and the desires of other individuals' humanitarian actions, will help us all to be able to separate and to begin to discern the reality of our very own true motives and own desires, that are all in existence, and rooted into the core fundamental platforms sourcing and fueling people's humanitarian planning and activities.

Reaching the maturity of this divine achievement in return it will enable us all humans to be able to distinguish between all the people that are driven by their sincere and genuine humanitarian values, and all the people that are being motivated and driven forward by their very own search for personal gains and self-benefit factors, that can, and it will open the doors and foster the growth to the strong active existences of many harmful and dangerous foundations that can, and it will hold on their very powerful structures, strong and deceptive waves of corruption and their destructive abuses of power at the expenses of other humans, and while when we all do indeed know that the people's very realistic humanitarian efforts are often designed, established and associated with many positive and many real humanistic changes for better in other people lives, we also do need to know that there in the reality of our true and living world, there are truly in existence many instances and examples where some individuals and groups, some communities and denominations are being very actively using the fear and guilt factor for the implementations of their many different deceptive and manipulative techniques, that are birthing and also fueling religious, political and economic programs that will help and enable them to start the process of exploiting other people wellbeing for their very own self-benefit search and personal gain results without any given remorse, thus it is making it imperative and very crucial for us the humans to start and consider and recognize the need to start searching in truth for different ways of achieving divine understanding that will guide us to be able to search, and to reach, and to develop a sincerely strong, and a divine and reliable internal mind functions and its prevent mechanism systems, that will also help us to start in truth to distinguish and to identify our very own true powered motivations that are being very actively expressing their released influences of power, and that exists deeply behind the shadows of our very own true motives and our very own true desires.

The Realistic Assessments involves the critical learning processes that are need it to be sincerely recognize, accepted and activated within our internal functions of our mind processor, helping us to apply a proper and genuine objective evaluation towards all of the situations, the actions and the circumstances that are being part of our daily living and activities and are pertaining to our own selves and also to others that are surrounding and interacting with us all, without distorting the reality of the factual truth that so many times we and others are being exposed by our own natural defects and defaults, to bypass it and to let it slide due to our confirmation biases and also due to our preconceived notions that have the powers to mold and to shape our character and behaviors, and that can be deeply rooted and then released into their own living existences from the fundamental depths of our own social experiences and cultural backgrounds that at times it is close to impossible to escape their influences, and by start using the applications of the Realistic Assessments Factors towards the process of "Developing an Advanced Internal Mind Mechanism System for Evaluating Our Humanitarian Actions", it will allow us all to see the things as they are, and how they are, and for what they are, at their face value, thus enabling us to gain a deeper understanding of ourselves and also of others, and without a doubt it will definitely help us all to be able to recognize our very own strengths and also our weaknesses in everything that we are prone to express and manifest within our own lives, while navigating through the complexities of life.

The Value Analysis that is required to be implemented while reaching and tapping into the processes that can enable and assist us humans on the pathway towards achieving and developing a matured and advanced internal mind mechanism systems for proper analysis and functions involves and also encompasses our fundamental realistic approach towards our very own driven motivations and their desires, without any influenced prejudices or any other self-biases and their confirmations, when we are being actively embarking and sailing the waves of our own lives explorations and evaluations of the many fundamental underlying strong living principles and robust belief systems, their ethic characteristics and their moral values that drives our very own human being's humanistic behavior, and by sincerely reaching and also by delving into all of our own primal and original divine values that were being once bestowed by the Almighty creator deep inside the very fabric and the fiber of our humanistic DNA line, we will be able to gain a true and a sincere insight and a divine realistic value understanding of our very own human beings essences of life and their living fragrances that emanates forward to life from within our very own characteristic behaviors that truly does guide our humanitarian actions and their actual and consequential motives that are all being reflected from behind the curtains and the mirrors of our myriads of choices, and by being enable to start exploring, evaluating and examining the moral values that encapsulates our being, we will be able to develop a real strong understanding of the consequences of our very own choices and their proper alignment with our divine core values.

    The Holding Accountability processes that really needs to be embraced by us all in our search quest of exploring the vast working landscape of our humanitarian desires, emphasizes the critical importance that makes us all at all times to be on our best active responsive mode, sensitive, and also to be aware of the many various situations that are surrounding our daily living, and by being able to take proper responsibility and hold to account our own actions and decisions, it will help us to develop the internal mind mechanism system for evaluating our humanitarian motives, that in return it will help us all acknowledging the powerful realistic impacts that can be rated as positively or negatively, based on our very characteristic behaviors and function attributes, by affecting our own selves overall health and wellbeing, and also by impacting and affecting the overall health and wellbeing of those around us that are living and also that are interacting with us and with our own humanistic and also humanitarian activities, and moreover Holding Accountability's strong views extends way far and behind any individualistic levels of manifest expressions and can be bridged into the essential life's applicable tools that if they are used properly will allow the humans to fundamentally build trust and to foster absolute transparency, internally and externally in regards of their activities with one another, by actively promoting and by encouraging true fairness and true justice for all, that are the natural leading causes that's helping us the humans to march forward on together as one, towards reaching and achieving an actual humanitarian society that openly invites into their very own built structures and ranks, and also that profoundly embraces the vital critical importance and the imperative implementations of our must need humanitarian, social and cultural accountability functions in a strict and proper order.

Reviewing and summarizing the importance of the above paragraphs that were being writing in the context of helping all of us that are striving in our own lives to move forward by focusing our energy towards reaching and achieving a mature and developed "Advanced Internal Mind Mechanism System for Evaluating Our Humanitarian Actions", and also to be able to evaluate the actions of other individuals that are also actively releasing their own humanitarian programs that are being revealed forward by their very own strong humanistic motives and their desires for the greater good, learning and embracing the living power of these strong three key subjects that I previously wrote and mentioned about it, under the phrase" The Three Humanitarian Capital Letters -A-", Assessments, Analysis, Accountability, indeed does play crucial roles towards helping us reaching and expanding our very own understanding of who we really are as human beings with a breathing and a living soul, and also helping us humans to realize who really are the people that are surrounding us, interacting with us, and that can also very deeply influence us on daily bases, and by the process of incorporating them internally and making them part of our lives and functions, the true signals and their operative senses being released by these very three powerful key subjects, will be able to equip us with all the necessary tool applications that we all so desperately need them to be all activated within the frames of our own human mind, while we are all navigating the strong turbulent waves of our own life's true challenges, by helping us the humans to also be able to make realistic informed decisions, based not on our temporary emotions and deceitful feelings, but based on the power and the capability of Holding Realistic Values, when we are ready to start exploring and start learning the necessary factor attributes that are to be recognized and accepted as part of our living lives, in order for successfully to start the processes of developing our strong internal mind mechanism systems that needs to work properly to be able to sincerely discern and distinguish between the actions of people's active motivations and their driven desires, using the power of the Assessments, Analysis and Accountabilities factors as being the fundamentally building blocks for all of our, and others humanistic and humanitarian evaluations.

As we near the conclusion of this very chapter, which is called" Deceptive Platforms," I wish to offer and to leave for the readers of my book " The Truth Shifters" a few more additional thoughts that I will write as a summary of the topics and the subjects that were being presented and layout on these pages to provide real enjoyment, learning, and also inspiration, by encouraging the readers to apply these ideas to their own living lives, and by doing so, we the humans can better equip and better navigate on our very own journey of life, individuals, groups communities and denominations, when we are moving forward with divine purposes and functions, aiding us in our desire for the pursuit of life's freedom explorations, leading to realistic personal growth, propelling us towards the wondrous landscapes of true absolute freedom and liberty that can be indeed recognized, expressed and manifested only through the truth of the Almighty God for all humanity.

We must earnestly seek and desire the truth to embark on this powerful, transformative life journey. It is through this genuine search and sincere longing that we truly can achieve the actual profound fundamental transformations of our lives that we are all seeking, even as we actively confront the myriads of challenges when safeguarding our souls during the turbulent waves of our life's trials, that will never stop coming against us and will always keep arising from the spring of the cultural background expressions and social experiences that have the power always to influence us and to shape our very own existence, which is all dominated by compelling institutions and platforms activated by the religious, political, and the economic views towards our humanistic and humanitarian future.

However, as we strive for positive personal growth and understanding, we must always remain active, vigilant, and aware of these powerful forces that seek to influence and control us. Only by recognizing and confronting the powerful grip that these institutions and platforms hold over us can we genuinely start implementing the processes of being able to liberate ourselves. In that way, we may fully embrace our living and desired freedom that awaits us all, which has already been revealed to humanity by the truth, grace, and mercy of our Creator and Almighty God.

We must be sensitive and aware that the path to freedom, led and guided by the powerful manifestation of truth, is challenging. However, by learning, reaching, and applying these shared insights, we can equip ourselves with the necessary tools and applications to transcend our limitations and sincerely embark on a transformative journey toward divine realization and spiritual fulfillment.

As we are navigating the turbulent seas and the challenges of our life, let's not be confined by the solid and powerful influences of corrupt religious, political, and economic institutions while we are actively navigating their platforms, but rather, let us embrace the boundless potential that lies within the power of each of us, waiting to be released and set free by the absolute truth of the Almighty God revealed to all humanity in the image of his only begotten son Jesus Christ, and let's embrace deep within all of our inner being these powerful words revealed by the Scripture for us where this so powerful truth the Word states it; Who the Son sets

Free it is Set Free Indeed.

The topics and the subjects of this chapter's insights are part of three powerful complex combinations and active processes that I wrote for the readers and can be individually explored and added together or in partially, as developing and supporting tools towards our very own human beings' comprehensive thoughts and fundamental structural functions of our own human mind's active properties.

They are being reviewed below in closing:

1). **"The Power of Enhancing Human Understanding and Development Through Our Life's Realistic Processes."**

Learning and mastering this first process will help us to:

a). Recognize -it will lead to - Awareness!

b). Develop –it will lead to - Understanding!

c). Reach Out –it will lead to - Communications.

d). Navigate –it will lead to - Experiences!

2). **"Surviving Corruption and Abuses of Power."**

Learning and mastering this second process will help us to realize the harm and destruction produced by corruption:

a). Corruption the Leading Impact on Human Expressions

b). Corruption is the Cause of the Erosion of Human Values

c). Corruption the Cause of Human Clouded Judgment

d). Corruption is the Cause of Human Selfish Desires

3). **"Developing anAdvanced Internal Mind Mechanism System for Evaluating Our Humanitarian Actions."**

Learning and mastering this third process will help us evaluate the motives and desires behind our and others' humanitarian actions.

a). The Realistic assessment of Power
b). The Value Analysis Evaluations
c). The Holding Accountability Factor

I am praying that the implementation of these accurate complex combinations and their active mechanism processes that were presented in this chapter will enable us all to achieve a more substantial and positive maturity growth and understanding while we are altogether actively engaging in our own life's living pursuit towards reaching and also completing the realistic and the divine highs of our Almighty God's designed and revealed purposes for our own human being's physical and spiritual freedom that we are so much longing for, to be able to achieve it and to possess it, and to experience it in our lives. And I firmly encourage us all, no matter what may come our way, challenges, influences, temptations, and trials, never waiver to pursue it, never stop searching for it, and never give up on the truth's powerful principles of life that have been bestowed initially upon us all the humans. It has the undeniable and ultimate power to define our entire accurate and actual humanitarian purposes and functions.

Conclusion

Psalm 12: 6-8:" The promises of the Lord are pure, silver refined in a furnace on the ground, purified seven times. You, O Lord, will protect and guard us from this generation forever."

Humans are all travelers together on this pathway of our life's expressions. This alive and living road of our existences does indeed have the real power to encapsulate within its structural built-in frames alongside the limited borders, signals, and live signs, all of our entire journey that also defines our human being's realistic existence and its very living expressions, that are being all truly and indeed manifested and forwarded into active actions by our very humanistic characteristics and behaviors, from within the deep grasps of our built-in mind capacity and ability to be able to comprehend, and to understand, to accumulate and to possess a fundamental actual knowledge that will guide us all in the absolute Truth, to be able to achieve our life's true meaning.

I started to write this book because of this very short, simple introductory inspiration received from a quote from the Holy Scriptures from the Gospel of John, chapter eight and verse thirty-two where our Savior Jesus Christ said," Then you will know the Truth and the Truth will set you free", and what dropped deep into my spirit was the real burden and the intense heaviness of this very powerful reality that was presented by the Lord at the beginning of this verse that it is so often being bypassed and neglected by people, and while they are keeping themselves busy running back and forth, stomping on their chest and proclaiming and declaring promises and decrees for and against other beings, by searching to elevate themselves somehow above others, by trying to establish their little self-righteousness, and active spirited kingdoms, where strong waves of corruption and abuses of power take priority, but are missing on this very short and critically vital and essential words spoken by the Lord," Then you will know", and this very reality of the Truth it is being tight and linked strictly by the actual living words also spoken by the Lord in the very previous verses that say," If you hold to my teachings", and also some other Scriptural word translations are using the sayings," If you remain in my word," or " If you abide in my word, or if dwell in my word", Then you will know the Truth, and this is the valid key and the door that can open our pathway to be able to reach and achieve the necessary divine knowledge of the absolute Truth that can genuinely set and make us a free people indeed.

    I want to say that these very passages of these Scriptures and the reality of the words of our Lord Jesus that stirred very deeply my own spirit with heaviness, was indeed the leading cause that guided me to start writing this very book that it is called," The Truth Shifters", in these challenging times when strong and very powerful influences of our lives and their living uncertainties that are surrounding humanity are working nonstop to keep the humans away from the very Truth of the Almighty God and from his true revealed power of deliverance and freedom for the Soul of the humanity, and by releasing and also by using many various and multiple deceptive informative methods and applications with the intent to captivate and to bound the very life and the very living expressions of all of those that are actively pursuing and are searching for the Truth in their quest for freedom, by creating very powerful schemes and also web influences and hidden labyrinths that also are the producing leading causes for the humans' s confusions, and by trying to always keep the humans in a total darkness, without any realistic understanding or any knowledge of the Truth, and by their design, they bypass the true meaning of the Living Word of our Lord Jesus the Christ that has been revealed to our entire humanity when he spoke these true-life-giving words, "Then you will know the truth."

But the enemy of our living and breathing souls, it is also actively unleashing upon the face of humanity expressions of compelling and influential opportunities that will enable their very own corrupt living existences to start proclaiming and declaring their very own words and their powered express decrees to bound the humanity with the chains of these very words," Then they will never know the truth."

By going forward and start working on this book project, and sailing together with you the readers the waves of these inspirational words that have been all written and released within the frames of these very pages, it has been truly a real blessing to be able to discussed and to cover together with you the very topics and these important subjects and their own matters, regarding the applicable processes of our own human being's very powerful and strong real driven strives and desires that we all have and possess, and by starting preparing ourselves and by embarking in this important journey of our living lives for the quest of discovering and exploring our true and realistic humanitarian pathway that we do need to walk on together as human beings, that it may lead us, and guide us all, towards the finish line of our own humanistic motives and desires while actively searching for God's absolute Truth and his freedom that has been released and bestowed upon the humanity from within the depths of its own breath of life, so that we humans may be able one day to really know the power of truth, and because of that we can never afford to stop traveling and searching for the truth and for his true powerful freedom, and in despite the many influences and the many strong efforts of all of those that are possessing very strong and powerful physical and spiritual entities, that are being so actively trying, and that were always been trying from the beginning of the creation's time, to hold captive and to strongly chain bound the very human beings and their living souls far and away from the very presence of the Creator, and far and away from his divine absolute truth, let us all be open to the power and to the revelation of the word of God that carry the instructions that can truly help us all the mere humans to mature and also to grow stronger in our received from above pure and divine understanding and its realistic comprehension, while we are actively searching and pursuing the knowledge of the truth for the freedom and for the liberty that it brings upon our very own human souls, and also for the overall health benefits for all of humankind expressions in the physical and also in its spiritual being.

Together, we stood shoulder to shoulder while embarking and navigating this majestic journey of our living lives, through the powerful waves of these inspirational words that rolled and became unfolded within the frames of these very pages, and through this powerful endeavor, we did together delved into the life of these very crucial topics, by exploring the depths of our breathing and living human being's soul's expressions and their actively powerful manifestations that are taking place physically and spiritually, by discovering the power of our very own human spirit's unwavering determination and continue the search for the unlimited and ultimate freedom, from the grip of all of the undeniable powerful limits and boundaries released against the soul of our humanity by the very enemies of our living and breathing soul and existence, and in a true sense of our collective pursuit towards reaching and also achieving increased knowledge and understanding, we have strived to cover the most of these significant topics and subjects that have the power from within, to shape in a positively way, or many times to shape in a negatively way our own humanistic existences, our own true life characteristics and expressed behaviors, and starting from the very beginning pages of this book with the very first chapter when we covered the vital importance and the need to be able to open ourselves up and to start recognizing the realistic processes of understanding the truth with a sincere, clean and pure heart, and mind, not only with a clear mind, because a clear mind does not always defines and evolves into a clean mind, and because of this we can be expose to so many different life opportunities factors that we can embrace with a very clear mind, and many times because of that, the very end results of our humanitarian process functions and their real life applications can cause at times more harm than good for us and for all of those that are around us, because our humanitarian actions have been clearly performed and completed, but without the true and the sincere comprehensive and divine understandings that must continually flow forward from a clean and pure mind and from a clean and pure heart.

  As we prepare ourselves and venture together forth on this deeply profound search for the purpose and the meaning of life, we uncover the authentic and realistic pathway of our living lives that can hold and bind us all together and lead us towards reaching the resting landscape of our greater human understandings for our own humanitarian and humanistic actions and quests, by the power of the true revelation that has been released upon all humanity by the word and by the absolute Truth of the Almighty God.

Then in our journey traveling the pages of the significantly following few chapters we went ahead and discussed and also covered the critical and vital importance pertaining to our lives, to be able to truly differentiate and to discern between the power process applications of the absolute Truth's divine purpose and functions for our humanitarian lives, and the many real opportunistic process applications of our own living lives that are being revealed and released forward into their own active existences by our own relative Truth or by our own planned, designed and activated projected Truth, that many times we are all exposed to pass it all along to ourselves and also to many others that we are interacting with in our lives, as being the true and the indispensable absolute Truth of the Almighty God, thus enabling the processing of creating many different and various leading causes that are all establishing very strong harmful strife, arguments, and ideological, and doctrinal fights, that are indeed so many times really hurting the very human being's overall physical and spiritual health, expressions and functions, and these robust dysfunctional and detrimental processes has nothing to do, or little to do, with the absolute Truth of God, and indeed, more or less, has everything to do with how we the humans are exposed to perceive it, to accept it, to receive it, and to understand it.

Within the pages of this book, we have sought together to be able to grasp the power of the absolute truth, the true and sacred essence of God's divine everlasting love that truly permeates our very own human being's existence, that it is releasing and granting us the freedom and the liberty that every single human soul's breath of life it is searching and aspire after, that heavenly and divine gift that has been deep breathed into the fundamental foundation and the structural depths of our humankind's existence by the Creator himself, that we may be able to unravel the majestically mysteries of our very existence and purpose within the vast paramount landscape of God's own creation, and in the face of myriads of influences and their strong waves of deception, we went ahead and together explored the powerful topics and their subjects, regarding the ability and the capacity of our very own mind's power functions, that has the power of enabling the true reality that surrounds us all when we need to start processing the signals that have been revealed by the truth when we are actively being exposed to so many various and different temporary realities, and also when we need to start processing the very impulses of the truth when we are being exposed to our very own humanistic thought applications and their nonstop moving and shifting shadows, that was then followed by another topic and subject covering our very existence and that has been discussed in more details in the chapter that is called the transcendental realm, allowing us to really be able to recognize and to be aware of our own real strong enemies of our living souls that are all from the very beginning of time operating very actively within their own manipulative quest and manifested expressions to start to hinder and to break the true and divine relationship and bond that exists between us the humans and our Creator, and also within the pages of the truth shifters's chapter, we did deeply explored and discussed in more detailed views about their strong and harmful methods and destructive techniques that have been released upon the humanity, using as a battlefield location for their own search end results the very human being's own power of the mind that it is active operating its executive functions for the maintenance and the sustainment of our own entire humanity while we are navigating the strong and the influential waves of our own living and breathing lives existences on these very powerful three major humanitarian platforms of life, that are known as religions, politics and economics, that are altogether carrying on their structural and fundamental foundations, and also that are encapsulating within the power grips of their frames, all of our humanistic living expressions and manifestations that have the power of truly revealing our very true own motivations, emotions, feelings and desires.

As I am bringing this book project to its conclusion, in a genuine humbleness I do want to be able to express my sincere and profound gratitude towards the readers with these few final encouragement thoughts, and may the comfort and the lead of God's Living Spirit, carry us all on our short journey and travel on this earthy realm, by helping us and propelling us towards a more profound comprehension of our own divine purpose and own life's meaning, united in our shared pursuit of the liberation and the freedom that it is revealed to us all the humans by the absolute Truth of God, and as we are setting our sights on the heights of the horizon, let us hold steadfast to the pure and divine knowledge, that we are never truly alone on this temporary journey of our living and breathing lives, and our Creator and God is always watching over us and carrying for us, and no matter how intense are our life's challenges and their uncertainties, He will never give up on us, and my sincere prayers for us all it is to stay positive and focus and never give up on ourselves, and may we all in the midst of challenging situations and circumstances that at times life presents for or against us, and in despite of all, let's stay true to our bestowed humanitarian moral values and humanistic characteristics, by choosing growth over complacency, and by selecting a true passion over apathy, and by choosing genuine compassion over indifferences, and by doing so we can draw strength from the very purpose of our life's meaning, making us all understand that an actual living human achievement is not an elusive hidden treasure of the past ages somewhere out of sight and out of reach, but rather it is a heavenly divine value that has been deeply planted by God within the depths of our own humankind's DNA fabric and complex structure, that can be genuinely rediscovered and restored to its original intent and proper functions only by the absolute Truth of the God.

May these words linger into the depths of our hearts and minds, and may the good Lord God Almighty help us, keep us, and guide us, and may his comfort and peace be absolute upon us and protect us all as we continue our own lives' temporary and short journey and quest on this earthly realm that for now we call home, until that day when he will receive us back home, in that majestic and eternal heaven where we will forever surrounded by the true power of his everlasting and steadfast love where we humans belong.

As I bid you, the readers, farewell, I do so with humbleness and gratitude; thank you for joining me on this beautiful quest of exploring the depths of life's meaning and purpose bestowed upon us by our Creator.

I am blessed to dedicate this poem I wrote at the end of this book just for you, the readers.

"For Truth, For Justice, For Freedom"

As human beings with a forever-living soul
Let's march all together in the sounds of unison!
In a forward motion toward the heights and apogee
Free from all indoctrination and ideologies.

And despite the struggles in our life situations
Let's never lose our hearts and their pure palpitations!
As the eagles soar high in the sky above all the clouds

So, we can remove through faith in God any seeds of doubt

Searching for the Soul's freedom and the human liberty
That has the power to transfer us from here to eternity.
It is the true quest of our human beings' deep explorations.
And can be indeed achieved with the Truth's interventions.

Indeed, this is our journey, sailing our living life's mighty seas
Fighting for survival through the storms and many fears
Waves of turbulences and powerful dark influences
But let's keep the faith in God with a smile on our faces.

We are not alone in the search for our own end's destination.
The Creator that guides us all is already preparing our rest location.
All we must do is to return and embrace the power of his Truth
That will free us humans forever, giving us a new root.

Planted deep inside the firm rock of our human salvation.
We will never be thirsty or suffer the plagues of starvation.
On that beautiful day when our living Soul will be set free
By the Creator's own powerful hands back into eternity.

Oh, my Soul, keep fighting, keep pushing, and never give up!
For Truth, justice, and freedom, do raise and stand up.
When coming that moment on earth to take one last breath.
At the end of your journey, to enter in heaven without regret.

By Mihai Ilioi

About The Author

To the Readers:

My name is Mihai Ilioi, and I am humbled and thrilled at the same time to be the author of this book called The Truth Shifters. I sincerely pray that all of you who read it will be blessed and the messages revealed within the frames of these pages will resonate with you.

A few words of introduction about myself: I was born in Romania on July 25th, 1969, during the height of the communist regime. Growing up in such an oppressive society, I constantly searched for political, economic, and religious freedom of expression. On June 12th, 1988, when I was 18 years old, I decided to take matters into my own hands and escape the oppressive communist regime by swimming across the Danube River, the borderline frontier between Romania and Yugoslavia. On the banks of the Danube River, I first encountered a supernatural presence that watched over me and guided me. At the same time, I was ready to start swimming in the Frontier River. I am praying that later, I will be able to write about this unforgettable, powerful encounter that happened in my own life, of that moment and day when I understood that it was the presence and the comfort of the Holy Spirit that came to strengthen me and to help me as I was starting a new journey of my life.

After spending some time in Yugoslavia refugee camps,

I eventually made my way to New York City with the help of the UNICEF department of the UN, which at that time was involved in processing the refugees that ended up within those camps from different parts of the world. Starting a new life in a new country was challenging, but I pursued the freedom I always craved. Over many years, I have been fortunate enough to be able to experience many different types of privileges, including expressing the freedom of religion, the freedom of speech, and the freedom to continue the steadfast pursuit of my passions with the focus and drive to reach a deeper understanding of our very own human reality that can encapsulate within its firm grip so overwhelming our entire living humanity, and our very own human being's truthful aspirations and desires for freedom.

On April 4th 1990, I married my beautiful wife Carla, and we have been blessed in our family life with five children and nine grandchildren, and many times when I talked to them and explained to them the subject thoughts about the true power of freedom and liberty, being individual freedom or being a freedom at the various levels of a community that in order to be reached and achieved and understood, it must be searched, pursued and protected at all costs, because once the freedom and the liberty it is becoming corrupted or it is deemed lost it will be very hard to reclaim it, and they all are looking in amaze, but also confused at times, trying to figure out what I am talking about, because many times this reality subject it does not make any sense to them, because honestly they have never been exposed to the life's brutality that it is being caused by losing the expressions of their freedom, but nevertheless my family has been consistently for me a nonstop and genuinely a constant source of inspiration and real support throughout my entire life, and I am grateful for their love and for their encouragement and blessings.

As an Author, I am passionate about sharing my experiences and insights with others, and I hope this book's message will inspire and uplift you and help you on your journey to the freedom you are searching for. I have always been drawn and encouraged to express life through poetry and song writings that reflect the daily realities of our breathing and living lives. There is something powerful about living expressions that can capture and process our experiences and emotions in a way that nothing else can and hold them tight within the depths of our human location and a divine place called Active Memories. Writing has always been a passion of mine, and I am fortunate to be able to share my work with others.

In addition to my writing, I have been blessed to be able to work in the Aerospace Industry as the breadwinner for my family. It has been a challenging and rewarding career that has taught me the value of hard work and true dedication. In addition to my career in the Aerospace Industry and my passion for writing, I am also an Ordained Minister and the Pastor of Phoenix Worship Community, and the founder of The Expressed Thoughts, a podcast dedicated to bringing in a front view the covering of the daily living reality of our internal and external life's meaning and true purpose.

Our ministry and movement have been established with the view and focus that we may be able to reach out to other people and their communities around us with the love message of the Gospel of our Lord and Savior, Jesus Christ.

It is a great volunteering effort, and we feel deeply called to serve and be there for others in this way.

Through our work at Phoenix Worship Community, we

aim to create a safe and welcoming space where people can explore their faith, participate, ask questions, and find support for their spiritual journey. Everyone deserves love, compassion, and proper divine understanding, regardless of their cultural and social background and beliefs. I am deeply grateful for the opportunity to serve.

This volunteering work has only deepened my desire and search toward reaching a genuine and realistic understanding of the interconnectedness of all things within our expression of life.

It has helped me see the world with a greater sense of empathy and compassion, and this journey of my life as a human traveler has inspired my writings to a more profound level.

I have always been fascinated by the different political, economic, and religious expressions of freedom. I realized that despite their differences, these multi manifestations of freedom are indeed bound together by their solid fundamental and structural foundations, which have the power to influence and mold our humanity's moral behavior and their forward manifested and expressed actions.

My genuine and sincere search for a deeper understanding of these actions and their behavioral attributes led me to write this book. The message and the insights within these pages will be an eye-opening experience for all those searching for a greater understanding of our world.

With a humble and sincere heart, I extend my thoughts and prayers to all of you who will be reading this book.

The message and insights within these pages will inspire and encourage readers on their journey toward the freedom they seek. True freedom is a universal longing that we all share, and it is something we all strive for in our pathway of life. This book will help you discover new paths and possibilities for your search. As you read these words, my prayers are with you. May the blessings from heaven above surround you all and give you strength, comfort, and peace on this temporary journey of your life's purpose and search. May you find the courage and the wisdom to overcome any obstacles that come your way, never lose sight of the hope and possibilities that lie ahead, and do not give up; never give up on yourself. Thank you for taking the time to read these words and for allowing me to share this book's message and its perspective with you. God bless you all, and may you find the freedom, liberty, and fulfillment you always seek as a human traveler on this beautiful earth's majestic landscape and its beautiful paramount scenes.

DITAT DEUS - AD DEI GLORIAM!

Notes:

Notes:

Notes:

Notes:

www.ingramcontent.com/pod-product-compliance
Lightning Source LLC
Chambersburg PA
CBHW070632160426
43194CB00009B/1441